# Michael Chekhov Technique in the Twenty-First Century

# Michael Chekhov Technique in the Twenty-First Century

## New Pathways

Edited by Cass Fleming and Tom Cornford

methuen | drama

LONDON • NEW YORK • OXFORD • NEW DELHI • SYDNEY

METHUEN DRAMA
Bloomsbury Publishing Plc
50 Bedford Square, London, WC1B 3DP, UK
1385 Broadway, New York, NY 10018, USA

BLOOMSBURY, METHUEN DRAMA and the Methuen Drama logo are trademarks
of Bloomsbury Publishing Plc

First published in Great Britain 2020
[This paperback edition published 2022]

Copyright © Cass Fleming and Tom Cornford and contributors, 2020, [2022]

Cass Fleming, Tom Cornford and contributors have asserted their right under the Copyright,
Designs and Patents Act, 1988, to be identified as authors of this work.

For legal purposes the Acknowledgements on p. xi constitute an extension of this copyright page.

Cover design by Louise Dugdale
Cover image © Katerina Kotti

All rights reserved. No part of this publication may be reproduced or transmitted in any form or by any means, electronic or mechanical, including photocopying, recording, or any information storage or retrieval system, without prior permission in writing from the publishers.

Bloomsbury Publishing Plc does not have any control over, or responsibility for, any third-party websites referred to or in this book. All internet addresses given in this book were correct at the time of going to press. The author and publisher regret any inconvenience caused if addresses have changed or sites have ceased to exist, but can accept no responsibility for any such changes.

A catalogue record for this book is available from the British Library.

A catalog record for this book is available from the Library of Congress.

ISBN: HB: 978-1-4742-7318-3
[PB: 978-1-350-18537-1]
ePDF: 978-1-4742-7321-3
eBook: 978-1-4742-7320-6

Typeset by Deanta Global Publishing Services, Chennai, India

To find out more about our authors and books visit www.bloomsbury.com
and sign up for our newsletters.

*We dedicate this book to Michael Chekhov and those who have led the revitalization of his work in the UK since the 1980s: Franc Chamberlain, Graham Dixon, Sarah Kane, and Martin Sharp, and to Jerri Daboo, who brought us together in 2011 to consider how we could creatively engage with the Michael Chekhov Theatre Studio Deirdre Hurst du Prey Archive and envisage new pathways for the future of the work it documents.*

*We also wish to honour the Chekhov matriarchs for keeping his work alive in the twentieth century and into the twenty-first: Marjolein Baars, Georgette Boner, Liisa Byckling, Diane Caracciolo, Jessica Cerullo, Alice Crowther, Lisa Dalton, Dorothy Elmhirst, Deirdre Hurst du Prey, Mariana Ivanova, Sarah Kane, Nancy Kindelan, Maria Knebel, Kim Lane, Felicity Mason, Joanna Merlin, Margareta Morgenstern, Mala Powers, Fern Sloan and Beatrice Straight.*

# Contents

| | |
|---|---|
| List of illustrations | viii |
| Notes on contributors | ix |
| Acknowledgements | xi |
| Introduction: Chekhov technique: Past, present and future  *Cass Fleming* | 1 |

## Section One  Chekhov technique: Processes of theatre-making

1. 'Theatre of the future': Chekhov technique for devised theatre and catalyst direction  *Cass Fleming* — 29

2. Actor-dramaturgs and atmospheric dramaturgies: Chekhov technique in processes of collaborative playwriting  *Tom Cornford* — 64

## Section Two  Chekhov technique: Beyond acting

3. The expressive voice in performance: Chekhov's techniques for voice and singing  *Daron Oram* — 93

4. 'The moment you are not inwardly moving and inwardly participating, you are dead': Chekhov technique in actor-movement and dance  *Roanna Mitchell* — 107

5. Feeling space, making space: Michael Chekhov's approach to theatre design  *Sinéad Rushe* — 132

## Section Three  Chekhov technique: Beyond the theatre

6. 'If the new theatre is to have meaning, the audience too must play its part': Chekhov technique in applied, therapeutic and community contexts  *Caoimhe McAvinchey* — 153

Cross-currents and conclusions  *Cass Fleming and Tom Cornford* — 174

| | |
|---|---|
| Glossary of Michael Chekhov's terminology | 185 |
| Bibliography | 190 |
| Index | 201 |

# Illustrations

## Figures

| | | |
|---|---|---|
| I.1 | The *Balladina* sketch | 2 |
| I.2 | Typed front page of notebook | 3 |
| I.3 | 'Never try to touch the heart itself' | 6 |
| 1.1 | Advice to students on 'The Fishers' Scene' | 48 |
| 1.2 | The Chart of Exploration, 1937 | 53 |
| 1.3 | A 1937 rehearsal plan for 'The Fishers' Scene' | 56 |
| 3.1 | 'All qualities come together in the actor' | 96 |
| 3.2 | 'All qualities come together in the actor', revised by Daron Oram | 105 |
| 5.1 | Character sketch of Toby Belch by Michael Chekhov | 138 |
| 5.2 | Character sketch of Feste by Michael Chekhov | 139 |
| 5.3 | Character sketch of Fabian by Michael Chekhov | 140 |
| C.1 | Seated participants in a 2016 New Pathways Praxis Symposium (Katerina Kotti) | 179 |
| C.2 | Participants in a movement exercise in a 2016 New Pathways Praxis Symposium (Katerina Kotti) | 183 |

## Table

| | | |
|---|---|---|
| 1.1 | The Chart of Exploration | 57 |

# Contributors

**Tom Cornford** is Senior Lecturer in Theatre and Performance at the Royal Central School of Speech and Drama, an editor of the international, peer-reviewed journal *Studies in Theatre and Performance* and a director and dramaturg. His research focuses on relationships between the practices of theatre-making and contemporary politics and culture in Europe and North America since the early twentieth century, and the politics of representation in contemporary theatre. Publications include a special issue of *Contemporary Theatre Review* on the director Katie Mitchell, and *Theatre Studios: A Political History of Ensemble Theatre-Making*.

**Cass Fleming** is Lecturer in Theatre and Performance at Goldsmiths, University of London, a theatre director, and trainer of actors and directors. Her practice and research centres on the use of play in the actor training and theatre-making processes developed by Michael Chekhov and Suzanne Bing (2013). Cass is the founder and co-director of the Chekhov Collective UK; has written on the work of Jacques Copeau and Bing, with Mark Evans in *The Great European Stage Directors*, Vol. 3; and with Evans is editing a special edition of *Theatre, Dance and Performance Training* (2020) exploring non-canonical actor training. https://chekhovcollectiveuk.co.uk/.

**Caoimhe McAvinchey** is Professor of Socially Engaged and Contemporary Performance at Queen Mary University of London. Prior to this, she established the MA Applied Drama: Theatre in Educational, Community and Social Contexts at Goldsmiths. Her publications include *Theatre & Prison* (2011); *Performance and Community* (2013); with Fabio Santos and Lucy Richardson, *Phakama: Making Participatory Performance* (2018); and *Applied Theatre: Women and the Criminal Justice System* (2020). She is currently working on a research project with Clean Break, considering over four decades of the company's innovative theatre practice with and about women who have experience of the criminal justice system.

**Roanna Mitchell** is a performance-maker and movement person, co-director of the Chekhov Collective UK, and lecturer at the University of Kent, UK. Her work explores performance and training in the intersection between acting and dance as well as applications of Chekhov technique beyond the theatre, especially in mental health contexts. Roanna has published on the body politics of acting, the actor's aesthetic labour and on Susie Orbach's work linking performance and body activism. She has directed/created/movement-directed performance internationally, often working site-responsively, including collaborations with Richard Schechner, Platform-7, Accidental Collective and others. www.roannamitchell.com.

**Daron Oram** is Principal Lecturer in Voice at the Royal Central School of Drama, where he teaches on the BA Acting Collaborative Theatre and the MA/MFA in Voice Studies. Daron's practice research focuses on equitable approaches to actor training and the synthesis of psychophysical acting and voice methods. Daron's published work discusses approaches to psychophysical training and the neurodivergent actor, with a specific focus on dyslexia and dyspraxia. Daron has also written about decolonizing/decentring listening practices in speech, accents and dialect training. Daron is a designated Linklater voice teacher, a Senior Fellow of the Higher Education Academy and in 2019 was awarded a National Teaching Fellowship.

**Sinéad Rushe** is a director, performer and teacher. She is Senior Lecturer in Acting and Movement at the Royal Central School of Speech and Drama, specializing in Michael Chekhov Technique and Meyerhold's Biomechanics. She has directed *Concert* (The Pit, Barbican, and Baryshnikov Arts Centre, New York; Gradam Comharcheoil TG4 2018 Award); *Night Just Before the Forests* (Macau Arts Festival, China); *Diary of a Madman* (Sherman Cymru, Wales); *Out of Time* with Colin Dunne (The Pit, Barbican, and Baryshnikov Arts Centre; nominated for 2010 Olivier Award), among others. Her publications include *Michael Chekhov's Acting Technique: A Practitioner's Guide* and co-translation into French of four plays by Howard Barker. www.sineadrushe.co.uk.

# Acknowledgements

This book represents the culmination of a lengthy process of both archival and practice research, which would have been impossible without the support of a large number of people. We would like, in particular, to thank all of the presenters and participants at the 2016 New Pathways event at Goldsmith's. Without your enthusiasm for both teaching and learning Chekhov's approaches, this project could not have happened. Caoimhe McAvinchey would like to extend special thanks to Zoe Brook, Hartley Jafine, Effie Makepeace and Martin Sharp for their contributions. Thanks also to Goldsmith's Department of Theatre and Performance for hosting and supporting the event, and to the Chekhov Collective UK, the University of Kent, Michael Chekhov UK, Queen Mary University of London, and the Royal Central School of Speech and Drama for funding and in-kind support for the event.

Fleming and Cornford's respective practice research was entirely dependent upon the companies of performers and theatre-makers with whom it was undertaken, whose enthusiastic and insightful participation contributed enormously to the findings presented in this book. We would like to thank the members of the Chekhov Collective UK who were involved in this project: Tom Bostock, Francesca Castelbuono, Sian Clarke, Derek Elwood, Bryn Fitch, Alistair Foylan, Rebecca Frecknall, Katja Hilevaara, Hanna Junti, Joshua MacLellan, Saskia Marland, Joe Mercier, Roanna Mitchell, Phoebe Naughton, Melody Parker Grome, Holly Shuttleworth and Chloe Stephens, as well as everyone who has worked with Common Ground Theatre in York, most particularly Hannah Davies, who made it happen.

We would also like to thank the archivists of the Devon Records Office for their help with numerous queries and requests for support. Chapters of this book were read by Tony Fisher, Johanna Gjersvik and Katja Hilevaara, whose insights have helped a great deal to shape it, as did the generous report of the manuscript's anonymous reader. Erin Lee also provided valuable research assistance in the final stages, for which we are very grateful.

Finally, we would like to thank our loved ones. From Cass: deepest thanks to Lorelei who has travelled down these new pathways with me and has been so patient, inspirational and playful on the journey, and also to Enid and Johanna for their encouragement and love. From Tom: thank you to Anna, Bella, Jacob and Nute for your unfailing love.

# Introduction

# Chekhov technique: Past, present and future

CASS FLEMING

## 1 A hidden treasure trove

Tucked away in a series of neatly organized and deceptively drab-looking archive boxes in Devon lies a treasure trove of ideas and material for the twenty-first-century practitioner. The brown cardboard boxes belie the imaginative, radical, social and experimental nature of their contents. Much of the material held within these boxes details the progressive work of Michael Chekhov's (1891–1955) Chekhov Theatre Studio, first based at Dartington Hall in Devon (1936–8), and later in Ridgefield, Connecticut, in the United States. It also holds records about the Chekhov Theatre Players, a professional company formed by members of the Chekhov Theatre Studio (1939–42). The Michael Chekhov Theatre Studio Deirdre Hurst du Prey Archive was created by Hurst du Prey (1922–2002), Chekhov's student and assistant teacher, who was to become his lifelong collaborator and friend, and is held by the Dartington Hall Trust.[1] Opening these archive boxes is an invitation to creatively engage with the world of the Chekhov Theatre Studio and its members through many different media. In addition to discovering a plethora of written sources, a visitor to the archive will uncover some intriguing props, costume items, sketches, paintings, diagrams, charts, index cards and categorization systems, photographs and recordings (e.g. the *Balladina* sketch; see Figure I.1).

The written records held in this archive are extensive and include early drafts of Chekhov's seminal book *To the Actor*, letters, rehearsal notes, teaching timetables, interview transcripts, lecture notes, devised play scripts and adaptations of pre-existing play scripts, sketches and non-scripted scenarios for performance, scores, cross-cultural research, reflections on practice, the Studio brochure and publicity material, newsletters, teaching aids, letters, biographical materials on a number of Chekhov's close collaborators, the teaching notes of Beatrice Straight and Alan Harkness, along with other materials gathered by Hurst du Prey during her lifetime. However, the heart of the written records are detailed transcripts of Chekhov's classes given at the Chekhov Theatre Studio (1936–42), which are titled 'The Actor Is the Theatre'. These records were diligently made and maintained by Hurst du Prey who, along with Straight, was involved in the creation of the Studio with Chekhov. She explains that prior to the opening of the Studio she '*worked with* [Chekhov] *on selecting group scenes, dialogues, soliloquies etc., from plays, to be used in class work*' (TAITT, 1936: 6–7) and when the Studio opened on 5 October 1936,

Fig. I.1 The *Balladina* sketch, photograph. The Michael Chekhov Theatre Studio Deirdre Hurst du Prey Archive (hereafter CTS-DHDPA), MC/S8/13.

> [I] began the work of taking [shorthand] notes of every class, lecture, rehearsal, recording everything that Chekhov said except when I was participating in the activities themselves. The problem of transcribing and typing the notes was a greater one, because I was taking the full acting course, acting in scenes, directing student scenes, assisting in teaching new students, and as one of the directors of the Studio dealing with problems concerning its artistic and social life, being present at auditions and all meetings regarding policy. (TAITT, 1936: 6–7)

Due to her work on these transcriptions, Hurst du Prey became known affectionately as 'The Pencil'. Jonathan Pitches has pointed out that she invested care not only in gathering materials but also in cross-referencing and constructing an archive of them over the course of her life (2013: 221). Ultimately, she became an archivist of Chekhov's practice both in relation to the gathering of sources and publications (1978, 1983, 1985) and in the embodied sense as a practitioner, a gift she bequeathed later generations through the materials and her own teaching (see Figure I.2).

Significantly, Hurst du Prey's archive does not focus on the end products of the work of the Studio, for example, the productions presented to public audiences, or completed play texts; rather, it charts a complex, relational and imaginative process of pedagogy, research and experimentation. As a consequence, 'The Actor Is the Theatre' outlines the evolution of Chekhov's pedagogy and practice in dialogue with, and in response to, the work of his students, collaborators, other artists and the social issues faced at that point in the twentieth century. The way in which it documents the experiments undertaken, and the exchanges between the students undertaking various roles, Chekhov and the other artists and teachers at the Studio, creates a polyvocal record of the work. The transcripts and other materials reveal discoveries, successes, ideals and dreams, but they also show the challenges,

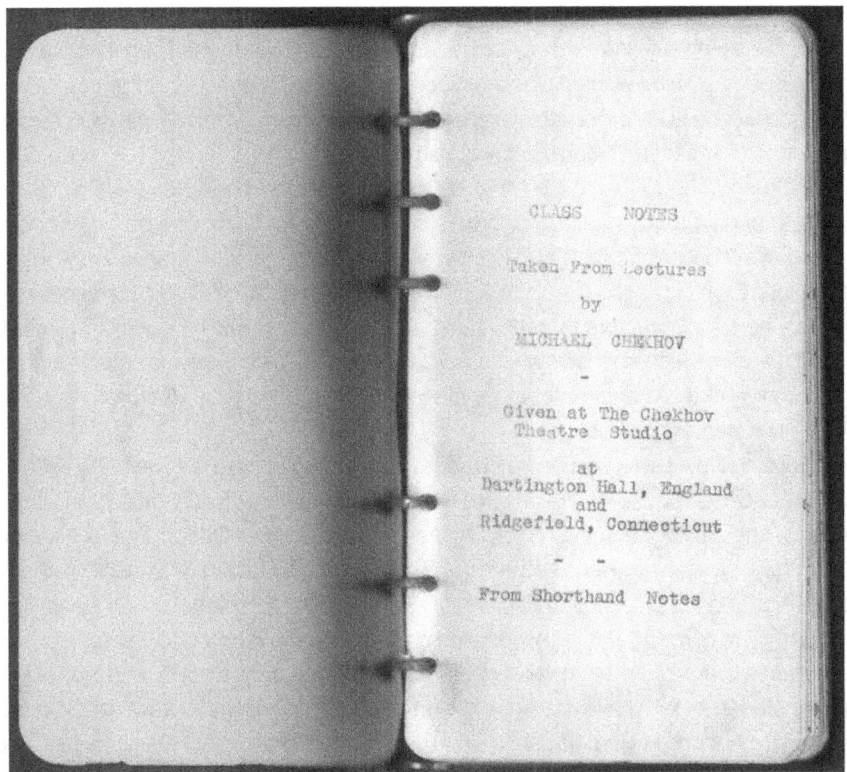

Fig. I.2 Typed front page of notebook, photograph. CTS-DHDPA, MC/S8/8.

failures and frustrations encountered by Chekhov, his students and collaborators. Indeed, the Studio was engaged in what we might now term practice research in relation to different modes and styles of performance and radically new ways of making theatre through collaborative processes. The students and teachers explored historical and contemporary theatre practices, such as *Commedia dell'Arte*, and forms of popular performance such as clowning, through practice and experimentation. In essence, the archive shares the creative, intellectual and spiritual journey undertaken by Chekhov and his collaborators.

## 2 The genesis of the New Pathways project (2013–16)

In 2011, Professor Jerri Daboo organized a symposium at Exeter University entitled 'Michael Chekhov and the Dartington Archives'.[2] This event sparked discussion and debate about what these rich archives created by Hurst du Prey of the work of the Chekhov Theatre Studio might offer contemporary practitioners and scholars and how we could make some of these important, but geographically inaccessible, materials more widely accessible. The genesis of our research project was an exchange that took place in 2012, which was followed by a series of interviews within the membership of Michael Chekhov UK (MCUK), a network of practitioners of Chekhov's work, about how it has developed and how we might explore new pathways for this practice in the future. The founding members of MCUK, Sarah Kane,

Martin Sharp and Graham Dixon, were interviewed by the younger Senior Associates, Tom Cornford, Cass Fleming and Sinéad Rushe.[3] Parts of these intergenerational conversations were published as 'The Michael Chekhov Centre UK Past, Present and Future' (Cornford, Fleming and Rushe 2013). From this exchange, the idea of the *Michael Chekhov Technique in the Twenty-First Century: New Pathways* project was born.

As Chekhov famously explained that his techniques and principles should always be explored through practice (2002) in order to achieve a certain type of '*wise body*', or embodied awareness (LTT: 23 May 1936), we knew that our research needed to be rooted in a symbiotic form of practice and scholarly work. Moreover, at the Studio, Chekhov told his trainee teachers and directors that they must not mindlessly follow his exercises but should experiment and make them their own, so we decided to follow this advice and playfully delve into the archive to try to encounter the materials in different ways in relation to our realities as twenty-first-century practitioners.

*Michael Chekhov Technique in the Twenty-First Century: New Pathways* (hereafter New Pathways) became a multi-institutional research project that involved Goldsmiths University of London, the Royal Central School of Speech and Drama, Queen Mary University of London, the University of Kent and the professional organizations Michael Chekhov UK, Bazooka Arts and the Chekhov Collective UK.[4] The lead researchers were Dr Cass Fleming and Dr Tom Cornford. All Senior Associates of MCUK were involved in the project,[5] along with a diverse team of twenty practitioners and scholars from the UK and abroad. New Pathways started in 2013 and culminated with a series of Research Events at Goldsmiths, University of London, in September 2016. The collaborative project drew on the archival material held by the Dartington Hall Trust as a creative springboard to explore new uses of the technique in the twenty-first century. The outcomes from the various different strands of the practice research form the basis of this book.

## 3 Who was Michael Chekhov?

Michael Chekhov was a Russian actor, director and teacher whose life has been discussed in a number of publications (Black 1987; Byckling 2002; Chamberlain 2004, 2010; Marowitz 2004) and in his own autobiographical writings, extracts from which were published in English as *The Path of the Actor* (2005). Chekhov originally trained and worked as an actor in Russia with Konstantin Stanislavsky, Leopold Sulerzhitsky and Evgeny Vakhtangov at the Moscow Arts Theatre and its associated studios before leaving the country to avoid arrest for being what the Soviet regime saw as a 'sick' artist because of his interest in idealist philosophy (Gordon 1985: 15). Chekhov had been one of the most acclaimed actors of the company during this period but importantly he had also established his own studio where he started to experiment with his own actor training, directing and theatre-making methods (1918–22). The development of his technique continued when he became artistic director of the MAT First Studio in 1922. After his exile from Russia in 1928, Chekhov lived and worked as an actor in theatre and film, and a director, theatre-maker and actor-trainer in Berlin, Prague, Vienna, Paris, Latvia, Lithuania and England before finally settling in the United States. Significantly for this project, Chekhov was invited, in 1935, to establish the Chekhov Theatre Studio at Dartington Hall in Devon by Beatrice Straight and Deirdre Hurst du Prey. Chekhov ran this studio between 1936 and 1938 before relocating the organization to Ridgefield, Connecticut, in the United States, in 1939 in the light of the impending war. Chekhov further developed his methods, teaching and ideas, in particular in relation to the different areas of theatre practice that this project and book explores, while he was working at Dartington Hall. In 1940, the Studio established the Chekhov Theatre Players, a touring theatre company mainly consisting of graduates from the Chekhov Theatre Studio, which presented five productions. In 1941, Chekhov opened an additional studio in New York. However, by the end of 1942 many of Chekhov's actors and students had been required to undertake military service. He closed the Studio and moved to Hollywood in 1943, where he was to act in various films and finally settle, but never taught in a studio context again. Interestingly, Chekhov started to teach professional actors in Hollywood, mostly on a part-time basis, who had been trained in diverse acting methodologies. Many of these actors worked in commercial theatre and film and subsequently his methods were to start to influence a generation of film actors, directors and teachers in the United States, and Gordon argues that '[i]ndirectly, Chekhov provided the strongest intellectual counterweight to Strasberg's much criticised Method' (1985: 17). In 1946 he restaged *The Government Inspector* for the Lab Theatre, and this was the last production he directed. After a second heart attack in 1954 he gave up acting but continued to teach, lecture and mentor artists until his death in 1955.

In addition to the influence of his early teachers and collaborators in Russia, Chekhov was also influenced by the work of François Delsarte, Émile Jaques-Dalcroze, Max Reinhardt, Rudolf Steiner and Uday Shankar, along with his close longer-term collaborators and the other artists who worked at Dartington Hall. Chekhov argued that artists 'have the freedom to make the most of the best in all techniques' and claimed that this approach only required 'a little wisdom, imagination and courageous experimentation' (1963: 48). His experiments led to the evolution of a technique that was indeed courageous and highly imaginative in the early years of the twentieth century and remains so now.

## 4 What is Chekhov technique?

Chekhov's techniques make up a holistic and synthetic approach built on a number of key principles, briefly outlined here and discussed in more detail later in this book, and a wide range of imaginative methods that can be used in myriad ways. Chekhov described his approach to acting as fundamentally psychophysical,[6] in that it is based on a model of an integrated body and mind. His techniques creatively explore the constant interplay between an actor's body and psychology, clearly indicating an opposition to the Cartesian, dualistic perspective that still dominated during his lifetime.[7] More specifically, his techniques were based in the development of the actor's 'embodied imagination' (Daboo 2007). Consequently, imaginative movement is the core of the practice (Petit 2010: 5). Unlike Stanislavsky in his early years, Chekhov refused to use the actor's personal emotional memories and in contrast developed what he termed objective techniques that indirectly stir the actor's inner life through a playful and rigorous awakening of the embodied imagination (Chekhov 2002) (see Figure I.3). Chekhov considered this form of embodied imagination equal to intellectual and analytical thought, and his approach is based on the belief that this multidimensional

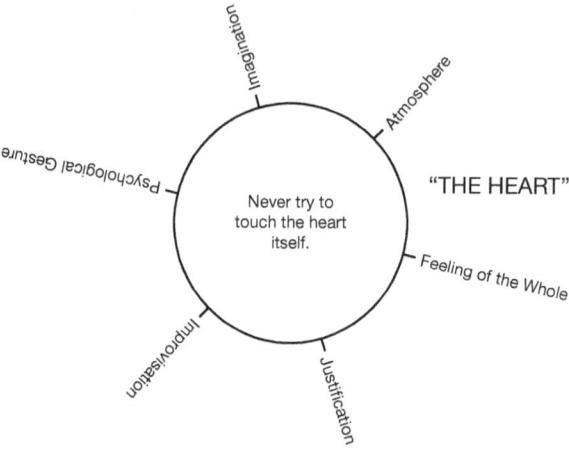

Fig. I.3 'Never try to touch the heart itself', diagram. TAITT: 12 July 1937, CTS-DHDPA.

embodied self is a medium of creative learning, knowledge and wisdom in its own right (Chekhov 2002). These methods therefore provide a radical contrast to acting techniques that he believed were overly dependent on 'dry' analytic thought (Chekhov 2002: 25), that is, practices which foreground an analytic and highly intellectual understanding of the text. Although Chekhov's practice does not disallow analytic thinking, he argues that it is better to delay its use until later in the process to ensure that it does not dominate.

Chekhov's techniques seek to facilitate a creative transformation of the actor, and he explicitly sought to free actors from their everyday sense of self by encouraging them to engage with their characters as distinctly other to themselves. Indeed he argues: 'It is a crime to chain and imprison the actor within the limits of his so-called "personality"' (2002: 27). His methods include the **psychological gesture, archetypes** and **qualities of movement, rhythm, images, imaginary body, imaginary centres,** dynamics, **polarity, directions in space** and **atmosphere**. All of the techniques are rooted in the principles of concentration and improvisation, are both playful and pleasurable and should embody what Chekhov terms the **four brothers (the senses of ease, wholeness or entirety, form and beauty)**. **Improvisation** as a fundamental principle not only underpins the training exercises but is also the key to the creation of performance material and is retained in public performance. Actors were encouraged to develop the 'psychology of an improvising actor' (2002: 4). They also sought to develop what Chekhov termed a **divided consciousness** at later stages of exploration or in a rehearsal process (1991: 155), when an actor has the ability to be fully engaged within their performance and to have empathy for, and deep connection with, their character, but also retain a level of distance so that they can 'see' and 'direct' their performance from the outside and see the production as a whole (2005: 147)[8].

Chekhov's practice also draws on the energetic,[9] relational, ethical and spiritual dimensions of what Phelim McDermott has described as 'Embodied Theatre' in which the 'performance also has a relationship beyond its own body-in-the-space and is in energetic dialogue with other performers, the design environment and light, and the audience' (2007: 204–7). McDermott argues that, in this type of practice, the 'whole energy field is a system in constant flux as it relates to itself and organises the system of emotions, impulses, intellect and storytelling' (2007: 204–7). Chekhov explains that many of his techniques are 'intangible' in that they may work with these types of energetic dialogues and imaginative processes and impulses but that once the actor has incorporated them in their embodied imagination, they bring about very tangible results in training and performance.

Chekhov's approach is renowned for being actor-centred, challenging the opinion that the actor exists merely to service the director's interpretation of the playwright's vision. Chekhov placed the actors at the centre of the creative process and provocatively claimed that '[t]he director, the stage designer, etc., are all accessories, but the actor is the theatre' (1985: 158). At the first class of the Chekhov Theatre Studio at Dartington, he spoke to his new students about this, stating, *'We aim to be actors and more than actors – artists'* (TAITT, 5 October 1936). This far-reaching perspective led to his use of collaborative working practices that were extremely progressive in the early decades of the twentieth century. He sought to give actors artistic freedom in order to help them develop what he termed their **creative individuality**. Chekhov's techniques were also rooted in, and dependent on, ensemble practice (Chamberlain 2013) and the notion of making **contact** with an audience. The techniques are flexible and holistic, in that each component can be seen to trigger other aspects of the method. It is also significant that Chekhov wrote a handbook for actors at a time when no other 'master' teacher or director had done so (Chamberlain 2004: 35). Nonetheless, in contrast to many of the acting teachers and directors in the early and mid-twentieth century, Chekhov was flexible about the way in which students used his techniques and indeed urged them to use any of the methods that resonated with them (1992). He also encouraged students to play with his techniques and invent new versions of his exercises for themselves once they had learnt those that he had outlined (2002). It is also important to note that none of Chekhov's methods were constricted by, or designed for, the rigid limitations of naturalistic theatre, and he embraced the theatrical aspects of performance, seeking to creatively explore the notion of style and form (Callow 2002). This was reflected in the wide selection of genres and types of performance that Chekhov used to teach the students at the Chekhov Theatre Studio and the fact that in addition to using pre-existing play scripts he also worked with sketches and scenarios, and devised original material. His creative methods and principles are therefore highly relevant for contemporary actors and can be used in various different modes and genres of performance, ranging from classical and contemporary text-based theatre to immersive performance, embodied performance, clowning and solo performance. They are also used in film and television.

## 5 Why do we need new pathways?

Since the late 1980s, interest in Michael Chekhov's technique has grown rapidly in the UK and internationally, and it has been recognized for its innovation and accessibility. Exploration of Chekhov's methods have primarily been limited to acting and actor training practice in the twentieth century, the development and use of which were well documented by him (Chekhov 1936, 1983a and b, 1985, 1991, 1992, 2002, 2005; Chekhov and Leonard 1963), his associates, his former students, and various scholars in Russia, the United States, United Kingdom, Canada, Finland and Israel. There have also been important preliminary explorations of other uses of Chekhov's techniques in practice around the world, some of which have been discussed in publications (Chamberlain 2004, 2010; McCaw and McDermott 2005; Pitches 2013; Bennett, L. 2013; Bennett, S.M. 2013; Rushe 2013). However, we felt that such explorations needed to be taken further and new avenues explored. Therefore, this project created a network of professionals, practitioners and scholars from various disciplines in the UK and overseas to investigate new uses of Chekhov's methods both within and beyond the theatre in the twenty-first century.

In addition to being taught and represented in Britain by three main professional organizations (MCUK, Michael Chekhov Studio London and Performing Arts International),[10] over the past twenty-five years, the technique has also been introduced as a practical methodology by a rapidly growing number of conservatoires and university drama departments. In 2013 the National Theatre Studio invited Cass Fleming to train, for the first time, directors in Chekhov technique. This was followed by a lecture and later a workshop for the directors in the Directors' Programme at the Young Vic Theatre in 2016. Sinéad Rushe also worked with directors and theatre-makers for Theatre Monkey in 2016. This growth of interest has been mirrored in academia, and consequently there is a growing body of literature in the field. Ashperger (2008) published an important survey of practice by the Michael Chekhov Association (MICHA) faculty in the twenty-first century, but it focuses primarily on acting teachers in the North American context and does not address practices in the UK. Daboo's (2012) analysis of the pathways and exchanges through which Chekhov's lineage has been used, developed and transformed since his death is particularly useful in an international context and will be considered in detail later in this introduction. She discusses the contrast between the embodied modes of teaching and cross-fertilization in the web of practices in North America and the very different forms of transmission in Britain, which she notes is 'one of fracturing and divergence and re-making' (2012: 80). A central aim of this project, therefore, is to explore Chekhov technique within the divergent and remade contemporary British context (2012: 80). Unlike these publications, and the valuable *Routledge Companion to Michael Chekhov* edited by Autant-Mathieu and Meerzon (2015), all of which are predominantly historical, this book, although drawing on a historical archive, is predominantly forward-looking, forging connections between practitioners and researchers with a view to generating new and innovative approaches to understanding and using Chekhov's techniques in the future.

## 6 Dartington Hall and the Chekhov Theatre Studio

The significance of the archival material has been acknowledged and reproduced in important but limited contexts (Chamberlain 2004; Daboo 2012; Kirillov and Chamberlain 2013; Pitches 2013),[11] but it remains inaccessible to a wider audience, and research has not thus far considered its application to contemporary theatre-making, areas of performer training other than acting, or therapeutic and social fields that extend beyond the theatre. This project aimed to gather and share archival material among the various researchers and participants involved with the network, dynamically exploring how the materials could be used, interrogated and transformed in fields outside of conventional actor training. This publication reproduces the selected clusters of archival and other harder-to-access materials that were used in the project.

A discussion of the socio-historic and artistic background of Dartington Hall is needed to place the archive in a broader context. Dorothy and Leonard Elmhirst founded the Dartington Hall community and project in 1925. To do this, they purchased and restored a derelict medieval hall and estate outside of Totnes in Devon. Leonard Elmhirst had previously been inspired by, and worked with, the Indian writer, progressive educationalist and artist Rabindranath Tagore, who had founded an experimental school linked to an ashram in Santiniketan (1901) and later a university, Visva-Bharati (1917), in the same area. The two men had set up the Institute for Rural Reconstruction in India in 1921. Dorothy Elmhirst was also deeply committed to progressive pedagogy, and after attending lectures by John Dewey, she sent her children to his experimental school in New York. She also built a relationship with Nellie Cornish, founder of the Cornish School of the Arts in Seattle, who was later to send a teacher to work at Dartington Hall. In 1926, Dorothy and Leonard, encouraged by Tagore, established Dartington Hall to build a self-supporting rural community bringing together artists, teachers, students, craftspeople and farmers. They aimed to explore new projects, ideas, pedagogy and forms of living for the betterment of society. It was a radical educational and social experiment that was to have considerable impact in Britain, although only some years after the experimented ended.[12] Daboo has described Dartington Hall as 'a translated model of Tagore's ideas of the ashram, but placed in the English countryside' (2015: 283). She also notes that in addition to the creative relationship between the Elmhirsts and Tagore, the Indian dance practitioner Uday Shankar spent time and presented work at Dartington, and that this represents an early form of intercultural exchange, in both directions, which was to also influence Chekhov's practice (285).

Dorothy Elmhirst's daughter, Beatrice Straight, and her companion Deirdre Hurst du Prey (who had previously trained at the Cornish School and the School of Dance-Mime at Dartington Hall), had been searching for a practitioner who could establish a theatre training school at Dartington. On the recommendation of one of Chekhov's former collaborators, Georgette Boner (Black 1987: 27), the two women saw Chekhov perform in New York and recommended him to Dorothy and Leonard Elmhirst. They were similarly impressed with his work and offered Chekhov the post. In 1935 he moved to England, opening the Chekhov Theatre Studio at Dartington in the autumn of 1936. Daboo argues that the work of the Chekhov Theatre Studio was 'a remarkable and virtually unique example of an attempt at establishing a residential actor-training centre in Britain' (2012: 62). Moreover, by the time that Chekhov opened his Studio, Dartington Hall had become a home to an extraordinary community of artists, educationalists and agriculturalists from different parts of the world. The Elmhirsts had given refuge to many performance artists who had fled from Nazi rule. The community also included visual artists and Uday Shankar's company on their frequent visits. Daboo (2012) and Cornford (2013) discuss in detail the way in which Dartington Hall facilitated a dynamic series of exchanges of practice and ideas during this time. Chekhov's students worked directly with Mark Tobey and Willi Soukoup in painting and drawing, and with Bernard Leach, the potter. They also had classes in movement with Lisa Ullman, Kurt Jooss and Sigurd Leeder (all of whom worked with Rudolf Laban, who was also at Dartington) (MC/S4/19/F) and the musician Hans Oppenheim. These interchanges also worked in the other direction, and Autant-Mathieu and Meerzon point out that the dancers Ullman and Leeder participated in Chekhov's acting classes (2015: 16), representing a crucial crossover of interdisciplinary practice. Daboo notes that this work at Dartington was in stark contrast to the actor training in Britain at that time, which 'tended to be very conventional, and geared towards producing a good solo actor, rather than an ensemble' (Daboo 2012: 66). The Studio opened on 5 October 1936 with a cohort of twenty to twenty-five students from America, Australia, Britain, Canada, New Zealand and students who had previously worked with Chekhov in Latvia.[13]

Despite Chekhov's Moscow Art Theatre background, his Studio received little attention from the British theatre community (see Daboo 2012; Chamberlain 2015). However, regardless of the establishment's lack of interest in the Studio, tucked away outside Totnes, Chekhov and his collaborators were carrying out innovative and revolutionary experiments. They were, in fact, exploring his principles and methods in relation to a wide range of theatre-making areas, in addition to actor training, and were often not working with pre-existing dramatic texts. He specifically sought to use and develop his techniques in close collaboration with playwrights, artists and designers who would work as part of an ensemble in distinctly alternative ways. He had hoped to create a touring company with the actors he trained. His proposals for this type of collaboration and shared ownership of work were radical during his lifetime, and we believe contain the potential to remain so in the context of contemporary practice both within and beyond the theatre in the twenty-first century.

# 7 The research project – seeking new pathways

## 7.1 The research questions

The central research question we posed in this project was: how can Chekhov's techniques be used in contexts other than actor training designed for the interpretation of existing dramatic literature in a twenty-first-century context? This overarching research question was split into five key areas:

1. Chekhov Technique: Processes of Theatre-Making. Exploring the possible uses of the techniques in devised theatre-making, in systems of catalyst direction and for collaborative writing practices.
2. Chekhov Technique: Beyond Acting. Considering the possible uses of the techniques for the training of performers in voice, singing, dance, actor-movement and for theatre designers.
3. Chekhov Technique: Beyond the Theatre. Experimenting with the possible uses of the techniques for applied theatre, therapeutic and community contexts.
4. Chekhov Technique: Cross-Currents. Investigating what new uses of Chekhov's techniques and approach are developing in other parts of the world and facilitating ways to share experiments and findings with international partners.
5. Chekhov Technique: Past, Present and Future. Identifying ways that practitioners and scholars can use archival materials as a living and creative archive.

Uses of Chekhov technique in relation to devised and writing processes of theatre-making, and the related forms of collaborative practice and models of what we are terming catalyst direction, are of central significance not only in a historical context of Chekhov's practice (see Chamberlain 2004) but also in the context of current practice, as these processes are now at the forefront of contemporary theatre-making in Britain and other parts of the world. Similarly, while Chekhov technique is now being used internationally for the training of actors, what these methods might offer voice, movement and dance training as a holistic and integrated practice is only just starting to be considered. Recent publications (Bennett, L. 2013; Bennett, S.M. 2013; Langman 2014; Haffner 2017) have identified this as an area worthy of further multidisciplinary consideration and interaction. What Chekhov's highly visual and spatial techniques offer to contemporary theatre design, and the growing interest in the use of non-theatrical spaces for site-specific or immersive performance, remains largely unexplored. Sinéad Rushe wrote about her directorial collaboration with a designer previously (2013) but has now written about the uses of Chekhov's techniques more fully in this publication. Chekhov's methods are rarely included in applied theatre-makers' or drama therapists' 'toolkits' yet they are particularly helpful, as they are fundamentally actor/participant-centred, experiential and holistic, and the systems of characterization are not based on participants' personal emotion memory. Concurrently, the possibility of using these techniques in a non-theatrical therapeutic context is starting to be explored by drama therapists, therapists and applied theatre practitioners and holds considerable potential, but had not been considered in detail, with the exception of Marjolein Baars's publications on its use in relation to dementia care in the Netherlands (Baars, Frayman, and Gener 2012; Baars 2016). There is a distinct need for innovative interaction between the areas of performer training and sociocultural and therapeutic practices in this respect, and this project was designed to enable a dynamic exchange across these disciplinary boundaries in order to increase understanding and the sharing of techniques. We therefore decided to connect a range of participants from different fields to explore innovative possibilities together, as a network of practitioners and scholars in Britain and the world. Concurrently, there was a need to survey and analyse these new pathways and issues in an international context. For example, there are practitioners working in other parts of the world that are using Chekhov's techniques in areas other than actor training and we sought to engage in dialogue with them.

A related aim of the project was to extend and diversify the existing Chekhov community by reaching out to new groups of practitioners from different disciplines. Consequently, the project was designed to offer free and inclusive events to a range of participants who had little or no prior experience of Chekhov's techniques as well as an introductory workshop for non-actors at the start of the events. The series enabled participants from different fields (e.g. therapists, theatre designers or teachers of voice) to try a methodology that was new to them and not included in training and provision in their disciplines. At the same time, we hoped that these exchanges with newcomers to the technique, from different disciplines, would help us interrogate the methods in innovative ways and help us consider the potential for further cross-fertilization with other methods and approaches in the future. We wanted to know what this wider group of practitioners felt held potential in their respective professional disciplines, and why. Lastly, we sought to identify a number of strands of this project to take further beyond the life of the New Pathways research project.

Concurrently, we realized that this collaborative project required the development of a new practice research methodology that worked symbiotically with scholarly writing and would allow for the polyvocality inherent in this project. This led to the development of this book with Bloomsbury Methuen's support and represents an exciting development in this field.

## 8 How we explored the new pathways

The research team was comprised of a group of scholars, researchers, therapists, clinicians, social/applied practitioners, theatre practitioners, designers and pedagogues, who explored, interrogated and valorized Chekhov's work in a twenty-first-century context. There were six central strands to the practice research addressing the use of Chekhov's techniques and principles, led by the following practitioners,[14] which explored the following areas:

1. Chekhov Technique for Devised Theatre and Catalyst Direction led by Dr Cass Fleming with Dr Roanna Mitchell and members of the Chekhov Collective UK.
2. Chekhov Technique for Collaborative Writing led by Dr Tom Cornford with Dr Hannah Davies, playwright.
3. Chekhov Technique for Voice Training and Singing led by Daron Oram, with John Gillett and Christina Gutekunst.
4. Chekhov Technique for Actor-Movement and Dance led by Dr Roanna Mitchell with Juliet Chambers.
5. Chekhov Technique for Theatre Design led by Sinéad Rushe with Aldona Cunningham.
6. Chekhov Technique in Applied, Therapeutic and Community Contexts led by Professor Caoimhe McAvinchey with Zoe Brook and Martin Sharp.

Each strand of the project drew on the archival materials and explored how they could be used in new and innovative ways in relation to different contemporary practices. The first two strands were longer-term practice research projects, conducted through sustained creative engagement with the approaches and concepts discovered in the archive, whereas the others took a more focused approach to exploring this material in workshops and discussions with practitioners. We explored the rich possibilities the technique offered to the new pathways but also reflected on the problems we faced when we used Chekhov techniques, and the archival materials, in our diverse areas. This involved an open consideration of the shortcomings of specific techniques and the sociocultural contexts that they were developed within and the challenges of adapting them to our current work. Consequently, we explored how we might reconsider, interrogate and develop Chekhov's metaphors and use of language in a way that stayed true to his principles and methods but engaged with contemporary perspectives and critical frames as well as the needs of the different disciplines represented in the project.

There were two phases of the New Pathways project. The first involved archival work to build a shared resource, practice research and early outreach events for practitioners from various fields. Phase two of the project led to a three-day public research event for 120 participants at Goldsmiths, University of London, in 2016. The first day of these events began with a workshop titled Chekhov Technique for Non-Actors led by Graham Dixon and Julia Krynke.[15] Practitioners working in a wide range of disciplines, including therapeutic practice, applied theatre and design, attended this session. It was fitting that Dixon's session launched the New Pathways research event, as he has taught each of the authors of this book over the past fifteen years and mentored Cornford, Fleming and Rushe. A Sharing of Practice Research carried out in relation to the two longer strands of the project was offered in the evening. Dr Tom Cornford presented on his collaboration with playwright Dr Hannah Davies that led to their adaptation of Dostoyevsky's *Demons* (2015), in response to the Chekhov Theatre Studio's version, *The Possessed* (1939). Dr Cass Fleming and the Chekhov Collective UK presented research and development material on Antoine de Saint-Exupéry's *The Little Prince* (1943), drawing directly on archival materials in relation to devised theatre-making and catalyst direction. The six strands of research were shared and explored in the praxis symposium sessions that took place over the following two days. These six strands of research, and the related praxis symposium sessions, are discussed in the main body of this book.

The afternoon of the last day included a plenary chaired by Fleming and two short papers by Brook and Mitchell, the contents of which are covered in Chapters 4 and 6 of this publication. Two Academic Auditors, Professor Franc Chamberlain and Professor Caoimhe McAvinchey, gave feedback on the events held over the three days.[16] Chamberlain's seminal publications (2004, 2010) represented the first wave of UK scholarship on Chekhov and have been a very significant resource for all of the authors of this book. He talked about his involvement in the remaking of a network of Chekhov practitioners and scholars since the early 1990s, and about the fact that he, Dixon and Sharp represented an embodied through line from this early cycle to the present day. Chamberlain noted that the older generation had held similar events to New Pathways and that these cycles of engagement and networking were organically growing the Chekhov community in the UK over time. For Chamberlain, the notion of the spirit and questions of spirituality in Chekhov's work remain significant, and he discussed this in relation to a number of the symposia. He reflected on the way in which Chekhov engages the spirit in his practice and writing, a term often seemingly replaceable by 'idea', but which Chamberlain considered particularly helpful as it combines imagination, embodied experience and intellect in the service of a higher purpose for art. McAvinchey fed back that she felt the research project had met its aims and had been exceptionally generous and generative. She argued that events being free of charge and accessible to practitioners from different fields, many of whom had not encountered Chekhov's techniques before, had been crucial. She applauded the event's embodiment of the principles of contact and generosity that Chekhov's techniques and principles nurture and advocate. McAvinchey felt that the collaborative nature of the project, involving a large group of practitioners and organizations working in partnership, and the fact that it was made widely accessible, pushed back against the neoliberal ideology that dominates higher education in Britain today. In this sense, she felt it was an important project and a model of practice research, outreach and knowledge exchange.

On the afternoon of the third day, there was a series of valuable international exchanges, chaired by Gretchen Egolf.[17] We were fortunate to have Ulrich Meyer-Horsch, co-founder of Michael Chekhov Europe (MCE) and a faculty member of MICHA, deliver a short paper about his work in person at the event. This was followed by Joanna Merlin, president of Michael Chekhov Association (MICHA), and her colleagues Ragnar Friedank in the United States and Marjolein Baars in Holland, who discussed via Skype their work and experiences of using Chekov's methods in new contexts. While these exchanges did not represent a comprehensive survey of the work of Chekhov techniques in new areas in the rest of the world, it offered us four important snapshots of current practice. These exchanges have gone on to build stronger and more diverse international links among the Chekhov community around the world since the end of the New Pathways project and paved the way for more partnership in the future. The contributions made by Meyer-Horsch, Merlin, Baars and Friedank are addressed in the conclusion to this volume. These formal events were framed by informal networking over lunches, viewing the archival materials presented in an exhibition and social events in the evenings. It was an exciting, provocative and creative three days and has led to further training, research and networking in the UK and beyond.

## 9 Past, present and future: The remaking of Chekhov's techniques

To contextualize the project further, it is necessary to return to Daboo's claim that the British lineage of Chekhov practice is one of fracturing, divergence and remaking (2012). There was a clear break in the lineage of Chekhov technique in Britain after 1938 largely because Chekhov's students and close collaborators moved with him to America, taking their expertise in the technique with them. After the closure of his Studio, Chekhov continued to teach artists in the United States, thereby growing the North American community of artists and teachers up until his death in 1955. However, at the time of his death – and for the subsequent forty years – his techniques were not widely known. Hurst du Prey, Straight and Blair Cutting had been awarded teacher's certificates, but only Cutting taught continuously following Chekhov's death (Citron 1983). Hurst du Prey, Straight and three American students of Chekhov (Mala Powers, Joanna Merlin and Jack Colvin) were using Chekhov's techniques in their professional work but were not consistently teaching the methods. Consequently, there was a gap in the training available in the 1960s and 1970s (Citron 1983; Daboo 2012). Beatrice Straight launched a studio in New York in 1980 with Deirdre Hurst du Prey, Blair Cutting, Felicity Mason, Eleanor Faison and Mel Gordon, and although it closed a decade later, it served as a training ground for a new generation of practitioners who would go on to teach Chekhov's work in the 1990s and beyond.

Daboo considers the 're-membering' and 're-making' of the Chekhov tradition in Britain in contrast to the North American context and argues that 'there was no continuous transmission of the work in Britain in the aftermath of the Studio. In fact, there is nearly a fifty-year gap from the end of the Studio until a resurgence of interest in his work in 1989 as a result of the effort of a former student [Felicity Mason]' (2012: 62). In Sharp's documentary film *Michael Chekhov: The Dartington Years* (2002), Paul Rogers, the only actor associated with the Studio who continued to work professionally in Britain after its closure, explains to Sharp that he did not fully understand all the components of the training during his time with the Studio, and that he decided not to tell theatre professionals in Britain about his early training with Chekhov. Rogers did, however, later emphasise the significance of Chekhov's work for his practice (Daboo 2012). Daboo argues that this reticence to talk about his early training reflects the 'way in which Chekhov was regarded with suspicion by the mainstream theatre world in London, and also the distrust of "foreign" teachers and approaches to acting, whilst contradictorily revering the Russian masters' (2012: 75). As a result of this, Chekhov's work was largely unknown in Britain for many years after his departure.[18] Daboo explains that the resurgence of interest in his practice happened through the 'drawing together threads from different parts of the world', and she argues that this 'raises questions about the notions of 'lineage' and 'tradition' within forms of actor training' (76).

In 1988 Graham Dixon, who had trained with Alice Crowther (the voice teacher at the Chekhov Theatre Studio at Dartington) in his native Australia, moved to London. At the same time Sarah Kane, who had been introduced to Chekhov's work and Steiner's Speech Formation in Germany and Switzerland, returned to England. Dixon and Kane became two of the principal teachers of Chekhov technique in Britain and have between them taught a new generation of practitioners in Britain. The workshop held by Felicity Mason[19] in 1989 is what 'truly began the revitalization of interest in Chekhov's work in Britain' (Daboo 2012: 78) and was attended by a number of former Dartington Studio students, including Hurst du Prey and Rogers. This was followed by another event on Chekhov's work organized by Sarah Kane and held at Emerson College in 1994.[20] Also attending this event were Franc Chamberlain, Bella Merlin and Martin Sharp, who had all first encountered the techniques through publications by Chekhov and who were to become key figures in the creative remaking of the lineage in Britain. Shortly after this event at Emerson College, Sarah Kane and Martin Sharp founded the Michael Chekhov Centre UK in 1995 (now MCUK), with Graham Dixon joining shortly after and opening the Michael Chekhov Studio London in 2003. In 2005 there was a second conference held at Dartington Hall, and in 2006 Chekhov's work featured heavily at a conference held at Exeter University.[21] A number of theatre practitioners in the UK, including Phelim McDermott of Improbable Theatre and some of the authors of this publication, initially encountered the techniques through Chekhov's publications that were available in the 1980s and 1990s. Simon Callow and other actors were also using the technique in their professional work.

This reconfigured British lineage is diverse and, as Daboo points out, the techniques are being used in different ways due to the broken, and reinvented, forms of transmission. For example, a large number of British practitioners blend Chekhov's technique with other methods, as do teachers based in other parts of the world. This includes Bella Merlin, Phelim McDermott and John Wright. Merlin explains: 'I don't adhere to any one theorist or practitioner, I use whatever might provoke my imagination at the time – Meisner, Chekhov, Stanislavsky, Knebel, Adler, Hagen, Brecht, Grotowski' (Daboo 2012: 82). Daboo notes that this has led to debate within the community 'as to ideas of "authenticity" and "purity" and the "correct" way to do his exercises' (2012: 80) and argues:

> The notion of 'tradition' is likewise problematic as this tends to imply a fixed object, rather than a fluid and changing form. This can also be applied to the sense of 'authenticity' in a practice. [. . .] The idea of 'authenticity' can create a conflict between the belief in a fixed and unchanging way of doing an exercise, and the process of fluidity and change which tends to be the experience of those who are actually working with or teaching the exercise. (80–1)

Like Daboo, we believe that the sense of lineage has been continued in a fluid and creative way in the British context. While Merlin's list of techniques that she draws on may be a broader mix than that used by the authors of this book, we do all draw on other methods in addition to Chekhov's approach, to a greater or lesser degree, as either a complementary approach or as a blend. Even when our work is primarily based in Chekhov technique we arguably carry embodied traces of aspects of our previous training and cultural practices within us. A number of the practitioners featured in this book bring with them training in different fields, such as therapeutic practice, design and dance, and this inevitably means that they are blending different approaches with their use of Chekhov's methods. We also need to remember that Chekhov clearly gives us licence to use the exercises that resonate with us, to invent our own versions of his exercises, and to stay responsive and in the moment in relation to the people and contexts we work in. Moreover, he insists that the work has to engage with the social reality that we are living in. '*The [Studio's] aim must be to find the connection to the whole world around us. [. . .] We are working for humanity and for society. [. . .] It means nothing to be an egotistical group. We will discover how to be useful to society, and we will grow in this way*' (TAITT: 1 February 1937). Our research into the archive materials, and other sources, demonstrated that Chekhov was deeply concerned with the potential of theatre as a social medium, an art form in which societies can debate urgent questions and begin the process of remodelling themselves. The authors in this publication feel that this social engagement in the twenty-first century now includes an active exploration of questions of identity, culture and politics along with the specific needs of the participants and places in which we work. Sharp suggests that the British 'lineage has been carried as an imaginative future, a projected image', and Daboo argues that 'there is an opportunity to see glimpses of this lineage embodied in its own terms in British theatre today' (2012: 83). This project and book therefore seeks to pull back this curtain to reveal this lineage and to explore these different imaginative futures.

Since 1990 the Chekhov lineage has been maintained and grown in the United States and other parts of Europe and Israel. In 1992 Joerg Andrees and Jobst Langhams hosted an important conference and workshops in Berlin designed to forge an international Chekhov community.[22] This was followed by workshops and events in Russia, in the UK and Berlin. In the 1990s Mala Powers, Lisa Dalton and Wil Kilroy took over the helm of the International Michael Chekhov Workshop and later founded the National Michael Chekhov Association in the United States. In 1999, Joanna Merlin, one of Chekhov's American students, co-founded MICHA in the United States with Sarah Kane and other younger generation artists and teachers: Fern Sloan, Ted Pugh, Lenard Petit and Jessica Cerullo. Joanna Merlin is President of MICHA and Jessica Cerullo is Artistic Director. They have a large faculty, and since 1999 they have led comprehensive workshops and teacher training programmes with participants attending from different parts of the world.[23] MICHA students and faculty have also formed organizations in other parts of the United States and around the world, including Michael Chekhov Europe (2008), Michael Chekhov Brazil (2010) and Michael Chekhov Canada (2012). MICHA faculty Fern Sloan and Ted Pugh also established the Chekhov-based company, The Actors' Ensemble New York in 1985. In 2018 MICHA held a retreat for Chekhov teachers around the world, and the countries represented included Australia, Brazil, Canada, Croatia, Denmark, England, Finland, Germany, Ireland, Israel, Italy, Japan, Netherlands, Portugal, Spain, Switzerland, Taiwan, Turkey, Uruguay and the United States. Cass Fleming, Roanna Mitchell and Gretchen Egolf represented England at this event and shared some of the outcomes of this project.

A vibrant and committed network of actors and teachers supported Chekhov's work during his life, and after his death, in different parts of the world. This included an important matriarchy of women, comprising Georgette Boner, Margareta Morgenstern, Deirdre Hurst du Prey, Beatrice Straight, Dorothy Elmhirst, Alice Crowther, Felicity Mason, Mala Powers, Joanna Merlin, Fern Sloan, Sarah Kane, Lisa Dalton and now Marjolein Baars, Jessica Cerullo and Kim Lane. In addition, two among the first wave of academics to address the work of Chekhov were women: Nancy Kindelan, whose presence is felt in the archive through various materials and her draft PhD thesis (1977), and Liisa Byckling, who has published on Chekhov, mainly in Russian. Between them, this Chekhov matriarchy financed his theatre productions and studios, supported publications of his books (and often helped to edit his material in German and English), built the archive of his work, published his recorded lectures and autobiographies, and established workshops and studios that teach his techniques and promote his work to new generations of students. In Russia, two other women played an important part in this matriarchy: Maria Knebel and Professor Marina Ivanova. Knebel committed to keeping the legacy of Chekhov, her former teacher, alive despite the Soviet government's attempts to eradicate his work and influence after he left his home country. Carnicke explains that in the last decade of her life Knebel worked hard to 'collect and edit Chekhov's books, manuscripts, and letters' and despite the heavy censorship of the resultant Russian publication in 1986, 'finally brought Chekhov home' (2015: 201). Professor Ivanova generously shared her knowledge and materials at the early conferences and for the publication of Chekhov's autobiography (2005: xi). There were a number of key male practitioners who were also crucial to this legacy and work around the world, but it is noticeable that this network of women became the central custodians of Chekhov's legacy and the innovators of new developments in the twentieth century, enabling new generations of practitioners to engage with his techniques and principles.

## 10 Past, present and future: The archive

In addition to detailing the classes and exercises delivered by Chekhov at Dartington Hall, the typed transcripts that make up 'The Actor Is the Theatre' also provide information on a wide range of collaborative projects (many of which were forms of early devised theatre), discussions held, questions posed, discoveries made and sociopolitical discussions about world events, the impending war and the role of theatre in society. The archive holds an outline of the syllabus, documents relating to class timetables and other valuable teaching resources. Hurst du Prey's archive also holds boxes of play scripts, including original devised pieces written by Chekhov and his collaborators as well as rehearsal notes for the Studio productions and the Chekhov Theatre Players written by various different people. The detailed cross-cultural Fairy Tale and Folklore files held in the archive were gathered by the Fairy Tale Committee that Chekhov established at Dartington Hall. The archive also holds various drafts of Chekhov's book *To the Actor: On the Technique of Acting*, which he had begun at Dartington and finished in 1942 (although this was not published in English until 1953), and cassettes of recorded lessons and interviews undertaken by Hurst du Prey with Chekhov's students. Also included is an important history of Hurst du Prey's work – 'The Pencil' – by Diane Caracciolo (1999) which forms the introduction to archive itself. The other records include photographs, props, costumes, costume designs by Chekhov and Mstislav Dobujinsky, and rehearsal diagrams. There is also Hurst du Prey's correspondence and personal reflections along with documents from former students. The general files also contain a mixture of original correspondence with Chekhov, records from the Chekhov Theatre Studio and some from the Michael Chekhov Studio founded in New York after his death. There are also press cuttings, course prospectuses and playbills.

Chekhov's decision to train Hurst du Prey and Straight as his teaching assistants and trainee directors at the Studio was also to become a crucial aspect of their work and creates a double layer of materials and readings in the archival sources. In the spring of 1936, Chekhov delivered a series of eighteen classes referred to as *Lessons to Teachers* specifically for Hurst du Prey and Straight and these form the first part of 'The Actor Is the Theatre' archive. These lessons were designed to train Hurst du Prey and Straight as teachers, although it is evident that their training continued during the lifespan of the Studio. As Jessica Cerullo has astutely noted, these lessons 'are organized and idyllic insofar as they are grounded in Chekhov's past experiences, with him entirely unaware of the unique challenges that would follow once the Dartington cohort arrived' (2018: xv), and she cites Straight, who explains that in practice he 'searched and worked with [his students], exchanging ideas, and changing with us . . . we all grew in the process' (xvi). These early lessons for teachers are arguably better understood in relation to the subsequent classes and specific theatre-making projects, and the associated approach to making and directing, that were developed during the life of the Studio. While Straight and Hurst du Prey were new to Chekhov's techniques, it is important to note that they both brought with them previous training and experience. For example, Hurst du Prey had already trained with at the Cornish School with Mary Wigman, worked with Martha Graham and had been a student at The School of Dance-Mime at Dartington Hall prior to joining Chekhov's Studio. Her early exposure to expressive gesture and embodied performance were undoubtedly important in terms of what she brought to her training and work with Chekhov, and Roanna Mitchell's chapter in this book discusses this in more detail.

This collection of different materials reveals a fascinating insight into Chekhov's processes and principles of pedagogy, and what is clear is that many aspects of his approach and teaching strategies also work as key components of his collaborative theatre-making and directorial methods. This is not to disregard the difference between the roles of pedagogue and actor, director, writer or designer, but to recognize a level of overlap in the use of the methods and guidance. Moreover, his pedagogic, social and spiritual philosophy also underpinned their experimental processes of theatre-making and the types of interpersonal skills, and related ethical and sociopolitical ideals, he felt were necessary for collaborative theatre practice. Various chapters in this book will therefore draw on aspects of his guidance to teachers, where appropriate.

Chekhov's pedagogic approach evolved within a rich genealogy of innovative artists and teachers. The influence of the establishment of a rigorous actor training programme by Stanislavsky and Vladimir Nemirovich-Danchenko at the Moscow Art Theatre, and in particular the work of Sulerzhitsky and the two related studios with their adaptation of non-theatrical texts for performance and practice of co-directing, should also be acknowledged as an important inspiration. Although Chekhov always had great respect for Stanislavsky and, as has been extensively discussed by numerous commentators, borrowed aspects of his system and the notion of a theatre studio and its relationship to training (see Autant-Mathieu and Meerzon 2015), he undoubtedly transformed this into an entirely different method and rebelled against his former director and teacher's pedagogic and directorial practice and also his interpersonal style. In *Lessons to Teachers* he argues: '*The tragedy of Stanislavsky was that he had no understanding of what it meant to be a teacher. He was never able to find the way in which to give his knowledge to others. He was a great inventor, but as a teacher and director, he was very ungifted. He could demonstrate, but he could not teach*' (LTT: 13 April 1936). He later claimed '*Stanislavsky tortured all the actors around him, and he tortured himself even more than us. He was a very difficult and strange teacher, and perhaps a very heartless and merciless teacher [. . .] he has perhaps not found the right way for his teaching*' (TAITT: 4 July 1938). This critique also extended to his directorial methodology and style, as Marowitz explains: 'The rehearsals for [*The Inspector General*] were many and, in Chekhov's words, "for the most part, excruciating"' (2004: 63). Marowitz reports that during one rehearsal when Chekhov and other actors slightly muddled their lines '[Stanislavsky's] stern, cold voice from the auditorium boomed, "Stop! You will repeat your lines thirteen times!" And with Stanislavsky tapping his finger on the desk to mark each representation, the actors duly recited them aloud like schoolchildren' (63). In marked contrast, Chekhov cites Sulerzhitsky's inspirational ability to lead a group of actors, retaining respect and authority while giving them creative freedom, as significant to the development of his own pedagogic and directorial style. Chekhov reflects that what he learnt from Sulerzhitsky was that 'to lead means to serve those who are being led and not to demand service on their part' (Chekhov 2005: 52). He similarly admired, and adopted, Vakhtangov's use of a visual and embodied working language with his actors which was not dependent on long intellectual discussions (70).

The pedagogic, directorial and theatre-making approach developed by Chekhov also drew on aspects of Rudolf Steiner's pedagogical approach in tandem with his spiritual ideas. Steiner had opened the first Waldorf School in Stuttgart based on anthroposophical principles in 1919 and, like other progressive pedagogues at that time (John Dewey, Caroline Pratt, Maria Montessori, Marietta Johnson, Margaret Naumburg, Émile Jaques-Dalcroze and others), challenged older models of education based on rote learning, strict discipline and rigid hierarchical relationships These progressive forms of pedagogy challenged the idea that pupils were empty vessels waiting to be filled with information provided by teachers who were the sole source of knowledge, and instead empowered the learner through processes of student-centred and experiential learning. This was built on the idea that students can learn through a process of creative trial and error and required attentiveness to the quality of relational exchanges between teachers and learners. Central to this was the idea that students have the capacity to teach and lead each other and work collaboratively, at times independently from the teacher individually or in groups. It also emphasized social responsibility, critical thinking and the need for students to pose and answer questions as a mode of learning. Working this way meant that both teacher and learner must be willing to take risks and to accept failure as part of the learning process. While teachers lead and hold the power in this relationship, they do not always control the outcomes of these forms of learning and experimentation and this required specific skills and forms of facilitation. Like a number of the other early twentieth-century progressive pedagogues, Steiner centralized play in this type of learning process along with drama, expressive painting and storytelling (Clouder 2003). He also believed in the importance of movement in a creative, expressive and spiritual learning process, and his schools taught his system of Eurythmy. Clouder also notes that Steiner believed that humour, laughter and joy were also important aspects of the teaching and learning experience and that teachers were creative and responsive artists in their own right.

The form of pedagogy and processes of collaborative and devised theatre-making that Chekhov developed reflected these principles, and he actively sought to empower and respect his students and actors in his teaching at the Studio. He explained: 'My ideal has always been not to be a despotic leader, but to lead with your help' (cited in Ashperger 2008: 95). Mala Powers, one of Chekhov's students and the executor of his estate after his death, noted that Chekhov often referred to his students as his 'colleagues' (1992), which is telling in this respect. Chamberlain notes that Chekhov was 'a very gentle' teacher who clearly challenged his students but 'did not torment his students or overly criticize them' (2004: 28). This approach and philosophy was to underpin the way in which Chekhov taught his students to work as small student-led companies, often carrying out auto-education through experiential discovery through a playful application of his methods to processes of collaborative theatre-making. The centrality of the learner within progressive pedagogy was applied to the actor-centred process of devised theatre-making, transforming actors from passive interpreters into active theatre-makers. This pedagogic approach was also applied to the directorial methods they used, and this led to a particular form of directing that is discussed in Chapter 1 by Cass Fleming.

It is important in the context of this book that we note Chekhov's invitation to his trainee teachers that they use their own improvisational skills and his methods to be creative and spontaneous artists in their own right. This principle was equally applied to his trainee directors, actors, writers and designers, when the Studio opened later in 1936:

> *You have limited yourselves in all your exercises by following the suggestions I gave you too pedantically. The meaning of my method lies in not one exercise or the other, but in the whole. You will only understand when you feel yourself absolutely free in all the exercises. You must understand the idea of my exercises, not only the exercises. [. . .] If you find other exercises beside those I have given you, please do them [. . .] after some time you have the right to re-create the exercises [. . .] you must be free to develop your individuality. You must be spontaneous and original instead of slavish in the way you do your exercises. If you understand this, you will always be free. You must allow yourself to be spontaneous.* (LTT, 23 May 1936)

This perspective is empowering, in that practitioners can use their own creative individuality in their practice, but it also carries with it a responsibility to be open and creative, in the same manner they expect from their actors, or their students. The authors of this book have likewise sought to be spontaneous and original in relation to the possible uses of Chekhov's technique in contemporary practice and also in relation to the use of archive materials.

## 11 Past, present and future: A living and creative archive

The complexity of archives as historical resources, and as a metaphor, has been explored by many different academic disciplines over the past thirty years. Derrida (1995) and Foucault

(1977), along with various feminist and postcolonial scholars, have challenged the notion that archives are objective, neutral, fixed, complete or truthful historical records. Instead Derrida, Foucault and others have argued that archives are contingent and are shaped by sociocultural, political and technological discourses and forces. Therefore, they point out, archival materials do not grant unmediated access to the past. Foucault also argued that archives function as systems of discursivity, which define their own truth criteria and therefore determine what might, or might not, be said (1977), and Derrida pointed out that archives are not fixed and that their meanings change over time (1995). Consequently, the way in which archives have been put together by Hurst du Prey and others – the information and objects recorded and presented, the decisions about what to include and exclude as well as the missing items and the acts of serendipity – can be seen as creative acts of interpretation rather than neutral and pure records of what has taken place and been experienced in the past. As Derrida and Foucault acknowledge, archives are also full of gaps, absences and contradictions. Our project, and in particular Daron Oram's chapter, directly engaged with various gaps and absences that we found in the archive and in the class records. We also actively engaged with the different voices represented either directly, or by association, in the records and noted the contributions of the different collaborators along with their own histories, training and approaches.

Carolyn Steedman argues that through this discourse about the archive 'the problem of diachronicity (in the realm of synchronic analysis and thinking) [. . .] was being raised. Or the problem of pastness, tout court' (2001: 1178). This suggests that a different conception of historiography might be helpful when exploring archives; a selective use of Foucault's (1977) notion of genealogy has been helpful to this project in this respect. Foucault, following Nietzsche, provides a useful critique of the way in which conventional history: 'reintroduces (and always assumes) a suprahistorical perspective: a history whose function is to compose the finally reduced diversity of time into a totality fully closed upon itself [. . .] a completed development' (152). He goes on to argue that the pursuit of 'origin' in a historiography becomes an 'attempt to capture the exact essence of things, their purest possibilities, and their carefully protected identities' which, he argues, 'assumes the existence of immobile forms that precede the external world of accident and succession' (142). Even if we are to try to search for an 'origin' or an 'essence', Foucault suggests one would invariably find something far more complex and less tidy, including the emergence by chance, reversals, repetitions and failures. The archival records are fascinating because they reveal the incomplete projects, challenges and failures that Chekhov and his collaborators experienced and which arguably fed into their innovation and success. Chekhov also passionately believed that a willingness to take creative risks, and engage with the unknown and failure, was something that artists needed to engage with in order to be fully creative. Importantly, Foucault's understanding of emergence within a genealogical study does not represent a 'closed field', and he claims that no one individual can be awarded responsibility for an emergence 'since it always occurs in the interstice' (1977: 150). A selective borrowing of this notion of genealogy allows us to approach the archives, and the related histories, as a complex web of practices and practitioners and to move away from a linear notion of history. This is valuable to us, as Chekhov worked closely with other collaborators in his Studio, and the work often existed in a type of creative and personal 'interstice'.

Women's and postcolonial studies supported forms of historiography that sought to write women and colonized people back into historical narratives. Both disciplines also challenged the limits of what is considered an official record and reminded us that there is always much that is silenced and distorted in the production of an archive. We have borrowed from feminist forms of historiography (Aston 1995, 1999; Rowbotham 1977, 2011; Case 1988; Hart 1989; Scott 1999) in tandem with a selective use of the notion of genealogy – notwithstanding the tensions between Foucault and feminism (Diamond and Quinby 1988) – in terms of bringing to the fore the work of Chekhov's close collaborators at Dartington, most of whom were women, and of exploring their contributions to this lineage of practice and the construction of the archive itself. This follows Crista Mittelsteiner's work on the collaboration between Boner and Chekhov (2018), and we believe it is in line with Chekhov's commitment to the notion of ensemble work. The chapters by Fleming and Cornford expressly explore Chekhov's collaborative practice and the way in which this developed new forms of theatre-making. Roanna Mitchell's chapter explicitly considers the contribution made by Hurst du Prey and Straight and links this back to earlier work by the female dance practitioners that Hurst du Prey was taught by, and worked with, prior to collaborating with Chekhov.

In order to resist what Derrida identifies as the coexisting drive of the archive as traditional and controlling (1995), the New Pathways research team chose to engage with our materials as a living and creative collection of historical materials. Sue Mayo and Caoimhe McAvinchey's work with the London International Festival of Theatre's living archive was a key inspiration in this respect. In this work, Mayo developed four creative approaches, including plunging in deeply to the archive; bouncing off the material to inspire new work; exploring a question or theme to create a trail through the archive and entering into dialogue with the archive (Shaughnessy 2012). The New Pathways team similarly employed a wide range of approaches to the archival materials in order to enter into different types of dialogue with them. Consequently, the research team took an intentionally creative, diverse and genealogical approach to the archive. One sketch, a transcribed lesson, an index card, diagram, list or letter was not seen as an origin, or something that existed in isolation, or 'belonged' purely to Chekhov but an invitation for exploration. We also enjoyed the random fragments we found, the incomplete records and palimpsests that we encountered, handwritten notes correcting or debating the contents of other documents, multiple versions, rewrites and materials that were never ultimately used. We took these materials as invitations, questions or possibilities that we interrogated and engaged with imaginatively and critically. There are obvious gaps in the material, and there are repetitions and variations in the classes and curriculum over the years that represent changes and developments. There is evidence of failed experiments, frustrations and a number of half-finished projects and dreams for the future that were not fully realized. The transcripts of the lessons are obviously more complete, but we have also sought to acknowledge that the embodied memories of the participants in these classes, which were then passed down and transformed through relational exchanges with other students and artists through body to body contact, oral history and stories, are an equal form of historical archive of this work (Schneider 2001: 105). Chekhov spoke no English when he arrived in England (and worked between four languages), and we can see there is an idiosyncratic use of language at times in the transcribed classes and lectures and a use of various metaphors related to embodied, energetic, imaginative and interpersonal states in the materials. We considered which aspects of Chekhov's work, assumptions or nomenclature might be unsuitable for contemporary use and we reconsidered and remade a dynamic form of language and metaphors that hold true to Chekhov's practice but clarifies his central ideas in the twenty-first century.

We further 'muddied' this process by jointly researching, sharing and debating the archival materials within the six research teams, among the wider team and ultimately with the participants at the Praxis Symposium sessions in 2016. This avoided universalist assumptions and the dominance of one person's interpretation of the archives as 'authority'; the meanings of the archive changed each time a different team engaged with it, bringing their passions, questions and disciplinary backgrounds to it. We celebrated all the possible ways of using this material as a springboard for contemporary practice and celebrated its innovation, but we also reflected on aspects of the work that did not work, or areas where we felt Chekhov technique needs adaptation to work in new contexts. The team approached the archive as a treasure trove, and the research included rigorous analysis of the material but also conjecture and experimentation. This resulted in a polyvocal weaving of work and scholarship rather than an attempt to give one definitive approach or singular understanding; instead, we used what Chekhov terms our creative individuality. Mala Powers claimed that Chekhov predicted that the Future Theatre would 'strive to enlarge everything – giving many points of view, many theatrical styles, many means of expression' (Chekhov 2002: xliii) and this is what we hoped to achieve. Each cluster of researchers and contributors were also considering how we might modify, blend and possibly transform the methods in our processes, and what questions this process raises regarding issues of 'purity' or 'authenticity' of Chekhov technique (Daboo 2012), and how it may challenge dominant historical actor training and directorial narratives.

## 12  The structure of the book

The authors in this book all approach their investigations into new uses and understandings of Chekhov's techniques in different ways, reflecting the variety of approaches to the archive material and research questions taken. The book is divided into three sections that look at new uses of Chekhov technique in relation to three key areas: Processes of Theatre-Making, Beyond Acting, and Beyond the Theatre.

The first section addresses the use of Chekhov's techniques in relation to processes of theatre-making and contains two chapters. Chapter 1 explores the use of Chekhov's techniques and principles for devised theatre-making and what Fleming defines as a form of catalyst direction. Chapter 2, authored by Cornford, focuses on the use of Chekhov's methods for collaborative playwriting processes and investigates what he terms actor-dramaturgs and a notion of atmospheric dramaturgies. Fleming and Cornford consider what the rich, but previously inaccessible, archive materials reveal about Chekhov's techniques in the contexts of devising and collaborative writing and what they offer devisers, directors, playwrights and dramaturgs working today. This first section of the book demonstrates the way in which Chekhov's radical theatre-making crossed the binary distinctions between 'theatre or performance' and 'writing or devising' (Radosavljević 2013a) and suggests that his techniques therefore offer much to modes of practice that resist these restrictive divisions that are emerging in the twenty-first century. The second section considers the ways in which Chekhov was using his techniques and principles for other disciplinary areas of theatre practice that went beyond acting. Chapter 3, written by Oram, considers Chekhov's approach to vocal training and singing and explores the ways in which his methodology can be used in contemporary practice and integrated with other methods. Chekhov's work also represents an important point of cross-fertilization with the work of the School for Dance-Mime and the Jooss-Leeder School of Dance that were also based at Dartington Hall, and in Chapter 4 Mitchell explores the use of Chekhov's methods in two key areas: actor-movement and dance practice. Chekhov's focus on real and imagined space, colour and light, form, architecture, objects, visual arts practices and atmospheres was central to his practice and his training of the student designers. In Chapter 5, Rushe considers how designers can use these imaginatively embodied techniques and what this offers collaborative theatre practitioners working in scenographically oriented and/or site-specific contexts today. Combined, these three chapters show how Chekhov's techniques offer a flexible set of tools and an accessible language that can be shared between different theatre-making disciplines. Section three takes the consideration of Chekhov's methods beyond the theatre and in Chapter 6 McAvinchey explores its use, and future potential, in applied therapeutic and community contexts. This chapter argues that these techniques are a valuable addition to applied theatre-makers' or drama therapists' 'toolkits' and is an area that warrants further development. In 'Cross Currents and Conclusions', Fleming and Cornford report on the international dialogue that took place at the New Pathway event and conclude by considering the overall research findings of the project's different strands and where work in this field may go in the future. In all, then, this book has a threefold aim: to broaden and deepen understanding of Chekhov's practice in the past by sharing archival materials and exploring techniques and ideas that reach beyond the realm of acting and actor training as they have been conventionally understood, to analyse the breadth and range of Chekhovian practices in the present, and to develop practical and theoretical articulations of his techniques that will inspire and facilitate their future application and exploration both in the contexts we explore and beyond them.

## 13 A note on the use of archival material and glossary of techniques

Quotations from the Michael Chekhov Theatre Studio Deirdre Hurst du Prey Archive are presented in italic font. Date references are given for all quotations and images, unless a date is impossible to determine. To help the reader distinguish between 'Lessons to Teachers' – the lessons that Chekhov delivered to his trainee teachers before the formal opening of the Studio[24] – and 'The Actor Is the Theatre' – the subsequent classes and rehearsals with all Studio members – the former are marked as LTT and the latter as TAITT, followed by a date reference. Archive box references and their corresponding date ranges are provided in the bibliography of the book. There is also a glossary providing brief definitions of some of Chekhov's crucial terms and techniques, and the first reference to these terms in any chapter is given in bold.

## Notes

1. After being housed at Dartington Hall for many years, the Michael Chekhov Theatre Studio is now held by the South West Heritage Trust in Exeter.
2. This event was funded by the Arts and Humanities Research Council.
3. The following members of the research team undertook training with Dixon: Brook (2005), Fleming (2005), Oram (2006), Chambers (2006), Rushe (2008, co-taught by Kane), Krynke (2010), Cornford (2011), Egolf (2013), McAvinchey (2016) and Mitchell (2019). Dixon, Kane and Sharp have also mentored this younger generation of practitioners in the UK. The research team have also been trained by Phelim McDermott and John Wright in the UK and many other artists and teachers using Chekhov technique from different parts of the world.
4. See the Chekhov Collective UK website for information about the organization and its ongoing work: https://chekhovcollectiveuk.co.uk.
5. This included Julia Krynke and Gretchen Egolf.
6. Stanislavsky developed an innovative system of actor training based on a psychophysical principle which recognizes an integral connection between the human body and mind, and relates to both what he defines as the actor 'experiencing' performance (the inner emotional/spiritual work which relates to the mind, will and feeling) and the incarnation of the role (i.e. the external exploration of this role) (see Carnicke 2009; Whyman 2008). Chekhov was introduced to the early form of psychophysical practice in Russia, and while his approach was built on this model, his methods and ideas developed very differently (see Whyman 2008: 28). Merlin argues that out of Stanislavsky's former students, it was Chekhov who was to most radically embrace and develop psychophysical practice in the twentieth century (2001: 4).
7. In recent years Chekhov's approach converged with the philosophical embodied mind thesis, which suggests that the human mind is determined by the human body and vice versa (Lakoff and Johnson 1980, 1999; Damasio 2000; Kemp 2012).
8. Chekhov linked this to an interpretation of Steiner's understanding of the 'Higher Ego'. He saw the higher ego as the actor's more creative self, which was different to their more 'everyday' self, or consciousness, because it was not 'closed off egotistically into itself' (2005: 147), and he believed that they worked dynamically together.
9. Chekhov's interest in energy is connected to Steiner's notion of the etheric body and notion of prana. Cristini explains Steiner's belief that there is 'a physical body, an etheric body (made up of energy and vital force), and an astral body (made up of sensations and feelings) – all of them guided by the ego' (2015: 70).
10. Kane also established Performing Arts International UK in 2018. This organization based in Sussex teaches speech and drama drawing on Chekhov technique and the speech work of Rudolf Steiner.
11. A small number of PhD theses addressing the work of Michael Chekhov from the late 1970s onwards have reproduced selections of archival material.
12. See Daboo (2012), Cornford (2013), Fleming (2013) and Pitches (2013) for a discussion of the significance of progressive educational movements on the Dartington Project and Chekhov's work.
13. Dorothy Elmhirst also took part in classes at the Chekhov Theatre Studio.

14. The institutional affiliation of the six research teams is as follows: Strand 1: Dr Cass Fleming (Goldsmiths University of London, MCUK, The Chekhov Collective UK), Dr Roanna Mitchell (University of Kent, MCUK, The Chekhov Collective UK) and members of The Chekhov Collective UK. Strand 2: Dr Tom Cornford (The Royal Central School of Speech and Drama, MCUK) and Dr Hannah Davies, playwright. Strand 3: Daron Oram (The Royal Central School of Speech and Drama), with Christina Gutekunst (E15) and John Gillett. Strand 4: Dr Roanna Mitchell (University of Kent, MCUK, The Chekhov Collective UK) and Juliet Chambers (Guildford School of Acting). Strand 5: Sinéad Rushe (The Royal Central School of Speech and Drama, MCUK) and Aldona Cunningham (The Royal Central School of Speech and Drama). Strand 6: Professor Caoimhe McAvinchey (Queen Mary University of London), Zoe Brook (Bazooka Arts) and Martin Sharp (University of Bournemouth, MCUK).
15. Graham Dixon runs the Michael Chekhov Studio London and is a Senior Associate of MCUK; Julia Krynke is also a Senior Associate of MCUK.
16. Professor Franc Chamberlain works at the University of Huddersfield and Professor Caoimhe McAvinchey at Queen Mary University of London.
17. Gretchen Egolf is a Senior Associate of MCUK.
18. Daboo suggests that the connection to the esoteric in Chekhov's work may have contributed to this gap of knowledge (2012: 72).
19. Also known as the writer Anne Cumming.
20. Emerson College is a Steiner educational organization in Forest Row, Sussex.
21. David Zinder ran training as part of 'The Changing Body' conference and various papers on Chekhov were delivered. Attendees included Phillip Zarrilli; Jerri Daboo; Cass Fleming; Cynthia Ashperger; Sol Garre; and Jonathan Pitches.
22. Andrees and Langhams founded the Michael Tschechow Studio Berlin in 1984. Since 1990 this studio has operated as a drama school. Andrees went on to found the Michael Chekhov International Academy in Berlin.
23. See the MICHA website for a list of faculty and information about the organization: https://www.michaelchekhov.org/.
24. These transcriptions have been recently published under the title *Lessons for Teachers* (Cerullo 2018).

# Section One  Chekhov technique: Processes of theatre-making

# 1 'Theatre of the future'

# Chekhov technique for devised theatre and catalyst direction

## CASS FLEMING

This chapter addresses the use of Michael Chekhov's techniques for devised theatre-making practice and the related directorial methods in historical and contemporary contexts. It shares, for the first time in published form, various important archival materials that illuminate Chekhov's work and offer contemporary practitioners many valuable tools and methods. The chapter discusses the archival, practice-based and scholarly research that took place over three years. It addresses these different modes of research simultaneously because they were continuously interwoven; in combination, they led to the research findings presented.

## 1 The actor is the theatre

The typed transcripts of the classes that Michael Chekhov delivered at the Chekhov Theatre Studio produced by Deirdre Hurst du Prey are entitled 'The Actor Is the Theatre'. This clear and bold statement recognizes actors as artists, frees them from servitude to the author, and places them at the heart of the theatre-making process. This perspective was intertwined with his lifelong commitment to ensemble and collaborative practice. The work that he undertook at the Chekhov Theatre Studio at Dartington (1936–8), and later at Ridgefield (1939–42), with students and colleagues was firmly built on these interconnected approaches, which he believed would lead to a newly configured *'theatre of the future'*. He explained to his student actors, directors, designers and collaborative writers that they were to *'carry out certain experiments with our future theatre'* (TAITT: 21 January 1938), which frequently began with skilled improvisation to produce original dramatic material, *'as if we are creators of the play'* (TAITT: 21 January 1938). In other words, Chekhov's techniques were also used for the creation of theatre, or what is now understood in the UK as devising practice, in addition to interpretive acting of dramatic literature. However, despite Chamberlain's identification (2004) of Chekhov's practice as a form of devised theatre, this central aspect of his work has still not been fully explored. Our research found it was the central thrust of the work of the Chekhov Theatre Studio.

At the Studio, Chekhov explained this new way of making devised performance must be based on a collaborative and relational exchange between all the different members of a theatre company whose roles and expectations would be radically challenged and reconfigured. In this new form of theatre, Chekhov suggests that the vision of the production, and the dialogue itself, comes from the ensemble as an act of collective creation. Indeed, in a later class he explains in more detail how this might work in practice and suggests it could be that '*a director will want to withhold the words of the play until he has produced some gestures*', and he goes on to argue that in the Studio '*[t]here must be absolute freedom. The play must be invented when the rehearsals are going on. It must not be written before. [. . .] Only this way will we get some new results*' (TAITT: 28 January 1937). Moreover, he argued,

> *The thing that is killing the theatre today is that we speak about beautiful words and a beautiful play, but nobody speaks about beautiful movements. But movement is the language of the theatre, just as much as words are. [. . .] Therefore, we must love such rehearsals with movements because we want to create a new language which will be a theatre language.* (TAITT: 14 December 1936)

However, he pointed out that they could also work the other way around and listen to the text being read in the first instance, and then respond to this through practical exploration. This theatre of the future therefore realigns the established roles and concomitant power structures in theatre companies and evidently empowers the imaginatively embodied actor and director to work as equals to the playwright in a devising process.

This model clearly challenges the Aristotelian hierarchy of theatrical elements dominant in theatre practice early in the twentieth century, which assigned the mythos (plot and theatrical text) and therefore the playwright, the primary status and authority in theatre-making. In contradistinction to Aristotle's position, Chekhov argued that the impulse, or the generation of material will come from the actors and directors in partnership with the writer, and from imaginatively embodied exploration. But Chekhov went even further and claimed that 'The director, the stage designer, etc., are all accessories, but the actor is the theatre' (Chekhov and Hurst du Prey 1985: 158), thereby liberating actors from the rigid dominance of directors, or designers, by placing them at the centre of his theatre-making practice. To some extent this position would seem to be the logical outcome of his focus on actor-centred practice. While this change in directorial role requires directors to find the generosity and humility to work more collaboratively with actors, in turn this reconfigured role permits directors to work in much closer collaboration with their actors, sharing the responsibility for, and the ownership of, the process and the work. At the time that Chekhov made this claim, it presented a considerable challenge to the dominant hierarchical structures that prevailed in Russian and European theatre. This model of actor as creator, and director as a collaborator who can lead through facilitation, fits Oddey's (1994) definition of devised theatre, which she describes as being 'concerned with the collective creation of art (not the single vision of the playwright)'. She goes on to argue that 'the emphasis has shifted from the writer to the creative artist' (4) and that this practice creates 'a freedom of possibilities for all those involved to discover; an emphasis on a way of working that supports intuition, spontaneity, and an accumulation of ideas' (1). While Chekhov was often working with some type of previously existing text, at different points in his process, and at times had between one and three writers working collaboratively within an ensemble, this does not preclude their practice from being defined as devised theatre in relation to much contemporary practice (see Heddon and Milling 2006: 6).

This realignment of roles, the empowerment of the actor and their equality in a theatre-making process, came with new responsibilities and skills. To create this new form of theatre that was more independent from traditional ideas of the dominant author, and to teach actors the skills and confidence to do this, Chekhov realized that they had to find another approach: *'We must start our new kind of exercises with an approach which will give us the possibility to work upon a small sketch, or many, many sketches in which each will have a part'* (TAITT: 14 January 1937). To develop a number of these devised sketches, scenarios and larger-scale performances, Chekhov placed the cohort into student-led theatre companies who were often engaged in self-led practice under his careful supervision. To enable an actor as an active maker of theatre also requires different skills from a director and the use of a devising methodology. The structure of the training delivered at the Chekhov Theatre Studio and Chekhov's pedagogic method and style were also to play an important part in their work and the development of a specific approach to devising and directing.

In twenty-first-century Britain there are a growing number of actors, directors and teachers who are drawing on Chekhov's techniques as a devising methodology as directors and makers working with, and without, playwrights. They include Graham Dixon, Phelim McDermott (of the theatre company Improbable), John Wright, Franc Chamberlain, Jerri Daboo, Christopher Heimann, Philip Weaver, Philip Zarrilli, all the authors of this publication and now a younger generation of artists. This represents an important and growing area of practice that this chapter addresses.

## 2 Playing with a living archive

This strand of the New Pathways project focused on the archive materials related to Chekhov's practice that involved work with fairy tales, folk tales, myths, verbally described scenarios, pieces that were made through a cycling process of devising and the projects which drew on the improvisational modes of performance as part of a devising process. At times, it drew on materials relating to projects on pre-existing play texts, where there was a level of fruitful overlap. It concurrently focused on the materials that related to directorial methods, principles and pedagogic exercises. To explore the treasures held in the archive, focus on the selection and rigorously interrogate them, I founded The Chekhov Collective UK in 2013 and was fortunate to work with a vibrant group of practitioners and scholars. I was first introduced to Chekhov's exercises in 1997, and after years of experimenting with the available books, I trained with Graham Dixon in 2005 and other Chekhov teachers thereafter. Since 1997, I have drawn on this technique as my central practice – in tandem with aspects of the French tradition of play developed by Suzanne Bing, Jacques Copeau and Jacques Lecoq (the original basis of my work) – and have incorporated it into my practice as a director, devised theatre-maker, teacher and academic. The first phase of the practice research began in 2013 when I was invited to run a workshop on Chekhov technique for directors at the Royal National Theatre Studio, with the assistance of my former student Rebecca Frecknall. Later that year, I brought together a group of practitioners trained in Chekhov technique who were using it in devised theatre-making and/or directing. Sixteen practitioners were involved at different stages of the practice research[1] and a core group – Tom Bostock, Sian Clarke, Alistair Foylan, Katja Hilevaara, Joshua MacLellan, Roanna

Mitchell and Phoebe Naughton – continued working on the project on a part-time basis over the next two years. Between 2014 and 2016 we shared the results of our practice research, led workshops for directors and gave talks, at various points prior to the final New Pathways research event in 2016.[2] This included three events at Goldsmiths, one at Queen Mary University of London and two at the Young Vic Theatre. This research fed into the final Praxis Symposium session in 2016 and into the writing of this chapter.

Our research was not concerned with a reconstruction, or contemporary restaging, of one of the devised projects created at the Chekhov Theatre Studio, or with producing a polished final production. Rather, this process-led project sought to carry out specific practice research experiments to explore and interrogate selected principles, approaches and projects carried out at the Studio to consider how they work in practice as a methodology, and the related critical issues, in a contemporary context. In addition to drawing on archival and other disparate or hard-to-access materials, this project also built on the important analysis of Chekhov's work on *The Possessed* and 'The Fishers' Scene' as forms of devised performance carried out by Chamberlain (2004) and Pitches (2013), respectively. Our methodological approach to exploring the materials was varied. As we did not believe we were trying to find one historically correct application, or a pure origin or essence of practice or a method (Foucault 1977), we playfully enjoyed a diversity of approaches in order to intentionally 'enter into a dialogue with the archive' (Mayo in Shaughnessy 2012: 214). The differences in approach outlined in the various archival sources were acknowledged and enjoyed. This resisted the idea of immobility, which can be seen as the antithesis of Chekhov's approach in that he actively encouraged artists to use whichever aspects of his method that work for them as creative individuals rather than following his methods in a rigid or formulaic manner. Instead of following one source pedantically, we decided to draw on the recurrent principles and tools that featured across these materials and used these as a springboard for our own practice research, following Chekhov's advice to '*take something and make it your own*' (TAITT: 16 January 1939). Obviously, many other avenues could have been taken through this archive, and the group, our sociocultural backgrounds, identities and interests determined this particular route. We hoped that our work would make Chekhov's archives accessible and relevant to contemporary devised theatre-makers and directors, and also help us imagine possible future forms of theatre.

## 3 'Propaganda against naturalism': Sources and inspiration for devised practice

A key feature of Chekhov's devised work, which provided specific tools for devised practice, is the use of non-naturalistic and non-theatrical texts, modes of performance based on improvisation, play and simple invented scenarios. A use of these types of story and narrative allowed for, and arguably required, a level of creative embodied play for the actors to 'discover' and 'invent' an embodied representation and performance material. In other words, it provided frameworks and stimuli that ensured that actors and directors would not be the servants of the playwright or the text itself and instead nurtured, and taught them to trust, their own creative imagination. This training of the actor and directors evidently taught them to perceive text as elastic in a devised theatre-making process and to feel confident to relate to it in an empowered and equal way when engaging with it to devise material. Throughout his lifetime, Chekhov expressed his desire to 'break the shackles of flat Naturalism' (Chekhov and Leonard 1963: 27) and argued that the 'actor-artist will understand that style is the most precious thing that he brings into his work' and that 'the artist cannot bring anything from himself into a naturalistic "work of art"' (2005: 42). Consequently, he advocated an exploration of a wide range of non-naturalistic genres and styles of performance, including tragedy, drama, melodrama, comedy, high comedy, farce, slapstick comedy, clowning, *Commedia dell'Arte* and theatrical grotesque, and this was built into the syllabi of the Studio which were often explored in devised projects. The planned end-of-first-year performances demonstrate this diversity: 'The Fishers' Scene' – devised from a scenario; *Balladina I* and *Balladina II* – a Polish tragedy, partly inspired by mask work; *Peer Gynt* by Henrik Ibsen; *The Golden Steed* – a performance based on a Latvian fairy tale; and *Two Kings* – a devised fairy-tale performance (TAITT: 2 July 1937).

## 3.1 Cross-cultural fairy tales, folk tales and myths

While still working in Russia with his first private studio (1918–22), Chekhov had experimented with staging productions of fairy tales and literary adaptations with his students. Later, Chekhov and Georgette Boner, in their devised production of *The Castle Awakens: An Essay in Rhythmical Drama* (in Gordon 1995), had explored Tolstoy's fairy tale, which had, in turn, been based on Russian folk tales. Chekhov had attempted to experiment with ideas partly inspired by Steiner's Eurythmy in this production, which signified primarily through movement, contained very little spoken text, employed a symbolist design and shared some surprising features with contemporary devised theatre. At Dartington Hall, Chekhov established a Fairy Tale Theatre Committee (1937–8), which carried out extensive research into fairy tales, folk tales, myths and legends. Chekhov and his students used this research and experimented with devising their own fairy tales and myth-like stories. There are multiple versions of these different scenarios in the archive, and many of their devised processes started with only a verbally described or brief written scenario, rather than prescribed scripts, as a springboard. The student companies also devised in close collaboration with writers, or multiple writers, at various different points, and in different ways, in the course of development of the devised performances.

To understand this approach and to utilize the devising and directorial tools that Chekhov drew from these sources, a closer examination of the archival materials is necessary. The Fairy Tale Committee's research was categorized in various ways and carefully recorded on index cards. The cross-cultural nature of their research is evidenced by the alphabetically arranged thematic series which includes, filed under 'A "Abducting"', *Tsar Saltan*, *Ramayana*, *The Mahabharata*, *The Bamboo Cutter*, and *Tonetto Busetto* (MC/S5/1). The choice of these stories as stimuli for devised processes is relevant on a number of levels. Many of these stories, originally intended for adults, are dark and disturbing. Alison Lurie notes the oral history of fairy tales and that '[t]he storytellers that the Brothers Grimm and other folklorists collected their material from were almost always women' (14 October 2009: 34). These stories were also shared orally in other parts of the world, rather than being written and formally 'owned' in the first instance. Although there are cultural and historical differences between them, fairy tales, folk tales and myths share key features that make them particularly suited for the use of devised theatre-making: they are all dramatic stories rather than prescriptive play scripts, and frequently they exist in multiple versions, written or told by different authors, meaning there is an inherent polyvocality and flexibility in the telling of the story itself. When Chekhov worked with these stories with the students, they were using what was often a previously known, or familiar, story or narrative, but there was no requirement for them to follow a pre-existing scripted plot, rigid character descriptions, stage directions or scripted dialogue.

This type of material also facilitated Chekhov's desire to explore movement as an equal and expressive language in theatre-making in important ways. Following one of Boner's lectures on *Commedia dell'Arte*, the students worked on *The Golden Steed*, a long-term project based on a Latvian fairy tale, and Chekhov explained '*[t]he dimensions of a fairy tale are bigger than the dimensions of an ordinary play*' (TAITT: 10 December 1936). This notion of an extended dimension in relation to these non-naturalistic stories broadened the possibilities of the physically expressive, transformative, stylistic, imaginative and fantastic acting. It also provided a space to develop embodied, visual, spatial, energetic and affective forms of dramaturgy in their devised work. The following year, Chekhov explained to students who were working on a fairy tale (*Two Kings*) what he felt these stories required in stylistic, psychological and ego terms. He comments: '*This play is very good propaganda against naturalism. In the majority of cases we could very clearly see that these were not the feelings of the actors*' (TAITT: 27 September 1937). Not only did these stories actively challenge naturalistic acting, they also forced the actors to engage with types of character, or representation, that were markedly different – and other – to them. However, this did not mean that the work was not imaginatively justified by the actors. In feedback on the student's work, he commented: '*This is a great achievement – a real demonstration for the feeling of truth. Here we have a fairy tale without any naturalistic approach – without any reason – and yet it is absolutely believable. The whole play is one big archetypal performance*' (TAITT: 1 June 1937). The archetypal aspect of these stories, particularly in relation to psychology, appealed to Chekhov and connected to his interest in Steiner's religious philosophy. The term archetype could be seen as problematic if it is understood in strict Jungian terms, that is, as something universally inherited that comes from a Eurocentric notion of the collective unconscious. However, for Chekhov this archetypal quality was also seen to be culturally and historically specific, and he quoted Rudolf Meyer in one of his classes in this respect, '*The fairy tale and its ancient motif comes through the rise and fall of people, and through the rise and fall of different world-outlooks*' (1942 version of TTA MC/S5/4) and, as the archives show, he was exploring archetypes from different parts of the world. Indeed, Chekhov expressed doubts about whether the term archetype best expressed his ideas (Colvin in Aspherger 2008: 244), and he therefore suggested we name it our own way. Crucially, this idea correlates to his use of 'archetypal' **psychological gesture** (opening, closing, pushing, pulling, wringing, etc.) and how a fully embodied exploration of these movements in relation to rhythm, quality of the movement and direction in space triggers the actor's embodied imagination in strong psychophysical terms – and when used in relation to a character, it helps the actor to discover their dominant desires or motivations. This relates to a basic level of sensory-motor coupling being shared between animals and humans from different cultures, although beyond this shared core of movement, cultural variation becomes inevitable. It is therefore important to note that Chekhov believed that actors and directors would work through, or bounce off, these archetypes to reach 'an individual and unique character' (1985: 145). These prototype characters (and gestures) enabled the actors at the Studio to start more simply with a clear form, but with an openness generated through creative play with various aspects of technique and other performers. This meant these prototypes evolved over time, and in surprising ways, without actors seeking intellectual or emotional 'sophistication' at the start of their character work. Chekhov explains we must not censor ourselves out of an intellectual snobbery, saying: '[W]e must not be afraid of the cliché, because cliché has form and without form we cannot express ourselves [. . .] but [cliché] must be filled with life' (TAITT: 23 June 1937, cited in Aspherger 2008: 88). So it is this dynamic and playful process of filling archetypes, or clichés, with 'life', in our own way, that prevents them from being reductionist or affirming hegemonic ideas about identity, and enables an exploration of this extended dimension of theatre-making and performance.

As the practice research undertaken by The Chekhov Collective was engaging with Chekhov's propaganda against naturalism, we chose to use Antoine de Saint-Exupéry's *The Little Prince* (1943) as a stimulus because the narrative is clearly non-naturalistic and shares a number of important features with fairy tales, folk tales and myths, including the characters of the Rose, the Snake, the Fox and also the ethereal Little Prince. It is a short, concisely worded book that we felt had the potential to be engaged with elastically in a devised process, and we were drawn to its social critique which had led to it originally being banned by the Vichy government in France. It also seemed full of movement and magic, which we felt held a celebration of difference and otherness. This seemed an appropriate stimulus to ensure that there was space for 'beautiful movements' in addition to 'beautiful words' to create what Chekhov defined as a 'new theatre language'. In relation to this, we considered what non-naturalistic performance styles and aesthetics a use of Chekhov technique led to in this context and sought to retain a visible 'poetic dimension' of the use of gesture (Rushe 2013: 306) in aspects of our work. We intentionally followed Chekhov's belief that casting should not be to type, which led to cross-gender casting in the roles of the Little Prince, the Pilot and the Rose, which in turn resulted in a queer take on the piece and an exploration of various sociopolitical issues raised in the text, questions of identity, and the politics and ethics of love. This decision also led us to explore materials on the early female pilot Amelia Earhart and additional texts by Saint-Exupéry. In our practice research we found that a use of archetypes, or prototypes, was not any less effective when artists were working from their own sociocultural springboards and sense of identity. Through a provocative and playful process of filling them with 'life' we found them to be simple but powerful tools that transformed, resisted and also challenged socially constructed ideas in our practice research. As a company made up of actors from different cultural backgrounds and various different gender/sexual identities and family-formations working in the twenty-first century, we often preferred less gender-specific terms for certain archetypes – for example, 'the care-giver' in place of 'the mother' – but found they were no less effective because of these changes in nomenclature and varied cultural understandings. However, regardless of whether or not you view these stories in purely archetypal terms, from the perspective of structuralism, or as flexible culturally specific prototypes or character types/masks, it is clear that playing in this type of frame frees the actor, director and devised theatre-maker from the ordinary and enables an imaginative engagement of the extraordinary, fantastical and transformative, and new forms of dramaturgy but in justified terms.

The Fairy Tale Committee analysed other aspects of the material such as natural phenomena, which are related to aspects of Chekhov's acting technique but were also to become central tools for their creation of devised performance, the invention of characters, atmospheres and the development of the dramaturgy. One document lists fifty categories, including '(14) Elemental beings: i.e. Water, Earth, Air, Fire (15) Animals and birds, fish, etc. (16) Plants, flowers and trees (17) Elements: Earth, Air, Fire and Water (23) Transformations [. . .] (40) Half-humans, i.e. centaurs' (MC/S5/1). This personification of the non-human, animal and elemental allowed actors and directors to freely and physically play with the fantastical, magical, non-naturalistic, non-human, animistic and grotesque character types or beings, and use them as sources for the creation of alternative forms of atmosphere and dramaturgy in a process that inevitably led to the invention of non-naturalistic devised material. Indeed, there is something inherently fluid and non-normative in some of these non-human representations, which transgressed the borders between a human and animal, or plant, or element and or material objects, destabilizing some dominant ideas about identity and the centrality of the human. The generation of devised material therefore occurs in a less rational and logocentric context, and is based in the embodied and intuitive imagination. This can be read in the light of Hélène Cixous' notion of *écriture féminine* (1975) which, as Segarra notes, has often been described 'as "writing the body", meaning [it] does not rely mainly on rationality but incorporates the body's rhythms, humors, and moods' (2010: 12).

Significantly, Govan et al.'s survey of devised theatre practice (2007: 89–90) points out that contemporary devising companies still often opt to work with known texts such as fairy tales, folk tales and myths in many different ways. They note that these contemporary devised practitioners are often 'interested in changing the status of the original artefact' (90) as Chekhov and his students had intentionally done early in the twentieth century through a process of liberating themselves from the text as a dominant component and in order to relate their performances to the social and political world that they lived in, which he believed was their responsibility as artists.

### 3.2 *Commedia dell'Arte*, mask and clowning

In addition to this fairy tale work, Chekhov drew on a wide range of non-naturalistic theatrical styles and genres, often explored in different student-led projects, running in parallel at the Studio. Students also developed 'sketches' or scenarios based on simple structures and concepts that were primarily explored through physical improvisation, such as 'The Meeting,' 'Work' and 'Clowns' (TAITT: 26 April 1937). Studying markedly different genres and dramaturgies simultaneously meant that they could apply the technique on a continuum of theatre practice that erased binary distinctions between devised practice, collaborative writing practice and work on pre-existing theatrical texts. A use of these types of stimuli and genres, combined with Chekhov's belief that an ensemble should always feel free to take 'liberties' with text, including pre-existing play texts (Chekhov 2005: 157; Hurst du Prey 1978: 14) and that actors need to be empowered to 'move beyond' the text and the director's vision to find their character (Gordon 1987: 119), taught his students the principles and confidence to devise their own theatre. As we have seen, these choices were not only propaganda against naturalism; they also actively prevented the actors and directors from being passive interpreters, who are servants to the text, and instead demanded a level of creation and invention.

The focus on *Commedia dell'Arte*, mask work and clown at the Studio was crucial to the further development of the skills, capacity and type of consciousness needed to become a deviser of performance, as they are all modes of performance that are inherently playful and improvisatory, and Hurst du Prey explained how Chekhov linked this to the development of the skills of ingenuity and originality. 'When exploring the Commedia style, the actor had always to be original, always inventive, always fresh, never repeating' (1978: 13). Various devised projects were closely connected to the papers given by Boner as part of the 'Lectures on the History and Development of the Theatre and Playwriting' addressing *Commedia dell'Arte*, Marionette Theatre and Style (MC/S4/6/A). Her lecture on *Commedia* (10 December 1936) addressed the use of masks and types in this improvised form of theatre, and the work of Goldoni, which Chekhov's students explored and fed into their work on various devised projects, including *The Golden Steed*, *Balladina* and *Two Kings* – and later *Spanish Evening* (1938) and *Troublemaker-Doublemaker* (1939). Boner explained to the students that *Commedia dell'Arte* used basic scenarios as a **spine** for the generation of original material through a process of improvisation and how this develops a specific type of consciousness:

> [With] the Commedia dell'Arte we come into the presence of a new conscience [. . .] which plays with the relationships, with the living changing interdependent relationships. At the same time we are in the presence of a new liberty, liberty of improvisation which creates relations between one movement and another, between one word and another, between one being and another. We are watching jugglers who are using their skill in juggling with regard to mental objects, who have adapted their art to the material. (MC/S4/6: 2-3, emphasis original)

Boner goes on to encourage the students to explore the genre and this type of juggler's consciousness through their own practice. We also know the students were using masks at the Studio and a sketch of masks in relation to the tragedy *Balladina* is held in the archive and reproduced in the introduction of this book, although it is hard to know if they were worn in performance. Sadly, references to their use of real masks in classes are not extensive. However, the metaphor of the invisible mask, the use of real masks and the functioning of Chekhov's methods as imaginary masks are all crucial features of his technique and each of them increases a specific type of creative play that appears particularly conducive to devised theatre-making.

Chekhov also discussed character types or representations found in fairy/folk tales and myths in relation to clowning (2002: 128–9). He believed that clowning operated on two levels concurrently – tragedy and humour – and that '[c]lowning, extreme though it is, can be an indispensable adjunct to the actor' (TAITT: 19 January 1937). This interest in clowning clearly correlates to a much freer and expressive type of physical play and the development of a sense of humour (and the capacity to laugh at oneself) that Chekhov felt all actors and directors should have but is also of fundamental importance in relation to the ways in which they learn explicitly about playing and making contact with an audience. He also suggested that actors 'consider the humorous retinue of the clown as consisting of *subhuman* beings' (2002: 128), demonstrating an affinity to a more overt play with animality featured in the fairy tales, and a correlation to the masks of *Commedia*. He argued that the clown's 'transitions from one emotion to the other do not require any psychological justifications' but that '[h]e has to *believe* in what he feels and does' (129). Importantly, he also argued that clowning would awaken within actors 'that eternal Child which bespeaks the trust and utter simplicity of all great artists' (130). In his autobiography (2005), Chekhov reflected on how the types of physical comic 'tricks' that he and Vakhtangov had played outside of formal rehearsals in Russia had developed very particular skills and the capacity to devise original and ingenious material. Consequently, clowning, slapstick and lazzi were important to the actor and director training and provided specific theatre-making tools at the Studio, and this was underpinned by his particular interest in, and use of, play and games. In our practice research we drew on these forms and principles and found they were key to a more nuanced understanding, and fuller use of, Chekhov's techniques in a devising process. They also acted as an important bridge to the development of other skills and an understanding of the various devised methodologies.

## 4 Devising and directorial methods

Thus far, the chapter has considered the way in which Chekhov's methods of devising and directing drew on various non-naturalistic and non-theatrical and flexible sources used as stimuli and improvisatory and embodied performance modes, and now I shall turn to devising and directorial methods that were used at the Studio – and in our practice research – and the politics of the social dimension of collaborative practice.

### 4.1 Directing: The politics of who, what and how

In addition to being an actor and teacher of actors, Chekhov also worked as a director for much of his career (Black 1987; Chamberlain 2004, 2010; Byckling 2002, 2015; Cornford 2012; Fleming 2013; Chamberlain and Kirillov 2013, 2015; Meerzon 2015). He began directing in Russia and went on to direct productions in Berlin, Paris, Latvia, Lithuania, in the studio context at Dartington and later in America. Chekhov directed a range of productions during his lifetime, including classical and contemporary plays, operas and experimental devised theatre productions. At the Studio he directed many devised performances and trained directors to work on these types of experimental projects. While Chekhov's circumstances and era were not conducive to the experimental strand of his practice and the related directorial methods, the rise of devised, physical and visual theatre in the past forty years in Britain have now created the space to better recognize his technique in these contexts.

Chekhov talked extensively about how his technique was concerned with not only what actors, directors and devising makers do, but also how they do it. Chekhov's methods of collaborative theatre-making and his approach to directing at the Studio were heavily influenced by his use of progressive pedagogy partly inspired by Steiner's schools and philosophy. This included the centrality of the actors, or participants, who are perceived and facilitated as artists capable of creation rather than passive interpreters of material. The notion of experiential learning, the centrality of play, the belief that artists can function as collaborative communities, and the principles of auto-education were all central to the methods he developed and used in the making of experimental work. Crucially, these principles of pedagogy can, in part, be read as methods for devised theatre-making and direction at the Studio, and they offer contemporary devised theatre helpful tools. Finding non-oppressive ways to collaborate has long been a part of the history of devised theatre-making and when discussing 'The Role of the Director' after the formal opening of the Studio, Chekhov explained his different approach to directing:

> *The director and the cast must be open to each other so that the time will come when they fall in love with something mutual. In other words, they must infect each other. The director must infect his cast, but he must take all their ideas too. There is no mechanical way. A director can be a despot like Meyerhold, but this is another way.* (TAITT: 25 January 1936)

Chekhov stressed that this is dependent on 'cooperative, collaborative and co-creative ensemble feeling' which requires an 'openheartedness' towards each other and these connections (1963: 78–9), which he defines as making significant **contact**.

For Chekhov, the role of director carries with it social and creative responsibilities and power which required artists to '*have a good style to be able to work as workers*', and this relates to a '*social approach to life*' (TAITT: 30 January 1939). Chekhov's approach was built on an attentiveness to the quality of the interpersonal relationships between the director and actor/student, or any collaborators, and he articulated the personal qualities and interpersonal skills he felt were needed to achieve this and how a use of aspects of his technique could help them to achieve this other form of directing. Entering the rehearsal space as a director is also performative; it is a role, and it rests on these interpersonal relationships and a specific use of energy. The director is encouraged to use his technique of **radiating** – the identification of their own psychophysical energy, life force and the capacity to both radiate it out strongly into space to others and the world around them, and receive others' energy into themselves – in just the same way as the actors. At the same time, Chekhov believed that directors – and teachers – need to be honest with themselves about whether or not they have made significant contact with those they are working with. This requires a level of self-assessment and the capacity to identify their own strengths, weaknesses and habitual patterns, not just those of their actors (LTT: 15 May 1936). This idea dismantles the notion of the director, or teacher, being all-knowing and infallible and requires humility and flexibility. While the director is earning the trust of their actors, they too have to trust the capacity of their actors as artists.

The specification of personal qualities by Chekhov could seem to bestow, or require, guru status on directors or teachers. However, Chekhov offers a number of crucial guiding principles that help the director or teacher avoid this. He perceived this as a relational process in which a teacher, or director, leads by serving those who are being led, not by demanding service (Chekhov 2005: 52) but by being prepared to empower the actor as an active maker of theatre, leading to a markedly different model of practice. Central to this model is the use of humour and a less aggressive style. Chekhov believed that

> to be able to laugh means to get a more objective point of view of oneself. If I laugh at others, it is not very beneficial to me, but if I laugh at myself, it means I am growing. [. . .] The more we can look objectively upon ourselves, the more our artistic abilities are flourishing, because the thing which keeps us contracted at times is our selfishness and our concern with ourselves. (1985: 129)

Rather than shying away from the personal attributes, qualities and skills that Chekhov required from his directors, in our practice research we realized that we needed to embrace this requirement and consider what it brought to our practice in the twenty-first century and to develop concrete techniques to achieve working in this way. We found that the actor-centred methods that directors can use with Chekhov technique, along with play, humour and his notion of love, offered an empowerment that provided space to welcome and negotiate difference and allowed varied interpretations and expressions to coexist in more polyvocal processes and the eventual performance material. Our research also highlighted just how significant Chekhov's centralizing of both play and pleasure in training and theatre-making is and the way in which these principles help to develop a sense of *ease* in a devising process and to support a more equal, pleasurable, relational and collaborative dialogue.

## 4.2 The juggler psychology for devised theatre-making

Chekhov did not distinguish between process and performance. He argued instead that actors would not 'notice any substantial difference between the exercise and your professional work' which confirms their 'belief that dramatic art is nothing more than constant improvisation, and that there are no moments on the stage when an actor can be deprived of his right to improvise' (2002: 40). Chekhov's own application of improvisation led to performances that were famously different from night to night and Hurst du Prey noted his performances were like 'a game between him and his audience' (1978: 13). He argued that the actor's 'compelling desire and highest aim can be achieved only by means of free improvisation' (2002: 35) and that this right allocated to the actor is central to their transformation from a passive interpreter into a co-creator of original material in a devising process.

Improvisation is of course a central feature of most of the devising processes that evolved in the twentieth century. However, for Chekhov this centrality of improvisation also requires the development of a particular disposition by both the actor and director to treat anything as potentially a springboard for improvisation and the generation of original material. This disposition and skill Chekhov termed the **juggler's psychology** (Hurst du Prey 1978: 13), which both required and concurrently developed advanced improvisational skills based on ingenuity and originality, facilitated by a very particular use of his technique. This creative juggler's psychology was to be applied to everything: '*If we grow accustomed to considering our simple exercises as wonders, we will get from them much more than if we consider them something dull and ordinary. We rob ourselves of a certain power. We reject something which is very necessary for our creative work. We must do our simplest exercises with love and care*' (TAITT: 16 December 1937). This approach requires a particular type of directorial and devising process – the how – built on this capacity to turn even simple exercises into wonders that could lead anywhere, including the generation of original performance material. Indeed, he explained to the students that '*by our exercises we are creating scaffolding on which we will build our play*' (TAITT: 10 November 1936). However, this did not mean that directors only facilitated the development of the juggler's psychology in their actors; crucially, Chekhov believed they needed to develop this principle and skill in their own directorial practice and seek to be spontaneous and original instead of slavish in their use of his techniques. In order to develop an effective juggler's psychology, and to embed this in a devising process, directors need to develop the capacity to give and receive, which in turn requires an openness and ability to observe, listen, sense and be interested in and attentive to their actors or students and their work. This form of contact aims to give *'the feeling that you are with them in what they are doing'* (LTT: 13 April 1936). While these skills seem obvious for directors, the emphasis on textual analysis and dramaturgy and the status awarded to the role of director often marginalize the development of these tools in contemporary practice. Combined, these methods can arguably build a sense of security and of being understood. In order to be open, actively improvise, give, radiate, receive and exchange in this context to make contact, Chekhov argued that teachers need to relate to their students with their *'whole being'* and distinguished this from merely engaging with them on an intellectual level (LTT: 11 April 1936) – and he later tells the directors just the same. Consequently, he required the directors to direct, using their juggler's psychology, embodied imagination and energy in addition to intellectual and verbal processes.

## 4.3 Devising and directing with grounds and spines

Hurst du Prey explained that Chekhov *'called the points of [his] Method* **grounds** *on which the actor stood'* (1992, MC/S9/2). This was not merely a metaphor but a significant and concrete methodology. Chekhov advised Hurst du Prey and Straight to select and use grounds in their teaching: '[you] *must direct the student and tell him what to look for. You must ask him to be attentive to the form, colour, quality, shape, texture, relation, etc.'* (LTT: 11 April 1936). Being attentive to these points of the method as potential 'grounds' offers a specific way of working by channelling the focus and engagement of actors. Crucially, this use of grounds also formed the foundation of a distinct directorial method that Chekhov taught at the Studio, as he explained, *'one of our methods of approach when rehearsing even the smallest scene, is to be led by something definite, and this we call a "ground"'* (TAITT: 8 December 1938). Moreover, mining the archive revealed just how significant the use of grounds was in relation to catalysing and harnessing the creativity of the devisors that was needed to generate original devised performance. On 8 December 1938, the Studio shared work they had developed on *Spanish Evening,* inspired by *Commedia dell'Arte* and featuring a number of classic character types from this genre, made through a process of devising in collaboration with author Henry Lyon Young *'who has made an offering of his play for our experiments (this is what we call collaborating with the author)'* (MC/S1/17: 1). This was an open rehearsal of their experiments, and in his draft speech Chekhov explains this specific technique to the audience:

> We shall start by demonstrating to you that part of the Method which we call 'Rehearsing on Different Grounds'. That means when we are rehearsing scenes we always define for ourselves the aim or leading idea which is like a spine running through the main scene. The ground can be atmosphere, for instance, or character, objective, psychological gesture and so on. (MC/S1/17: 1)

The rehearsal plan for this event detailed the selected grounds that the actors would work with in relation to specific scenes so that there was a shared understanding of these points of focus and retention of the juggler psychology in performance. As these quotations demonstrate, the use of grounds was often, although not always, related to Chekhov's concept of working with what he terms the 'spine' of a class, rehearsal or process of devised theatre-making. In relation to teaching and directing he argues: *'If you try to find "the spine" in everything you teach, without losing details, you will get a very interesting feeling which can help you to teach and be taught'* (LTT: 25 April 1936). He discusses the notion of the spine many times, and in different ways, over the life of the Studio in relation to acting, directing, devised theatre-making and writing. In a later class for Hurst du Prey and Straight he explains it thus:

> 'THE SPINE' (RHYTHM) – *'The 'spine', or essence, or fundamental quality, or essential character of a thing. You must feel and sense this essence – there is no law about it. [. . .] You must find 'the spine' in every feeling, every act, every idea. In some cases it is good to have 'the spine' as intellectual idea, and in some cases it must be a sensation or feeling.* (LTT: 2 June 1936)

Because Chekhov argues there is no 'law' in identifying the spine, or the more fluid and embodied notion of an essence (as lifeblood, the core, a heart) in sensations, feelings, or an intellectual idea, this discovery and exploration of a spine is open to multiple interpretations. It can be based in imaginatively and intuitively embodied, rhythmic, sensory, intuitive *and* intellectual impulses. The holistic nature of working in relation to spines, with an application of different grounds, also changes the conception of the spine itself, as exploration and development of the material in a devising process evolves.

This provides a flexible frame discovered, developed and redeveloped in a cyclical process and owned by the ensemble. This cyclical frame concurrently underpins Chekhov's technique of the ensemble and directors identifying and exploring what he calls leading questions about their work and characters. These leading questions are explored through an application of grounds, and spines, and this practical exploration then leads to the identification of further questions, ad infinitum. Consequently, these grounds and spines are specific, yet flexible and imaginatively embodied, tools for directing and devising practice. Chekhov believed that *'imagination is the language which the director and actors speak to each other. Instead of intellectual understanding – imagination. This is absolutely necessary, not only for speaking but for creating'* (TAITT: 22 February 1938), and he taught his trainee directors to use grounds and spines to develop and share this language of imagination. He explained in the first term of the Studio, *'the director will only give small pieces of what he has in mind. The actors must take these with imagination'* (TAITT: 13 November 1936). This process of selection, reduction and intensification of focus was facilitated by a use of different grounds:

> [W]e should never start our performances, and even rehearsals, without having chosen a special point of our method which will become a starting point, a springboard, for our rehearsing and for our performances. It can be anything: Radiation; Atmosphere; Objective; Feeling of the Whole [. . .] having in mind this particular point of our methods, our attention will be concentrated on it, our interest will be awakened, and the feeling of being 'dry' or uninspired will disappear immediately. (Chekhov 2004: Disc 3)

In addition to grounds and spines being used for acting, teaching and directing, they also acted as a catalyst for the generation of original material in devised rehearsal processes. Hurst du Prey recalls that in January 1937 *'Chekhov announced that we were to be divided* into groups which were given a scene which would be performed at the end of the term. The purpose was to involve the "points" of the method as "grounds" for our rehearsal' (MC/S9/2). Later that term he notes the accessibility of grounds to the student directors working on *Balladina*: 'It is very simple for the director to ask himself, has the actor a ground? What ground shall I give him? To find the ground for today's rehearsal is enough – it does not need to be a revelation about the play' (TAITT: 16 March 1937). This takes considerable pressure off directors and at the same time intensifies their work. The following year, he expressed concern that the student directors had not sufficiently used grounds in their work and, crucially, stressed that directors need a clear method as much as their actors. He argues that if the director gives some suggestion, in the form of a ground, it will appeal to the actor's imagination and is therefore an artistic method that allows the actor to 'receive the directions and instructions with inner action' and that 'the director is able to describe things that will never be turned into dry intellectual content' (TAITT: 22 February 1938). Grounds, therefore, offer a method for directors and devised theatre-makers that keeps them anchored in an imaginative and actor-centred process but ensures that there is a clear and strong focus for the creative work.

However, a use of grounds also requires the director to trust their actors' capacity as equal creators in the process and develop the capability to share the creative space with them. While the director is still very much in control of the process, their role does have to move away from hierarchical concepts of the director, and this requires particular creative, technical and interpersonal skills. Chekhov also wanted his directors to allow themselves the freedom to work playfully and believed that doing so further enabled the actors and co-devisors. He also believed that the use of grounds facilitated working in this way. Chekhov argued that 'it is only by experiments, by attempts at innovation, that [the director] can bring his ingenuity fully into play' (1963: 78). He explained to the students that if a director 'does not know his aim he must experiment' (TAITT: 16 March 1937) and that '[b]y doing many experiments which may be wrong, the director will find the right way. A poor director will cling to some of his ideas, but the good director will try everything. Don't be afraid of experiments which can be wrong' (TAITT: 28 January 1937). Chekhov therefore advises directors to 'let everything happen. Let it be right or wrong and don't worry about it' (1985: 46) and highlights the need for artists to be open to 'accidental discoveries' in improvisation (2002: 38). This experimentation obviously carries with it a risk of failure in this engagement of the unknown, but the use of grounds (with or without spines) removes the pressure and pretence of being the all-knowing director, and it shares the responsibility of creation of material with the actors as fellow artists. Chekhov realized that directors are as prone to inhibitions and nerves as actors and claims that an effective method for overcoming this is 'the application of the ensemble feeling in rehearsal' (1963: 78–9). In his suggestion to the trainee teachers, he notes they should not dominate the process or rush the actors: '*Deirdre spoke too much to the students while they were working. She explained things too much. You must think of yourself as leading each individual through certain experiences [. . .] which may be of use to them as actors*' (TAITT: 1 May 1939). Chekhov also applied this pedagogic approach to the facilitation of an 'experience' to their directing methodology and work ethic as ensembles of collaborative artists. This led to a method that enabled directors to facilitate and guide the work of actors/devised makers without over-directing them and provided a way to relieve their own nerves, self-consciousness and unregulated ego drive.

As we have seen, Chekhov urges the young directors to use the grounds to help them feel confident enough to start more simply and trust that this simplicity in the hands of actors as creative artists in a devising process will lead to complexity and depth. This simplicity also enables the directors to remain authentic in their practice and to maintain their own sense of ease in their directorial process: '*At the beginning stages we must not force [our imagination] by pretending we have more to show than we have. Just the most simple steps are enough*' (TAITT: 30 January 1939). Moreover, Chekhov explained that '*every student will be required to give suggestions to the directors. [. . .] In this way the directors will receive many new ideas which they will be able to apply to their sketches*' (TAITT: 13 July 1937) and this identifies new grounds, and therefore questions, and reconfigured spines, for exploration in the process. One of the key findings of our research was that in Chekhov's approach, the director gives the actors more space to be creative artists, and to devise material, by giving them ostensibly less. The director is, therefore, often skilfully functioning as a creative and responsive catalyst. This catalyst director provides alternative creative pathways, leading to new discoveries and reactions by supporting, and improvising with, the ensemble in playing with these grounds, spines and questions in a theatre-making process.

## 4.4  Grounds, play and games in practice

Gordon (1985), Black (1987), Chamberlain (2004, 2010), Merlin (2001), Ashperger (2008) and Petit (2010) refer to a notion of play when discussing Chekhov's technique, although they do not offer an expanded discussion of this dimension of his practice. Related to the use of grounds is the way in which Chekhov talks extensively about these points of his technique operating as 'games' to be played by actors, directors and theatre-makers (2002). For example, he suggests actors approach **imaginary body** and **imaginary centre** from this perspective: 'Consider creating and assuming a character as a kind of quick and simple game. "**Play**" with the imaginary body, changing and perfecting it until you are completely satisfied with your achievement' (80). He advises engaging with his technique of the imaginary centre 'freely and playfully' to create characters, and performance material and explains that if actors play with this 'game' they will find that innumerable possibilities will be 'opened up' (82). Chekhov goes on to argue that he does not need to specify further exercises relating to these points of the method, as once the actors and directors have learnt how to 'play' with these games, the act of playing itself will automatically enable them to devise new forms of the game (84). He also points out that possibilities will emerge for the actor, director and theatre-maker, if they are willing to engage freely with the various 'games' and that if they are able to trust this process, and enter into it fully, they will appreciate both the enjoyment inherent in playing this game and its considerable practical value. Directors, therefore, need to learn how to design, set up and lead 'games' using grounds and spines to catalyse such play.

Chekhov also explicitly talks about how his technique can be used as grounds for creation with or without an existing play text, or even a stimulus or spine, of any kind. In a class held on 27 September 1937 he explains to the students that they will work on small sketches '*no more than one minute, perhaps even less*' (TAITT: 27 September

1937), teaching them to quickly and spontaneously invent and create performance and how devising artists may become 'playwrights' in their own right. He also encourages the students to devise characters from real and visualized objects, animals, structures or natural forms, such as trees, through a use of grounds that can be creatively used for devising, instead of, or in addition to, non-theatrical text. Indeed, this form of freer play with only a ground can lead to the discovery of a spine through the process of improvisation itself. In this context, Chekhov's use of grounds functions like the rules of a creative game; led by the director, it takes the actor into a state of creative play and simultaneously teaches the ensemble how to devise new games and approaches for themselves. Significantly, the actor can also facilitate this play-based process for themselves. In addition to working with different grounds as a type of game, or frame for creative play, Chekhov also advocated the use of children's games without any adaptations made for adult actors (1919, in 1983b: 54–5) and the ball games his technique is now well known for. These were used in both training and devised rehearsal processes to develop their creative imagination and their capacity to create, rather than merely interpret, material and to develop a specific type of energy, focus and form of ingenuity.

The methods developed by Chekhov drew extensively on these 'games' and play frames for both individual and ensemble work. However, these games are varied in nature and are not often concerned with the notion of a winner or loser. The 'rules' or 'frames' or 'grounds' can be flexible, which means they can be internally or externally imposed, changed, broken, dropped or reinvented. Play socializes relationships and engagements in general, but Chekhov's play also draws on the ways in which the actor experiences themselves in relation to their own imagination and inner life and also in relation to all the experiences external to them, such as making contact and energetic exchanges with other performers, the audience and, importantly, the natural world (including nature, elements, animals and the environment identified in the fairy/folk tales and myths) and society. This relational dimension also applies to space, the scenographic world of the performance, that is, all the scenic pieces, costumes, objects, colour, use of light and sound as discussed in Chapter 5 by Sinéad Rushe.

This use of play and game structure as a trigger, and catalyst, for creativity and an underlying methodology for devised theatre-making is discussed in relation to the French tradition of devised performance (Suzanne Bing, Jacques Copeau, Marie-Hélène and Jean Dasté, Jacques Lecoq), but it is often overlooked in Chekhov's work. There are a number of important points of convergence between Chekhov's work and Suzanne Bing and Jacques Copeau's earlier practice (and Lecoq's later work based on this methodology) in this respect, which I have discussed in detail elsewhere (Fleming 2013), but in this discussion I will draw on some of the discussion of Lecoq's later notion of play, 'le jeu', to help to illuminate this aspect of Chekhov's devising and directorial practice. Murray's discussion of 'le jeu' and its relationship to actors working as co-authors/makers of material is helpful to our understanding of the principle of play and a use of grounds in Chekov's process of devising at the Studio:

> [P]lay is the *driver* of creativity. Without a disposition – and ability – to play it is impossible to produce the conditions whereby the actor/performer is a creator rather than simply interpreter. While the divisions between being a *creative* as opposed to an *interpretative* actor are neither rigid or impermeable, Lecoq is proposing a model of performing where

the actor is the (co-) author-maker of material whether it is physical, spoken, musical or imagistic' (2010: 223)

Frost and Yarrow note that for Lecoq 'le jeu' also '[signifies] the energy that is shared between performers on stage and in rehearsal – the ball that the game is played with – which is why for him improvisation is very much a matter of physical activation. "Play" also means the *inter-play* of this activity, emphasising the relationships that spark off or create new combinations' (2016: 71). Chekhov's work with energy and radiating, his commitment to what he defines as making contact and a clear use of grounds, play and game principles, along with the use of these tools in devised practice, evidence a clear correlation here in the use of play (Fleming 2013). There are, however, important differences between Chekhov's forms of play through a use of grounds and spines to Lecoq's notion of 'le jeu', and it is therefore important to reflect on how his methods work in a devising process and to consider why they remain such a valuable tool for the directors and actors in devised theatre-making today.

Despite a growing interest in play during the twentieth and twenty-first centuries, there has been no agreement on a singular definition of this ambiguous, culturally and historically situated, phenomenon (Huizinga 1955; Sutton-Smith 2008; Schechner 1993; Henricks 2015). Stuart Brown (2009) has suggested that play's significance is now being better understood as a fundamental biological and neurological process and argues that for humans 'play lies at the core of creativity and innovation' (4–5) and that contrary to the view of play in the West, '[w]e are designed to be lifelong players, built to benefit from play at any age' (48). A utilization of play and games can be seen as a way of harnessing and catalysing artists' creative and inventive potential in a devising process seeking to embrace the unknown in order to improvise, transform and invent original material in tandem with developing the skills to play with a wide range of stimuli. Play is also understood to be a motor-based, fully embodied activity which enables body-mind integration, what Caillois defines as a 'total activity' (2001: 175), or psychophysical, in Chekhov's parlance. So how does this use of a juggler psychology and play principle work in Chekhov's devising and directorial practice? Chekhov argued that when actors are 'occupied' in the specified ground, for example a particular gesture, 'our talent is freed' (1985: 11) and this becomes the trigger for this type of playful and creative experience. John Wright, a British director who draws on the work of Lecoq and Chekhov in his devised practice, also describes this principle in relation to games: 'All games, whether open or closed, inspire spontaneous physical reaction and they keep these reactions live. Games confine action to a simple structure; they impose limitations on us in order to make us do something; they restrict us and channel our creativity' (2006: 86). Victor Turner, the performance anthropologist, discusses play and games in relation to the 'flow' experience theorized by Csíkszentmihályi and MacAloon (cited in Turner 1982). They define flow as a holistic sensation that occurs when one acts with total involvement, removing a sense of duality. This correlates to Hurst du Prey's reflection on Chekhov's technique of **awareness** which required the actor 'being absolutely open to what is going on, so that it flows into you and takes you and lifts you and moves you' and notes that this must include every part of your being 'body, soul and spirit' (1978: 10). Turner explains that by abiding by types of limitations (i.e. the use of grounds as rule for a creative game, as Chekhov does) to trigger this flow experience 'our minds and our will are thus disencumbered from irrelevances and sharply focused in certain known directions' (1982: 56) and that the rules of a game 'dismiss as irrelevant most of the "noise" which makes up social reality, the multiform stimuli which impinge on our consciousness' (1982: 56). Therefore the intensification of concentration generated through the heightened engagement, the awareness, with the chosen ground in the making or rehearsal process results in the actor being able to exclude some, but not necessarily all, of their social 'noise' (and customary restraint) and find a different type of engagement in the moment of initial creation. Flow is seen as a way of heightening creativity and lessening the self-consciousness and self-censorship that the actor, and director, can often feel, and it is evident that Chekhov understood that this is an important tool for devised theatre-makers.

Chekhov's directing and devising methods were certainly limiting the stimulus field by using the principle of grounds, which can be seen to merge action and awareness in the moment. However, he did not dismiss anti-flow entirely, as he also required actors/directors to reflect on what they have experienced, and required directors to be able to view the work from the outside. The key to this is when this movement of anti-flow takes place in a devised process. Chekhov described the process of actors looking back on their creation after working with a chosen ground as keeping a 'spying eye' upon themselves (1991: 109) to see where their spontaneous play has led them. Later in a theatre-making process, after working with various grounds, spines and leading questions over time (what he describes as the fourth stage of exploration, 155), Chekhov also encourages artists to develop a sense of what he termed the **divided consciousness** (the capacity to be both inside, and outside of, the performance) so that they have a clear sense of their relationship of the whole composition and strong contact with their fellow actors and – crucially – the spectators. Chekhov notes that the 'answer' or discoveries may come in the moment of acting (or devising) or afterwards, but using this principle avoids intellectual reasoning dominating the early part of the process. This technique is particularly helpful when devising, as it ensures that actors/makers/directors do not self-censor their creativity too soon but ultimately achieve the capacity to be both inside and outside the work.

The advice Chekhov gave to support the directing and acting students in the development of one of their devised versions of 'The Fishers' Scene', based on an invented scenario, shown in Figure 1.1, is enlightening in this context, and we drew on it extensively in our practice research. 'The Fishers' Scene' is the story of a chorus of villagers awaiting the return of fishermen who are caught in a fierce storm and has been insightfully analysed by Jonathan Pitches, who argues that the students' work on this project exemplified Chekhov's use of progressive pedagogy in relation to the way in which it provides synthetic learning and a process-led, experiential training (2013: 227). The archive holds various visual scores (diagrams, paintings, sketches), including one for the entire 'Fishers' Scene' by Hurst du Prey, one in relation to composition by Rogers and two by Straight on her character. Some of these are reproduced by Pitches, and we drew on these valuable resources in our research. These scenarios were used to specifically train the students as devised theatre-makers, heeding Chekhov's advice that '*The play must be invented when the rehearsals are going on. It must not be written before*' (TAITT: 28 January 1937), meaning they often started to work without writers or written materials. Chekhov's decision to initially verbally describe this story as the springboard for the devising process in certain classes during the life of the Studio is significant here. Indeed, Chekhov proposed that it was only '*after the author has*

```
M. Chekhov                              January 14, 1937

        image is of a girl of thirteen or fourteen who loses her
        elder brother in the tragedy; she has kept house for him.
        Catherine's image is of a boy of ten or twelve, in love with
        the adventure of going to sea.  Felicity's image is of a sad,
        lonely figure:  a bride of eighteen, who has come from an-
        other village.

        General advice:

                1. The cast must follow the director with the
                imagination only.

                2. The feelings can be awakened through means of
                action, atmosphere, or imagination.

                3. The director need not use the results of some of
                the work at once.  Perhaps he can use it later on
                in the play.

                4. Repeat each exercise, each moment, many times
                until a good result has been reached.  Meditate
                upon it each time.

                5. It is wrong to ask your actors to act at once -
                they will only lie.  Begin by exploring, discovering,
                imagining, and doing.

                6. The actor's approach is with the body and the
                feelings - not the intellect.

                7. Ask your body what it can tell you; each muscle
                will tell you something.

                8. Try to find the spine of the sketch.  This can
                be done by finding the most important points in its
                development.

                9. Always jot things down or draw them because
                they will add to your material.  In later stages of
                your work you will be very happy to have these notes
                because they represent your first impressions and
                will inspire you.

                10. When you discover that your body can speak to you,
                you will be greatly enriched as an actor.  It will no
                longer be an enemy as it is with most actors today,
                but it will inspire you.
```

Fig. 1.1 Advice to students on 'The Fishers' Scene', photograph of class notes. TAITT: 14 January 1937, CTS-DHDPA.

*seen the sketch performed, [that] he must be able to re-write them because he has got new ideas, and the actors will re-act the new texts'* (TAITT: 18 February 1939).

This advice highlights the imaginative and embodied nature of his directorial method. The second point in the general advice lists key grounds that directors can work with (for example, objective atmosphere) as a form of play, and the material is developed through organic cycles of evolving repetition. Objective **atmosphere** is a central technique for Chekhov, who argues that 'atmospheres are limitless and to be found everywhere. Every landscape, every street, every house, room [. . .] every phenomenon and event has its own particular atmospheres' (2002: 48) and that in life we, often unwittingly, change 'movements, speech, behaviour, thoughts and feelings as soon as you create a strong, contagious atmosphere' (49). As the archival materials, and our practice research found, it is central to Chekhov's model of devising. The fifth point is significant as it relates to a more autotelic use of the grounds to facilitate this exploration, discovery and imaginative engagement in directorial and devised theatre-making processes. Chekhov explained this further to his trainee directors in a class the following week: '*The later [the director] allows his actors to act, the better the quality will be. After he sees that inspiration has touched his actors, he must let them be free. At the beginning the director must improvise, then later the actors will improvise for him*' (TAITT: 19 January 1937). This dovetails with another feature of Csíkszentmihályi and MacAloon's notion of flow experience, which is that it has an autotelic nature that is, there are no goals or rewards outside itself (Turner 1982: 56–8). While a use of these grounds in Chekhov's practice was not in itself purely autotelic – they were being used to develop material for a performance, an end result – they do require a paradoxical autotelic attitude to playing in order to function with efficacy. Chekhov points out that while the actor cannot attempt to play with these grounds with the intention of quickly achieving an end result or fixed goal, this equally applies to the work of the director facilitating this process: 'My whole interest is directed towards the process of the work itself, its results coming as something unexpected' (2005: 114–15). He explains that actors and directors must trust that these grounds of the method will be 'powerful enough to change your psychology and your way of acting without being "helped" by pushing or forcing of any kind' (2002: 138). This requires the directors to engender a sense of ease, patience and curiosity in a rehearsal process in order to not pressure their performers to 'act' too soon and to develop a sense of being open to discoveries that can 'drop' into their creative process if they are able to avoid rushing, or attempting to predetermine the end results. This opens the whole ensemble to chance, serendipity and accidental discovery and trains them to trust their own intuitive responses and be willing to take creative risks and make discoveries through failure. These are key skills for devising artists, particularly those who opt to generate most of their material through improvisatory processes. We also see Chekhov advocating a use of the spying eye and anti-flow, in the moments after the improvisation, when they 'meditate' on what they have done. The sixth and tenth points on the list recognize the body as a source of 'knowledge' and suggest that a director can facilitate the ensemble to play through a use of various different spines and grounds so that the entire ensemble can 'think in motion', a key feature of play (Brown 2009). In the ninth point, Chekhov advises that in addition to taking notes, directors and actors can produce drawings in relation to their impressions and explorations, and states that this is important in terms of finding non-verbal ways to be attentive to and express aspects of the work that can engage with image, gesture, dynamics, rhythm, qualities, shape, colour, texture and relation, all of which will then function as important grounds at some point in the making process.

Directors are encouraged to use the various methods, including grounds and spines, to discover the play principle themselves. It is this development of the juggler psychology – as a disposition rather than just an activity – that can turn any kind of work with a ground, or an exercise, into a form of play and a potential generator of original devised material. As Chekhov explains: '*[W]hen the director begins to play with the Method as with balls, that is the right use of the Method*' (TAITT: 4 March 1937). It is this capacity to direct using an improvisational and responsive use of grounds that will enable them to enter a flow state at various points in the making and rehearsal process, in order to be with their actors and to discover ingenuity and originality. This juggler psychology is something that directors have to establish and nurture in their actors but arguably can only be fully achieved if the directors have developed this disposition in themselves.

The archive holds other guidance, charts and diagrams that vary in terms of detail, and offer considerable variations in approach, but they all retain the central principles and the development of the juggler psychology, and the core use of grounds and spines as catalysts for play and invention, and cyclical work patterns. In *On the Technique of Acting* (1991) Chekhov outlines four stages of a creative process, but crucially points out that they do not have to be followed in a precise or pedantic way. This leads to original and playful ways of exploring the text or stimuli, and what he defines as a non-materialistic analysis (LTT: 4 June 1936). As we have seen, Chekhov suggests that early in a rehearsal process the companies explore a score of atmospheres that they have identified in the material in contrast to undertaking detailed, rational-intellectual textual analysis around a table. Indeed, he told his students to '*[l]isten and rely on the atmosphere and you will get more suggestions than you will from any director in the world*' (TAITT: 21 August 1939). It is also atmosphere that Chekhov believes enables real contact, reciprocal action, between actors and spectators. His suggestion that a director enables the same scene/section be played cyclically a number of times by the actors exploring different grounds for play (e.g. psychological gesture, imaginary centre) is reminiscent of 'toys' being available to play with in relation to the stimulus material for a devising process or a pre-existing script. In the context of Chekhov technique operating as a synthetic whole, often one ground or toy will bring the others into play. The director may remain with one 'ground' for a period of time, return to previous 'grounds' and later combine two, three or more together (Chekhov 1991: 53–4) as the work becomes more complex. As the process develops, different actors can focus on different grounds at the same time. As these grounds and spines operate as imaginatively embodied 'springboards', it moves beyond an application in limited or mechanistic frameworks and becomes a more synthetic approach.

An exemplar from our work on *The Little Prince* demonstrates the way in which the use of the juggler psychology, catalysed through a game structure to explore objective atmosphere and various grounds, led to the synthetic development of one of the devised scenes. The character of the Rose (played by MacLellan, a man) arrives unexpectedly as a seed and grows on the Little Prince's planet (played by Mitchell, a woman), who has never seen a rose. Chapter eight of the novella explores their subsequent complex relationship, which was explored in a compressed and symbolic time frame in our performance. Initial improvisational games were based on the ground of the objective atmosphere, the image of the rose and our intuitive ideas about the spine. Our initial map and diagram of objective atmospheres noted a shift between various different atmospheres. The first was one of everyday routine for the Little Prince, which shifts to one of discovery, excitement and anticipation when she notes the rose growing on her planet. As the Rose grows and opens, the atmosphere evolves into one of seduction and fascination, which reaches a point of closer intimacy between the lovers before there is a further change in the atmosphere to one of distance and regret as the relationship becomes disconnected and problematic. I gave the actors ground of atmosphere and added the exchange of juggling balls as a way to add in the ground of dynamics. This was then developed organically in cycles of playful exploration triggered by an application of further grounds and combinations. For example, MacLellan chose to work with the psychological gesture of wring – 'manipulate, bend, fascinate, unravel, fool, seduce, charm, trick, oil, twist, beguile, trap, mold' (Ashperger 2008: 320) – in relation to the objective he had identified for the character, so that as he physically grew and opened his petals he seduced the transfixed Little Prince. The dynamic of the seduction – the shift in atmospheres and the fact that the Rose remained in fixed space (as a rooted plant) while the Little Prince moved to watch him grow – emerged. In response to this and their subsequent use of space and dynamics, I improvised by introducing a hand touch game, retaining the work on gesture and adding exploration of **movement qualities** as additional grounds. The game also required the actors to fully trust and be led by an application of grounds, and it produced interesting results. In this game the Rose had to place his hand somewhere in the space around him and the Little Prince had to touch it. This game eventually brought them into close physical contact, and through working with the ground of movement qualities, the touches became intimate. When their relationship starts to falter, the Rose will no longer engage with their game and as his gesture moves to one of closing, they enter an atmosphere of disconnection, resignation and regret. This use of atmosphere, grounds and the game structure organically developed and became the metaphoric representation of the stages of their relationship. MacLellan's use of gesture in this scene had a higher level of 'poetic trace' in that it was visible in a direct sense, unlike the use of gesture by other characters in our performance, and meant that the movement language was foregrounded. Moreover, the fact that the Rose was played by a male actor who was working with these grounds led to interesting physical work that transgressed dominant ideas about masculinity. In this sense we felt the fairy-tale, non-human elements held potential to disrupt generalized socialized ideas about identity and representation creating a queer form of dramaturgy.

## 4.5 Play, games and naïveté in devised theatre

Chekhov's notion of play means that the actual structuring of the making process must also be based in an autotelic form of play. Chekhov connects this juggler's psychology, or play consciousness, with his technique and principle of making contact. His feedback to students explains this connection:

> *I have seen for the first time today the instinct for playing which children have. [. . .] I have seen you unafraid in contact, and there was a certain charm which is in the playing of children. Keep this in mind, because it is the best quality you can get. And how are we able to awaken this instinct for playing? Through just such pedantic exercises as we have been doing. The more [. . .] you pay attention to all the exercises [. . .] everything, then [. . .] flowers will open inside you, and you will get this ability to play as children, but the difference will be that children are doing it quite instinctively, while you do it with the knowledge which has become again childlike.* (TAITT: 22 October 1937)

In this context, the discussion about children's play turning the 'pedantic' into 'creative flowers' is not as romantic as it might seem. This feedback reveals Chekhov's interest in the notion of child's play, and naïveté, but was not suggesting that adult actors can ever return to being a child. Instead, they can regain a particular type of embodied knowledge, and juggler psychology, which is childlike. As Henricks explains, this 'cognitive style [. . .] encourages [people] to see many situations as play opportunities when others might see those same settings as occasions for drudgery or routine' (2015: 30). Achieving this imaginatively embodied capacity, or skill, in relation to devising performance relates to both the development of a play consciousness and a set of specific methods. Chekhov's work at the Studio evidences a very sophisticated set of practices and techniques used to teach and nurture this type of disposition for play. The rehearsal notes for the Commedia dell'Arte-inspired *Spanish Evening* are enlightening in this respect, and Chekhov explains that this mode of performance requires an engagement with the following form of consciousness:

> *Try to imagine a [very small] child who awakens [. . .]. Observe in your imagination how the child opens its eyes. Try to absorb the child's psychology – not the movements – only the spirit [. . .] we must have a child-like psychology [. . .] open to everything which you see, hear, or do. You absorb everything, being absolutely open. Get it through the psychological gesture.* (TAITT: 17 January 1939)

He believes that this is achieved when the actors are '*absolutely centred on something – absolutely in it, never floundering about*' (TAITT: 17 January 1939), which takes us back to the use of grounds and spines as a process of focusing and intensification in his technique. This equally provides a useful lens for a director in their work. It is particularly helpful in a devising process, as this type of play turns players, without even intending it, into 'agents of change' (Hendricks 2015: 2) and invention.

In 1919 Chekhov reflected on why children are able to use their imaginations more fully than adults and noted the difference in terms of the use of imagination in agrarian/tribal and industrialized societies. Notwithstanding the primitivism that is evident in his writing that our team strongly challenged from a postcolonial perspective, his comments in relation to children's play are useful here. He argues that the modern artist who has been 'brought up on exact sciences' – that is, certain types of post-Enlightenment rationalist and positivist knowledge, or frames of thought – must attempt to develop a certain type of naïveté that enables them to combine elements of their imagination without being dominated by rationalist frames of thought (1919 in 1983: 56). However, it is to his credit that he did not suggest that actors can completely return to some pure pre-adult, un-socialized state through a creative engagement with naïveté, but his methods indicate that it may be possible for adults to regain some aspects of the related disposition and skills for devised theatre-making. Brown argues that 'through movement play, we think in motion' (2009: 84), and Chekhov argued that everything happening in rehearsal can be interpreted by exploring playful 'gesture, action or movement' (1985: 107), which arguably becomes a form of thinking in motion. Chekhov understood that a specific making process was needed to enable this type of thinking and creativity in a devised process, and he told the students that '*we must not kill our intellect and become mere idiots, but we must postpone the work of the intellect until later on, when it will be very useful to us. It must be under the control of the artist, and not the reverse*' (LTT: 2 July 1937). The Chart of Exploration (MC/S8/12) shown in Figure 1.2 provides an exemplar of the naïve processes of theatre-making he developed to facilitate this.

This chart demonstrates a form of non-materialistic textual analysis, which is perhaps better defined as a process of accumulative and relational synthesis (Chekhov 1985: 11). Chekhov argues that while the artists must know as much as possible about the play, the important difference is 'how he knows it' (38), and as the guidance notes and chart reveal, the use of grounds in relation to spines enables the ensemble to know creatively by

CHART OF EXPLORATION
given by Michael Chekhov as a guide for using his method
Chekhov Theatre Studio – Dartington Hall 1937

| I. | IMAGINATION | ATMOSPHERE RADIATION | CHARACTERIZATION | LEADING QUESTIONS | IMAGING THE PLAY & ITS COMPOSITION AFTER THE FALL OF THE CURTAIN |
|---|---|---|---|---|---|
| E X P L O R A T I O N | 1. Reading play by creating images. 2. Enlivening images (people, situations, happenings, decoration) | To get through: 1. Imagination 2. Music 3. Colour and light 4. Sounds 5. Movements | Imaginary body and center in chest Entirely in Imagination | Directors and actors | Becoming acquainted with the composition of the play |

| II. | CHARACTERIZATION | LEADING QUESTIONS | PSYCHOLOGICAL GESTURES | WORDS & EXCLAMATIONS | MOVEMENT |
|---|---|---|---|---|---|
| EXPLORATION BY FLYING OVER THE PLAY AND ATTEMPTS AT INCORPORATION | Attempts at part Incorporation | Leading to incorporation | From generalization to detail as far as possible. TIME \| SPACE ACTIVITY \| QUALITY | 1. On the grounds of psychological gestures 2. In connection with atmosphere 3. Incorporation of that which was heard in the imagination. 4. In connection with characterization 5. Speech formation | 1. Incorporation of separate moments seen in the imagination (acting). 2 Characteristic mise-en-scene (motionless or with movements) Objectives Movement in connection with atmospheres and words |

Fig. 1.2 The Chart of Exploration, 1937, diagram. CTS-DHDPA, MC/S8/12.

playing how to develop what they collectively perceive as the essential structural, dynamic, atmospheric and thematic qualities of their work. In contrast to what Chekhov defines as cold, factual intellect he suggests that we can access a 'knowledge [which] is at the same time an imaginative picture' through the use of his methods (Chekhov 1985: 11). It is hard to know exactly how the Chart of Exploration was used, and in relation to what projects, as there is not a full explanation provided, but we found this intriguing and interesting in terms of it being a visual representation of a process of more naïve exploration. The layout of the chart shows that the process is not linear and that the development of the material is circular and organic and based on a process that can move forwards and backwards. The chart clearly facilitates a less prescriptive, creative and playful experience and helps a director to structure and guide a process in which the actors begin by 'not acting' and they start by not over-directing. For example, in the first phase of exploration on the chart, we see the use of the ground of objective atmosphere, which as we have seen, Chekhov argues can give more than a director's instructions, followed by another ground, imaginary centre, in the next column. The chart supports the empowerment of the actor as maker and foregrounds the playful and exploratory nature of the work as well as the capacity of the director to receive. Chekhov's ideas about working with the ground of imaginary centre exemplify this:

> Never ask anybody whether your idea about the centre is right or correct, use your own judgement; trust your intuition, your imagination, your talent. Of course you might take into consideration your director's suggestion and alter your ideal conception of the centre, but there is no need to doubt your own judgemental, logical approaches to it. [. . .] Enjoy it, play with it like a child would play with its ball. (2004: Disc 1)

In effect, this gives the actor's creative discoveries through play with different grounds as much weight as the director's ideas.

On the chart, the ground of objective is placed beneath the heading of movement, reflecting Chekhov's belief that psychological gesture was the most useful way of identifying, refining and exercising their character's main 'desires' (2002: 63) or 'objectives' (1991: 111), as discovered through intuitive and spontaneous trial and error, in direct contradistinction to an intellectual process of identifying an objective based on early textual analysis, which, he argues, 'cannot be of use to the actor' (1991: 108). For example, he explains to the students: '*If you will build the whole scene by means of your psychological gesture, you will at the same time rehearse the play, but on a level which is much richer*' (TAITT: 23 January 1937). This helps us understand the ways in which Chekhov extended exercises/games fluidly into performance-making.

In his published texts, and the archival materials, Chekhov argues that if the director and actors have an understanding of the play (or devised scenario or source material), there is no need to approach the material in a linear manner in rehearsal. Indeed, he argues that a linear process tends to 'codify and formalise everything into a monotonous pattern' and that 'these inflexible approaches often mean that important moments are neglected' (1963: 86). He proposes that a director 'upsets this orderly but antiquated rehearsal procedure' by approaching the scenes in a different order, 'or with just so many pages from anywhere in the script that he chooses to experiment with' (1963: 86). He notes that 'once a new beginning has been created' in this way 'the cast is out of the rut of repetition and on the alert' (1963: 86), and the different phases and stages of the exploration mapped on the chart demonstrate this. Further, he suggests that the director propose an exploration of the various different forms of **polarity** between the beginning and end of a section, sidetracking the middle section temporarily, in order to make new discoveries. These fresh beginnings operate as newly configured frames for experimentation with different grounds (and become grounds in themselves) through cycles of repetition and variation, requiring the use of the juggler psychology by the director and actors that leads to the organic development of devised material and keeps them in the moment. Chekhov argues that it is problematic to concentrate on one scene too early on and argues that the 'performance will ripen more organically if the cast is given the opportunity to fly over the whole play at each stage of work and even if possible, during rehearsals' (1963: 152–3), as shown on phase II of the Chart of Exploration. This helps the company gain an understanding of the composition and enables them to '*[imagine] the whole of the play when the curtain is down*' (TAITT: 25 February 1938) and identify significant moments that act as signposts and climaxes in relation to the evolving spine. Chekhov notes that an ensemble working in this way will have imaginatively, and collectively, found a clearer sense of the dynamics and direction of the material and a more imaginatively embodied sense of the composition than could be found in a more linear and conventional approach (1963: 87), and we certainly found this to be the case in our practice research.

The rehearsal plan for 'The Fishers' Scene' (MC/S6/3/R) (Figure 1.3) is particularly helpful in giving an insight into how this worked for the directors leading a devising process. There are evidently differences between the advice, chart and rehearsal plan reproduced in this chapter, but the same core principles emerge. In this plan we see the use of spines, psychological gesture (point 2) and grounds (point 3 and 7) and other grounds such as **rhythm and tempo** in relation to the composition of the work and his principle of polarity (point 11). What is of particular interest in this plan is the way in which the students are searching not only for a spine of the play and the characters, but also for the sea, the land and the chorus. In the same way, the director and actor are asked to find a gesture for the various elements. The climax of the scenario is developed through an application of various grounds (point 3), and they are asked to develop the text by using only a few essential words and then adding and developing the spoken dialogue/text in a holistic manner, thereby giving sufficient space for the embodied, spatial and atmospheric language. We also see references to the visual charts the students were asked to produce and the dramaturgical work they carried out through their process. Although contemporary devised work may not be divided into three main divisions or sections due to non-linear narratives and non-narrative forms of performance, the idea of developing dramaturgy as an experiential process, including the identification of climaxes, auxiliary climaxes, gestural, rhythmic and atmospheric patterns on a chart or visual diagrams, can be extremely helpful to the director facilitating a devising process and the development of many different types of performance in the twenty-first century.

The Chekhov Collective worked through four play-based, non-linear and holistic phases inspired by these resources. In each phase we were working cyclically with exploration and experimentation, creating and developing material and characters. We directly explored the archive materials and through this process identified the key methods and concepts that were being used by Chekhov and his students. The practice research was designed to be shared in process – mirroring Chekhov's approach to *Spanish Evening* – at the New Pathways event in 2016, but as a company we also discussed what would have been a fifth and final phase of work if we had intended to take the performance to completion (Table 1.1 shows our own chart of exploration).

To fully commit to this process as a director, I had to resist doing the preliminary selection and adaptation of the stimuli material in advance and allow this aspect of the dramaturgy to come from the imaginatively embodied exploration of the ensemble. We used the methods as a form of dramaturgy to 'audition' the sections of material from the novella and together we identified the images, atmospheres, spines and grounds in order to liberate ourselves

```
                REHEARSAL PLAN FOR "FISHING SCENE"      April 25, 1937.

        In order to bring the play to the point of production the following
        steps will have to be established and developed.

        1.   Establish the spine of the play and the relationship and importance
             of the following elements to the spine:  the Sea, the land, Mother Gillard
             and the people.

        2.   Establish the psychological gesture for the spine of the play - then
             the objective for the spine and the various elements.

        3.   Develop the climax of the play which is John's entrance, by means
             of the following:  MIS EN SCENE, IMAGINATION, ATMOSPHERE, OBJECTIVES,
             LEADING QUESTIONS, PSYCHOLOGICAL GESTURE.

        5.   From this point develop the text by using a few essential words   then
             adding and developing where necessary - always with the spine in mind.

        6.   Do this with each climax and auxiliary climax.

        7.   Work on the CHARACTERS by means of IMAGINATION; INCORPORATION,

        OBJECTIVES, LEADING QUESTIONS, PSYCHOLOGICAL GESTURES and MOVEMENTS.
        Find the inner characterization.

        8.   Through exercises in imagination, music, sounds, etc. the power of the
             sea must be expressed through the speech, movement and psychology of the
             characters on the stage.  This must also give a special quality to the
             voices and the speech, as well as a special significance to the relationship
             of the characters to one another.

        9.   Establish and show on the chart the three major sections - beginning,
             middle and end.  The major climax, the auxiliary/or sub-divisions.  For exampl

        1st Section:              2nd Section:              3rd Section
          Awakening                 Mother Gillard             John's appearance
          Sighting the boat                                    Realization

        (The Major climax, which is John's entrance, is in the 3rd or End part)

        10.  Establish the snecruze and metacruze for each climax and the auxiliary
             climaxes.

        11.  Find the different tempos in the 3 main divisions - the tempo of the
             beginning must differ absolutely from the tempo at the end.
```

Fig. 1.3  A 1937 rehearsal plan for 'The Fishers' Scene', diagram. CTS-DHDPA, MC/S6/3/R.

from the dominance of the text. Chekhov's techniques enable actors and directors to engage with, and 'see' play scripts in quite specific ways. He argued that while the non-actor simply reads the lines of a play script, 'the actor reads between the lines, sees beyond the characters and events of the play. These magic "beyond" and "between" places make up that kingdom in which the talented actor lives and moves freely' (1991: 71). He points out that from this position the actor 'sees the whole play as a stimulus, as a series of signs and indications behind and beyond the words urging and guiding him in his individual acting' (1991: 71), and this was the approach we took to the novella, which was, of course, even less prescriptive than a pre-existing play text. There is an interesting correlation here between Chekhov's ideas about reading the in-between and beyond in texts and a willingness to use a more intuitively embodied, and less rigidly rational, approaches to text and Cixous' later ideas about *écriture féminine* in which 'writing is precisely working (in) the in-between, inspecting the process of the same and of the other without which nothing can live [. . .] dynamized by an incessant process of exchange from one subject to another [. . .]

Table 1.1 The Chart of Exploration, diagram. The Chekhov Collective

| Phase I | Phase II | Phase III | Phase IV | Phase V |
| --- | --- | --- | --- | --- |
| • Making contact.<br>• Becoming an actor-centred ensemble.<br>• Development of the juggler psychology (play consciousness) by both actors and director.<br>• Learning to use the grounds (with and without spines) as catalysts for play and devising.<br>• Playful preliminary, non-linear, explorations of the archival material and the novella.<br>• Identifying initial leading questions about the novella explored through the grounds.<br>• Underpinning the rigour and discipline with humour and pleasure. | • Intuitive exploration of the novella: seeking imaginatively embodied, visual and sociopolitical responses and questions. Provisional selections of the novella.<br>• 'Not acting too soon': non-linear cycles of discovery working with autotelic play.<br>• Exploring the material using objective atmosphere and adding/combining further grounds and spines, creating large maps/diagrams for the chosen material. Flying over material.<br>• Over time identifying (and adapting) key moments, climaxes and spines and adding key words, or sentences, that the actors dropped in as improvised speech.<br>• 'Postponing but not killing the intellect': playing in flow and spying back.<br>• The director working with flexible palettes of materials, grounds, sound, music, objects in order to improvise with the actors. | • Flying over all the diagrams/maps of the objective atmospheres and spines/grounds from start to finish.<br>• Experiencing the emerging dramaturgy: the shifts in atmosphere, rhythm, tempo and dynamics in the piece in relation to a feeling of the whole and polarity (contrast).<br>• Experiencing the real and imagined uses of space, and scenographic elements (i.e. heights) in the composition.<br>• Spying back process: re-arranging the diagrams/maps (pinned to the walls) to change the overall composition and to identify gaps which needed original material or additional ideas from the novella.<br>• Spying back to identify bridges and transitions between the sections.<br>• Identifying the grounds needed for the next phase to develop the material, character work, bridges, transitions and dramaturgy. | • Building on discoveries made through flying over the material with a sense of the emerging (but still changing) composition as a whole.<br>• Further development of material and incorporation of new discoveries and original material made through playing with grounds/spines.<br>• Gradual development of a performance score which retained notes on objective atmosphere, spines and grounds.<br>• Developed scenographic elements become integrated.<br>• Development of the divided consciousness.<br>• Making contact with spectators through various public sharings.<br>• Two-day period to bring the whole piece together through use of grounds/spines.<br>• Sharing of the practice research experiments at New Pathways event and retaining a use of grounds and the juggler psychology. | • We shared our research and development work at the end of the fourth phase at the New Pathways event. If we had intended to take the work to final performance we envisioned a fifth phase would involve: concentrating on the development of the dramaturgy of the piece as a whole; more detailed incorporation of scene/character work and the retention of the juggler psychology; the further development of the chorus; and the involvement of a scenographer and musical director. |

a multiple and inexhaustible course with millions of encounters and transformations of the same into the other and into the in-between' (2010: 36). Consequently, I am arguing that an application of Chekhov's methods of grounds and spines act as liberating springboards that enable a company to 'see', 'encounter' and 'interpret' a text with a juggler psychology. The text becomes a flexible stimulus with a more porous frame of signs providing increased space for extended embodied play as a multidimensional form of 'writing' – or the embodied making of – devised performance.

An example of my improvisational practice as a director working on a choral scene of *The Little Prince* highlights other findings we gleaned from our practice research and how we worked in-between and beyond the text. The novella features a planet inhabited by a businessman who is counting and banking the stars above his planet as a system of ownership and is too busy to meaningfully engage with the Little Prince on her arrival. She eventually challenges the businessman's notion of materialistic ownership and control, before leaving the planet. We drew extensively on objective atmospheres and their associated tempo and rhythms as an initial ground to catalyse play. As we were freely devising from, and not simply staging the text, our initial intuitive maps of atmosphere for this particular scene (which we felt was one of greed, competition, arrogance and control) contained references to the current banking sector based in London and Wall Street and their aggressive late capitalist culture. These intuitive responses expressed by the company led to my decision to catalyse the initial play as a chorus. In order to explore Chekhov's belief that there is no distinction between exercises (and therefore warming up), making and performing, I introduced specific games and grounds for rehearsal from the very start of the warm-ups. For example, for this scene I focused on the staccato rhythm we had related to the objective atmosphere and games based in competition and forms of ownership of space or objects. These warm-ups offered moments of discovery that I then fed back into the later group movement improvisations exploring the grounds of atmosphere and sound, specifically two different sounds of clocks ticking. This was a particularly fruitful period of creation in a flow state. At a later stage in this process, I removed the sound of the ticking clock and introduced the central image we had identified of the businessmen's planet, which was the counting and owning of lots of glittering stars. Using key words from the text then helped us find the gesture of grasping, plucking or grabbing the stars. Without the need for lengthy discussions, and resisting being dominated by intellectual analysis, we determined that the chorus should be kept, and we consequently never cast an individual actor as the businessman. In the early improvisations, the actors remained huddled together, pushing to identify and count/claim the stars above them, but moving as a group that resisted the Little Prince's attempts to join them, although they broke apart and reconfigured during corporate mergers and when the Little Prince finally challenged their social order. This use of space and proxemics subsequently became a central feature of the scene and the dramaturgy, and the source of further grounds. We found that the work on this scene evolved fluidly and playfully, and it only needed a light touch of facilitation in the process itself. Chekhov's advice that '*if possible, the director should speak little and give only one or two suggestions to the actors, then have them repeat the scenes*' (TAITT: 15 December 1936) proved to be central to the effectiveness of this approach.

To achieve this more fluid form of improvisational flow, Chekhov's advice that directors use objective atmosphere themselves, in line with the work that the actors are exploring, became a key directorial tool. Chekhov explains that it is desirable, although very difficult, for a director to *'be in the line and style of the performance [. . .] because the more receptive the actors are, the more they will subconsciously assume the mood, tone, and key in which the director gives his suggestions'* (TAITT: 30 June 1937). Working with objective atmosphere as a directorial tool in this way required a careful consideration of this dimension in the rehearsal planning overall and in relation to the different phases of the devising process we were in, as well as the different social and interpersonal temperature of the ensemble at any particular point in time. By using this directorial ground as a key in this way, I was able to coexist in this shared atmosphere with the actors, to be with them in the devised process more fully and to more effectively able to feed into, and respond to, the improvisatory nature of much of the work and formulation of original ideas. The use of objective atmosphere as a key was also inextricably bound to the use of my juggler psychology, which quickly revealed the need to prepare for a very flexible and responsive approach, while retaining a sense of the spine of the rehearsal. To be sure I was able to enter the atmosphere and facilitate the juggler's psychology of the company and of myself, I prepared palettes of grounds as catalysts for play, drawing on exercises, **images**, sounds, music, colours (using lighting gels), rhythms, objects and games, in relation to our preliminary written and visual maps of objective atmosphere in order to genuinely respond to the relational exchanges and discoveries. This meant that I was able to rhythmically improvise around my rehearsal plan to *'free [myself] from bad habits and free [myself] from narrow ways'* (LTT: 17 April 1936) and to take us to new and unknown spaces.

If grounds function like the rules of a creative game to generate devised material and ideas, what does this mean for the director? How does this transform the role? Caillois (2001), Huizinga (1955) and more recently Henricks (2015) have emphasized the way in which play demands a simultaneous adherence to rules and also to spirited improvisation. In play, order and disorder commingle becoming both antagonists and allies. [. . .] Simultaneously, it "equilibrates" and "disequilibrates"' (Henricks 2015: 19). It was Chekhov's methods of grounds and spines in cyclical experience of creative play that helped me to navigate between free play (the unknown, unexpected discoveries, risk, and possible failure) and the discipline and constraints that are needed in a theatre-making process and as a facilitator of a creative process. These methods become a set of creative and social principles that are relational (in Buber's sense of the term, 2004) and anti-individualistic; nothing in this process exists in isolation, everything is connected and can be played with. While this still means that as a director I was leading the company and ultimately held power, the guiding is more tacit and flexible, and it required me to learn how to make contact with the actor-creators and to be with them in new, different and embodied ways. For us, it led to a new form of devised theatre and raised many critical questions about how this challenges, and what it offers to, contemporary practice and directing.

## 5 Conclusions

This exploration of the archival materials through intertwined practice and scholarship has revealed a number of key principles and techniques that provide valuable methods for contemporary devised theatre and directors. These tools also highlight a number of sociopolitical issues regarding the working relations of devised companies and ways of creating work through embodied processes. This research has demonstrated how Chekhov's work was built on the principle of an ensemble working as equal co-creators of the performance in a process-based and collaborative exchange. For Chekhov, this was inseparable from a need for attentiveness to social, sociopolitical and ethical working practices – that hold the potential to destabilize traditional hierarchies and power structures – in order to forge the genuine contact between the collaborators that is needed to create a polyvocal process and final product. This belief that the personal holds significance can also be read in relation to the later feminist position that the personal, and interpersonal, is always deeply political. The rise of the #MeToo movement in the United Kingdom and the United States has identified just how significant these issues are and indicates a pressing need to better train directors in the theatre and film industries. The approach Chekhov developed aimed to ensure that movement was an equal theatrical language to the spoken and written word and that the devised makers felt empowered to take 'liberties' with any text, or material, they might use in their processes. Chekhov also harnessed various tools from his work on 'propaganda against Naturalism' that develop and expand the non-naturalistic dimension of performance and facilitate the development of play. Underpinning the use of all the other Chekhov techniques in these devising and related directorial processes was the development of the juggler psychology and the related principle of play. This catalysed the work with grounds, spines, questions and autotelic processes and brought with it various other skills and embodied experiences that amplify the artists' capacity to generate ingenious and creative material. It also supported the approach to the devising and rehearsal process, retaining a more open and naïve approach not dominated by rational and intellectual analysis that enables practitioners to use Chekhov's techniques as balls in a game. The use of diagrams and charts captures impressions in non-verbal and verbal ways and provides loose frameworks for processes that reflect the development of a broader performance language. Variations to the approach taken evidenced in the different materials mean that the frameworks also evolve and can be responsive and flexible, and we have seen how this leads to an evolving form of embodied dramaturgy, a more 'feminine' form of making (or 'writing') performance with movement language, the sensorial, energetic, intuitive and non-rational, in addition to written or spoken words and intellectual thought. Lastly, we see that Chekhov advocates retention of the use of grounds (and therefore the juggler psychology) even in final performance, ensuring that the work retains a playful consciousness that keeps the work alive, responsive and able to make dynamic contact with an audience and the wider world.

With regards to directing, our research found that the work of this more 'feminine' catalyst can be discounted as not significant, or not perceived as a legitimate directorial method, and the radicalism of the practice is therefore often misunderstood and unacknowledged. Indeed, play and play-enablers viewed through the matrix of the Western post-Enlightenment rationalist tradition have frequently suffered from adult-centric, anthropocentric, materialistic, patriarchal and Cartesian prejudice (Cattanach 1992: 31). It is revealing in this context that Byckling argues that in his Habima production of *Twelfth Night* 'Chekhov did not lay down an exact mise en scène, but employed his method of improvisation, imagination and the organic birth of the role' (2015: 27). She goes on to cite a Habima company member reflecting 'perhaps [Chekhov] deliberately does his directing work in such a way that it goes unnoticed, that the actor does not sense it' (2015: 27). This comment reflects a specific form and style of catalyst directing, which was subtle and indirect but evidently very successful in this production. We therefore need to consider what this directorial model offers, challenges and questions in relation to the sociocultural practices of theatre-making in contemporary theatre. While Chekhov's working practices were inclusive and kind, in our practice research we also found them to be nonetheless profoundly radical. This resonated with Elizabeth Grosz's (1999) ideas about the radical nature of the newness, creativity and innovation, and she argues that when this newness is 'unpredictable, disordered, or uncontainable change – the idea of chance, of indeterminacy, of unforeseeability – that lurks within the very concept of change or newness, seems to unsettle scientific, philosophical, political and cultural ideals of stability and control' (16). In this context, Chekhov's methods are far more innovative and challenging than may seem at first glance – and overlooked – by more patriarchal and gendered ideas about 'Master Teachers' and 'Master Directors' and an acceptance of the continuing dominance of the dramatic text and playwright. Moreover, when observing a rehearsal of *The Little Prince*, Tom Cornford commented in feedback that our making process, and the way in which the embodied and visual language was given equality with the spoken word, was reminiscent of some forms of dance-theatre, and that the form of emerging dramaturgy was distinctly queer. We used Chekhov's methods to enable a creative indeterminacy, and hence the results were also unpredictable, and purposefully so.

The practice research revealed this process requires more investment of time in the early phases but reaps rewards in terms of how quickly the company can then generate high-quality material thereafter and develop a shared and flexible language that makes new developments and changes much easier and more productive. However, as Chekhov had argued, directors cannot be expected to navigate and manage the facilitations of these types of more fluid – and arguably more feminine and potentially queer – processes that do not necessarily produce results quickly in a linear manner, without having a method themselves. I found a use of his techniques in this context provided a flexible, transparent, creative and ethical toolkit that supported me in working as a catalyst in a devising process and empowering the actors as artists. Using this approach certainly requires an active resistance to the approach taken by large theatres in the UK and other parts of the world where there is pressure to produce a product in a tight timescale and to make it appear that a product is developing quickly and in a recognizably linear manner. To some extent this approach resists the Protestant ethic's reverence of 'work' that culturally dismissed creative play in the post-Enlightenment period as non-productive and frivolous, and resists the post-Enlightenment rejection of the non-verbal, non-rational and non-hierarchal aspects of in theatre practice. Using Chekhov technique, in this way, becomes a reclaiming of the artistry and ingenuity of performance-making in different, embodied, energetic and relational ways, and in relation to different cultural and political ideas.

Our research indicated points of convergence between Chekhov's approach and other devising methodologies. The most significant area of convergence was with the play practices developed by Suzanne Bing in France with Jacques Copeau and others, and later developed by Jacques Lecoq, as a key principle in devised theatre-making. Frost and Yarrow have also argued that Chekhov's principle of divided consciousness suggests a parallel with Copeau, Bing and Lecoq's notion of neutrality and non-Western actor training 'rooted in particular understandings of mind/body integration and models of consciousness' (2016: 13). This point of synergy is highlighted by the work of other UK-based devised theatre-makers. For example, Phelim McDermott draws on the practice of Keith Johnstone, in addition of Chekhov technique. Johnstone was indirectly a recipient of Bing's play practice through a complex genealogy stretching from Bing to Michel Saint-Denis, and from Saint-Denis to George Devine, who worked with Johnstone at the Royal Court Theatre in London. John Wright draws on aspects of Chekhov in his highly playful practice along with his use of Lecoq technique and mask work. In other parts of the world, Joerg Andrees also draws on Johnstone's methods in his playful practice with Chekhov technique, and Lenard Petit and Marjolein Baars work with the technique in relation to clowning. This helps to challenge the dominance of Lecoq's notion of 'Le Jeu' in relation to the discourse and understanding of the way in which play can function in devised theatre-making and demonstrates how Chekhov's methods add significantly to this area of practice in different and important ways. The use of holisitic cycles for the development of devised material using points of focus as a more limited set of 'grounds' was later echoed in various postmodern dance devised practices, which in turn fed into devised theatre practice. Examples include Anna and Lawrence Halprin's practice of RSVP Cycles, later developed by devised theatre director Robert Lepage and Ex Machina in Canada and Mary Overlie's choreographic system of Viewpoints, later extended and developed by Anne Bogart and Tina Landau. However, these approaches do not deal with areas such as energy and radiation, atmosphere, making contact and, crucially, the juggler psychology and the principle of play, as opposed to advanced improvisation. Moreover, Chekhov's use of grounds with – and without – spines provided a much broader and flexible palette than either RSVP or Viewpoints. The notion of an improvising director was later used by Eugenio Barba, but in a significantly different manner. Although different, these approaches offer fruitful blends with Chekhov's approach.

However, I would argue that there is a crucial and fundamental difference between Chekhov's methods of devising theatre, and the related form of direction, and the approaches noted above that are particularly relevant for contemporary practitioners. This is the way in which his commitment to actor-centred practice with the development of a juggler psychology catalysed through play with grounds and spines, but not overly dominated by a director, straddles a broad continuum of ways of playing identified by Caillois (2001), which ranges from Paidia (very free play) to Ludus (very structured play). As this chapter has demonstrated, it is possible to use just a simple ground to trigger free improvisation with no form of pre-existing spine – examples are McDermott and his colleagues' improv work with Improbable theatre, or Petit or Baars' Chekhov-based clown work. At the same time, this chapter has discussed how the exploration of a ground in improvisation can lead to the invention of a spine, or vice versa, with no reference to a pre-existing source material. In addition, many of the projects at Chekhov's Studio used some type of stimuli material for playful devising processes, which was the approach The Chekhov Collective took. This approach can involve a writer, at some points in the process, but crucially does not have to. At the other end of the spectrum, Chekhov was also using these techniques and principles in work on pre-existing play texts, whether modern or classical, representing a more structured, Ludic, form of playing. However, regardless of how structured the play frame was, Chekhov sought the retention of the juggler psychology and play principle in the work and final performance. At the same time, it would seem an inevitable outcome of using these techniques in relation to contemporary or classical texts that Chekhov was led to taking playful 'liberties' with them, adapting them freely and working in-between and beyond their texts.

What this suggests is that this approach works equally well with textual and non-textual, devised and non-devised performance, movement-based work and a wide range of styles, meaning that the method forms an expansive and elastic continuum of practice made possible through a shared language and flexible toolkit rather than a binary either/or approach. This spectrum of application also means that while Chekhov's approach ensures that movement is given equal space in this performance language, and the work is able to develop a significant level of dramaturgical depth through embodied play-based processes, there is fundamentally no division between these aspects of performance for Chekhov. This notion of continuum presents a challenge to many of the still-dominant ideas about theatre-making and direction that prevail in the UK today and offers exciting new pathways for practitioners. For example, in Rebecca Frecknall's production of Tennessee William's *Summer and Smoke* (Almeida Theatre, 2018; Duke of York's Theatre, 2019) she used Chekhov's methods and the development of a juggler psychology in the cast and herself as a director, as a way to explore the play, to generate sections of original staging and to retain a level of play in the final performance (2018). Equally, in recent years the technique has been used for devised performance art, site-specific theatre and dance-theatre in the UK. Chekhov's techniques consequently offer a rich portfolio of flexible, creative, transparent and shared methods for contemporary practitioners that form a bridge between these different types of theatre-making and between disciplines.

At the New Pathways event in 2016, I led a Praxis Symposium session with other members of The Chekhov Collective where we were able to practically share and debate the findings of our research with a large and diverse group of devised theatre-makers and directors. We hope this chapter has continued this process and will lead to many exciting and divergent forms of future theatre. The spirit of this research project lives on and The Chekhov Collective has continued to grow and develop as an organization since 2016, embracing other new uses of Chekhov's technique, in different ways and contexts, in contemporary practice.

## Notes

1. The other artists involved included Francesca Castelbuono, Derek Elwood, Bryn Fitch, Rebecca Frecknall, Melody Parker Grome, Hanna Junti, Saskia Marland, Joe Mercier, Holly Shuttleworth and Chloe Stephens.
2. See https://chekhovcollectiveuk.co.uk/portfolio/michael-chekhov-in-the-twenty-first-century-new-pathways-project/ for further information about the research project and organization.

# 2 Actor-dramaturgs and atmospheric dramaturgies

## Chekhov technique in processes of collaborative playwriting

TOM CORNFORD

## 1 Introduction

This chapter builds upon an analysis of the close connections between Chekhov's practices and those of collaborative playwriting that were developed later in the twentieth century, as well as the 'new dramaturgy' that has emerged in the early twenty-first. It proposes, in brief, a new pathway for Chekhov's technique in the training, study and practice of dramaturgs and collaborative playwrights and the theorizing of dramaturgy that underpins their work. In order to achieve this, I seek ways of both breaking open Chekhov's practice to reveal some of its essential dramaturgical principles and fundamentally transforming it by challenging some of the cultural assumptions that shape both his techniques and the language in which they are articulated. I aim, thereby, to effect a kind of Hegelian sublation of Chekhovian practice, so that it is both negated and carried over in the creation of the new pathway that I seek to establish with and for it.

This process unfolds in three phases in this chapter. The first asserts the basis for this new pathway for Chekhovian practice by analysing significant points of intersection between practices developed at the Chekhov Theatre Studio between 1936 and 1942 and those of twenty-first-century dramaturgs and collaborative playwrights. The second section develops a proposal for the development of practices in this new pathway by exploring the application of Chekhov's technique to the dramaturgical training and development of theatre-makers for collaborative playwriting. This section draws upon the materials gathered in the Michael Chekhov Theatre Studio Deirdre Hurst du Prey Archive and the findings of my own practice research. This was principally undertaken from 2014 to 2016 in collaboration with playwright and performer Hannah Davies and our company Common Ground Theatre, based in York. During this period, we made four new productions, written by Davies in collaboration with me as the director and the performers. Of particular relevance for this study is our 2015 production of *Demons*, an adaptation of Dostoyevsky's novel, which was created using some of the same techniques used by the Chekhov Theatre Studio in their adaptation of the same novel as *The Possessed* (1939). I also draw, here, on the findings of the 2016 New Pathways Praxis Symposium on Michael Chekhov, Collaborative Playwriting and

Dramaturgy (led by me and attended by a variety of playwrights, dramaturgs and collaborative theatre-makers). Following this proposal for a neo-Chekhovian dramaturgical training, the chapter's third section elaborates a theoretical basis for this new pathway: a conception of dramaturgy rooted in Chekhov's understanding of **atmospheres**. The material covered in this exploration of the phenomenon of atmosphere is, in fact, no less practical than the previous section, but my exploration of it here is framed as a neo-Chekhovian account of the theory of dramaturgy, to be read in partnership with the proposal for dramaturgical practice that precedes it.

In sum, this chapter argues that the excision of dramaturgy from accounts of Chekhov's technique has crucially limited our understanding of its potential and that, by bringing the two together, some crucial limitations of Chekhov's approach can be overcome. Furthermore, the discipline of dramaturgy stands to gain a great deal from both practical interventions and theoretical insights grounded in a reappropriation of Chekhov's technique for a form of dramaturgy that reflects not only the shifts in aesthetic tastes in the sixty-five years since his death, but the political and cultural specificities of twenty-first-century performance.

## 2 The authors of the new theatre: The Chekhov Theatre Studio, collaborative playwriting and 'new dramaturgy'

On 8 December 1938, just before the Chekhov Theatre Studio left Dartington Hall to take up residence in new premises in Ridgefield, Connecticut, its students gave a farewell performance. It included excerpts from Gorky's *The Lower Depths*, Ibsen's *Peer Gynt*, a monologue entitled *The Old Jew* and a play that was being developed at the Studio, entitled *A Spanish Evening*. Chekhov prepared a speech to introduce the public rehearsal of this final extract, noting that he would introduce the actor and writer Henry Lyon Young as '*the author who has made an offering of his play for our experiments*', explaining that '*this is what we call collaborating with the author*' (MC/S1/17). This form of authorial collaboration was extremely unusual in the 1930s but was central to Chekhov's vision for his Studio, as he explained in its 1936 prospectus: '[t]he new theatre, if it is to have vitality, must write its own plays', which 'must be constructed in such a way as to give the new theatrical principles their fullest scope' (Chekhov Theatre Studio 1936: 18). Such plays would be doubly new, in both their content and the form of their conception, and their creation would depend, as Chekhov realized, upon the Studio's capacity to 'evolve a playwright who, working with the group, will devote to it as much of his time and energy as do the actors themselves' (Chekhov Theatre Studio 1936: 18).

Chekhov's search for such a writer was not, however, simple. In 1936, arrangements were made to contact various playwrights so as to develop, across three years, 'a repertory which we can take on tour' comprising plays that 'must be written in close collaboration with the Group, and especially with the Director who is leading it' ('General Points to be Considered When Contacting Playwrights', MC/S4/14/D). One writer so approached was the Irish playwright Sean O'Casey, presumably both because of his increasingly expressionist style – in, for example, the allegorical *Within the Gates* (1934), a departure from the realism of his earlier plays – and his enthusiasm for Chekhov's 1930 Habima Theatre production of *Twelfth Night* (Levy 1979: 107), which he described, in a letter to the theatre manager Sidney Bernstein, as 'a great epiphany': 'as God is in the composition and colour of a great painting, [. . .] so He is in the acting of the Habima players' (8 January 1931, MC/S4/35/E). O'Casey and his wife, the actress Eileen Carey Reynolds, were also predisposed to Dartington, and moved their family to Totnes in 1938 so that their children could attend Dartington Hall School, 'the only school for the O'Casey children', as he reportedly said (Duchen 2014). O'Casey seems, however, not to have been willing to collaborate, possibly because Chekhov insisted (in some notes for a letter to be written to O'Casey) that *'the theatre must have its rights as well as the playwright'* (MC/S4/14/D). This was a clear indication that Chekhov was not willing to compromise on his principle that the Studio must *'have as much right to the play as the Author'*, meaning that the playwright would be unable *'to sell the play or to sell the cinema rights'* ('General Points to be Considered When Contacting Playwrights' MC/S4/14/D). It is also likely that W.B. Yeats's rejection of O'Casey's anti-imperialist play *The Silver Tassie* (1928) would have made the playwright suspicious of any arrangement in which he would be required to yield considerable artistic control to a director or company.

Chekhov was unambiguous that practising collaborative authorship would require a rebalancing not only of financial but of artistic control:

> *The author of the new theatre will be a person who creates the words for the play, not in the solitude of the study but working with and among the cast. He must know what it means to stand on the stage and utter the words. If he is an actor as well as an author he will know what words he must write down, and what words are possible for the actor to say. The director and the actors must be able to tell him what they wish to do and the author must understand and give the words for their purpose. The theatre is a great power but it must find itself. We must know what it means to be a member of the theatre – it doesn't mean to be the servant of the designer or the author. In the future the right impulse for the author and the designer will come from the actors and directors – they are the heart of the theatre.* (MC/S6/3)

This requirement of authors to allow actors and directors to dictate *'what they wish to do'* has been a consistently visible aspect of collaborative writing processes in the years since Chekhov's death. As Sarah Sigal has shown, authorship in a collaborative context 'is bound up with the "live" resources of other company members, so the dramaturgical process of a collaborative piece becomes an ongoing dialogue between the writer and the rest of the company' (2016: 11). Frequently, this 'ongoing dialogue' is, however, subject to considerable directorial control. In Joan Littlewood's approach, for example, which often involved, as her company members recalled, getting 'the author to work alongside the actors, rewriting on the spot where early rehearsals showed weaknesses' (Milne and Goodwin 1967: 118), afforded Littlewood 'a maximum of control' (Sigal 2016: 28). This pattern continues in the present day. Writing as recently as 2012, playwright Simon Stephens observed that the English actors in Sebastian Nübling's production of his play *Three Kingdoms* were 'used to using the playwright's text as a bible', whereas 'Sebastian had an instinct to tear it up. I had to let them know that I was happy with that' (Stephens 2012: vii). Collaborative writing sometimes involves exchanging one master for another.

Chekhov does not, however, ask that the writer become the '*servant*' of the actors and director but stipulates that the writer should work '*with and among*' them, accepting that their '*impulse*' will come from actors and directors. Chekhov describes this process by a tacit, metaphorical reference to his own technique. For Chekhov, impulses come from a **centre**, and – for him – a '*harmonious figure*' has her '*centre in the chest*' (TAITT: 1 July 1938). Writers must, in his approach, accept that their impulses will come from actors and directors, because their role sits closer to the 'heart of the theatre', as, for Chekhov, the theatre's fundamental language is not primarily verbal but a language of feeling, and feelings – in Chekhov's technique – are centred in the heart (1991: 53). For this reason, Chekhov uses the analogy of music to articulate his vision of 'theatrical expression' in the Studio's prospectus:

> The Studio will attempt to weld into one harmony all the elements of a theatrical expression. A production will be composed like a symphony following certain fundamental laws of construction, and its power to affect the public should be equal to that of musical composition. Composition, harmony and rhythm are the forces of the new theatre. Such a production should be intelligible to a spectator regardless of language or of intellectual content. (Chekhov Theatre Studio 1936: 13)

Again, a comparison with the making of *Three Kingdoms* reveals the close connections between Chekhov's conception of a performance's symphonic construction and the collaborative playwriting practices of the twenty-first century. Stephens explains that, in the 2012 production, 'my role was never authorial, [. . .] I had to dislocate my rehearsing-self from my writing-self'. Stephens's 'rehearsing-self' worked, by 'edit[ing] and cut[ting] the play' and writing 'new sections in the wake of [. . .] suggestions or my response to rehearsal' (sometimes, to the creative team's 'command'), to the end of 'refining the shape of the text' (2012: vi–vii).

Chekhov likewise described the dependence of a collaborative approach to playwriting on the '*flexibility*' of the author, who must watch rehearsals and then '*be able to re-write because he has got new ideas*' before giving the actors the opportunity to '*re-act the new text*' (TAITT: 18 February 1939). Through this process, Chekhov argued, '*[w]e will get better and better scenes*', provided that the writer is prepared '*to grope in the still dark world of the sketch*', and fundamentally question the construction of their work:

> Where is the climax, for instance? Is it right for this scene to climb up to this high point, taking so long to do it, or should it be shorter, etc., etc. Or the anti-climax should be reached in another way perhaps. The author must get the gesture of the whole picture – this is an invisible gesture – this gesture must be true and justified. (TAITT: 18 February 1939)

It is important to note here that Chekhov requires a writer not merely to be flexible but also to adopt the terminology of his technique and the working practices of his studio. Chekhov's notion of **gesture** is fundamental to those practices, since he used gestures '*to express [. . .] the idea, the interpretation, the action, the text, [. . .] the feelings, the atmosphere, everything*' (TAITT: 16 January 1937), and as the basis of a '*new kind of conversation [. . .] between actors, playwrights, costume designers, directors, etc.*', which would, he said, enable '*the feeling [to be] much more easily awakened than by describing it*' (TAITT: 11 December 1936).

In spite, however, of the fundamental importance for the success of his Studio of developing this '*new kind of conversation*' with other artists, Chekhov had limited success in attracting and retaining playwrights to work with him, which is perhaps hardly surprising given the radical approach he advocated. Henry Lyon Young and Iris Tree joined the Studio at Dartington, and the American playwright Arnold Sundgaard joined after the move to Connecticut and went on to collaborate with Chekhov on a play for children, *Troublemaker-Doublemaker*. Hurst du Prey recalls this play fondly, but the terms of her praise ('a very amusing, wonderful little play') are revealingly modest (1980: 14). She also acknowledged that 'Arnold Sundgaard was always flexible', to a degree that she expected 'very few playwrights would be' (1980: 14). Another playwright who proved himself flexible in collaborating with the Studio was the author of their 1939 adaptation of Dostoyevsky's *The Possessed*, George Shdanoff. He had, however, both previously worked in film (importantly, perhaps, a medium in which writers have not traditionally expected to have authorial control) and already had a detailed understanding of Chekhov's approach. It is possible, therefore, to read Chekhov's insistence on both the flexibility of collaborating playwrights and their willingness to adopt his technique as a means of tacitly asserting his fundamental control over the authorial process of collaboration. This argument is not without merit. The great majority of the archival material upon which this volume draws was, after all, created by a process of dictation: Chekhov's classes and rehearsals were recorded in shorthand by Deirdre Hurst and typed up by her, which can hardly be considered a process of collaborative generation. However, Chekhov also encouraged his collaborators to adjust and adapt the technique even as they learnt and taught it, so that it became a means for enabling their **creative individuality** to emerge: '*You must understand the idea of my exercises, not only the exercises,*' he told his trainee teachers Deirdre Hurst and Beatrice Straight. Further, he said, '*[c]hange the exercises I have given you, and if your idea is wrong, I will tell you. If you find other exercises besides those I have given you, please do them*' (LTT: 61). It's also important to remember Chekhov's use of different **grounds** for rehearsal, whereby he would give actors a shared concept or technique upon which to concentrate while improvising a scene. These grounds demonstrate the levelling intention of Chekhov's technique: it aims to offer, literally, a shared basis for collaborative work (as discussed by Cass Fleming in the previous chapter).

The importance of shared grounds in collaborative work is echoed by the Estonian dramaturg Eero Epner, reflecting on his role in the process of creating *Three Kingdoms*:

> I think a dramaturg is not a person, but rather a function. And it can be filled by different people. I've seen several times, over and over again, how great actors or video engineers or set designers [. . .] can be dramaturgs. [. . .] They simply lose their normal function and start to do something else. [. . .] Theatre is collective art. [. . .] And everybody in this process has an equal share. It's absolutely old-fashioned and useless to think, feel and underline the hierarchical nature of the theatre. There is no hierarchy. Well, of course there is in today's theatre, but it's a completely fucked-up system. *We did it all together*.
> (Stephens 2012: xi–xii, emphasis in original)

Epner is refreshingly open here about the ways in which collaborative writing today represents a compromise between two approaches to theatre-making. It draws, first, upon traditions of collective creation that emerged in the post-war period and attempted to reject 'all traditional theatrical structures that establish hierarchies of separated functions and entities', as Marianne

DeKoven wrote of the Living Theatre (2004: 144). Collaborative playwriting also borrows, however, from more conventional, delineated structures of theatre production, such as Joint Stock's 'director-driven' approach (Sigal 2016: 36), Filter's assertion of the company's control over the authorship of the productions that are scripted by playwrights (98) or Emma Rice's view that, as the director, 'the authorship [. . .] lies with me' (145). As Simon Shepherd has shown, the structures of theatre production became increasingly aligned, across the twentieth century, with principles of efficient economic management and thereby tended to reinforce the hierarchical superiority of the director (2012: 86–9). The collaborative creation of *Three Kingdoms*, for example, would have been impossible without the commitment of the director Sebastian Nübling both to 'find the producers' (Stephens 2012: xi) and to 'get actors to improvise text' as part of the process of generating an 'idea, image and action' from the 'starting point' of Stephens' play (Radosavljević 2013b: 265). In short, tensions between an egalitarian ethos and the centrality of a director are typical of collaborative playwriting and should not necessarily be assumed to be problematic. In fact, Sigal's analysis of a range of versions of collaborative playwriting suggests that much more damaging than directorial control is a lack of clarity about who is 'the guiding force within the creative process' (2016: 89). Collaborative playwriting, therefore, necessarily represents a compromised form of collectivity in which productions are collaboratively authored (though scripted by a writer) within a process for which a director usually has ultimate responsibility. It tends to balance collaborative principles with specialized functions – directors still direct, designers design, actors act, writers write – but the timescales and structures that define the process are arranged so as maximize opportunities for the group of artists collaboratively to shape parts of the creative process from which they would expect, in a more hierarchical system, to be excluded.

A further contemporary example of collaborative playwriting (to which I will return in the second part of this chapter) is the American SITI Company, co-founded in 1992 by directors Anne Bogart and Tadashi Suzuki. As Scott Cummings has shown, in the case of SITI's collaboration with playwright Charles Mee to create *bobrauschenbergamerica* (2001), '[t]hey all create everything together', though Mee retains ultimate responsibility for the text (in collaboration with dramaturg Tanya Palmer) and, 'when necessary, Bogart will exercise her directorial prerogative to resolve a situation or make a unilateral decision' (2006: 222). In general, however, Bogart's direction is attuned to the attempt to facilitate collaboration, and it is striking that, as Epner suggests, in this process her company members 'simply lose' (or, rather, suspend) 'their normal function, and start to do something else'. For example, Bogart describes her sound designer, Darron West, as 'the best dramaturg she has ever worked with' (Cummings 2006: 225). The flexibility of the SITI Company's roles reflects Epner's suggestion that a dramaturg is a 'function' more than 'a person', with responsibility for the entirety of the endeavour 'to create a stage reality' (xiii). Bogart's reflection crucially shifts the attention of this analysis of collaborative playwriting from the relationship between writer, director and company to the function of dramaturgy to underpin collaborative authorship.

The meaning of dramaturgy has shifted in the early twenty-first century, so that, as Katalin Trencsényi and Bernadette Cochrane have argued, it is no longer 'considered only as an attribute of a dramatic text and/or the textual', but has 'become synonymous with the totality of the performance-making process' and is 'now considered to be the inner flow of a dynamic system' (2014: xi). Dramaturgy sustains the dynamic system of a performance, in the words of Claire MacDonald, by engaging 'the space between the elements of composition and the unfolding of a performance in the presence of viewers' (2010: 94). Artists practising dramaturgy – who, as MacDonald observes, 'might not think of themselves as dramaturgs' – undertake a range of activities: they 'research, watch, gather and note strands of development, editing, curating and asking questions' (2010: 94). These activities are commonly – as Bogart implies, and Trencsényi and Cochrane confirm – to be found 'so near [to the centre of a production's creation] that the role itself dissolves and is taken on by the company' (2014: xiii). For MacDonald, dramaturgy is 'a mediating process par excellence' (2010: 94), and therefore – whether it is undertaken by an individual or distributed among a company – it occupies the spaces between traditional functions in the production process.

This expansion of the dramaturgical paradigm in theatre, dance and performance has been marked by the term 'new dramaturgy', which embraces 'ideas and practices that are sometimes contradictory' but nonetheless share key features, namely that they are '*post-mimetic*', will 'embrace *interculturalism*', and be '*process-conscious*' (Trencsényi and Cochrane 2014: xii, emphasis in original). These three features of new dramaturgy relate it more closely to what Epner terms the 'stage reality' than the play text. The new dramaturg must attend to the question of a performance's aesthetic form (since it can no longer be assumed to be mimetic); she must consider its multiple and intersecting cultural contexts (since its world can no longer falsely be assumed to be mono-cultural), and she must work critically to interrogate the process of its creation (since practices of collective creation have exposed the ways in which hierarchies of process replicate political hierarchies on stage).

Although these aspects of 'new dramaturgy' underline its specificity as a twenty-first-century phenomenon, they also demonstrate its emergence from the twentieth-century phenomenon of the 'production dramaturg', a role that was closely related, historically, to the development of Chekhov's technique. The production dramaturg has traditionally combined 'analytical interpretational and critical functions' (Trencsényi 2015: 125) and taken responsibility for 'the inner logic of the performance [. . .] and with strengthening the conceptual framework by considering the process, material and ideas from different perspectives and angles', including 'the perspective of the audience and the context in which the performance is presented' (Turner and Behrndt 2007: 166). Charting the history of this role, Trencsényi focuses on the correspondence between Stanislavsky and the co-director of the Moscow Art Theatre, Vladimir Nemirovich-Danchenko, and its revelation of what she calls 'a mutual, synergic, dramaturgical relationship' between the former's 'knowledge as an actor and theatre-maker' and the latter's 'literary mind' (Trencsényi 2015: 114). Chekhov would have agreed; he emphasized Nemirovich-Danchenko's 'genius [. . .] in going directly to the crux of the matter and immediately finding its main idea, the guiding theme' and his creation, on this basis, of 'a sort of scaffolding or skeleton, which he slowly and painstakingly fleshed out in every minute human psychological detail' (Chekhov and Leonard 1963: 45). Chekhov's use of his technique to develop detailed scores, representing what he called 'the composition of the performance' (1991: 129–45; 2002: 93–122) is directly indebted to Nemirovich-Danchenko's dramaturgical work.

Unlike Nemirovich-Danchenko, however, who wrote that 'I tend towards the conventional in form', Chekhov – like the 'new dramaturg' – was determined to develop 'post-mimetic' performance-languages (Trencsényi and Cochrane 2014: xii), which would 'leave the ways of mere imitation and naturalism and probe beneath the surface' (Chekhov Theatre Studio 1936: 12) and 'be intelligible to a spectator regardless of language or of intellectual content' (13). Also, like the new dramaturg, Chekhov was also exemplarily process-conscious: he was always deeply concerned with the way that theatre is made, closely reflecting the importance of process to new dramaturgy: 'the process's ethics, aesthetics, ecology, etc. become dramaturgical concerns, as they inform and shape the materiality of the production' (Trencsényi and Cochrane 2014: xii). Chekhov's tendency towards a universalist perspective that seeks to communicate 'regardless' of cultural difference is not well aligned with the twenty-first-century politics of interculturalism with which the new dramaturg is associated. However, his technique is unquestionably culturally expansive. It emerged from his ongoing practice of 'understanding and negotiating between different cultural systems', which is also central to new dramaturgy (Trencsényi and Cochrane 2014: xii), and offers further possibilities for such negotiations. This has recently been shown in, for example, Jerri Daboo's analysis of intersections between Chekhov's work and that of Uday Shankar (2015: 282–96), and Daniel Mroz's exploration of Chekhov's practice from the perspective of Yinyang Wuxing cosmology and the movement system of Zhi Neng Qigong (2015: 297–310). Chekhov's technique can therefore, as I will argue, be adapted as a dramaturgical and theoretical means to 'embrace interculturalism' as Trencsényi and Cochrane argue the new dramaturg must (2014: xii).

The intersections between Chekhov's work and the practices of collaborative playwriting explored in this section demonstrate the considerable potential of this new pathway for his technique. This case is further strengthened by the multiple points of connection between Chekhov's technique and new dramaturgy, which is both practically and conceptually central to processes of collaborative authorship in the twenty-first century. The remainder of this chapter therefore develops a neo-Chekhovian dramaturgy for collaborative playwriting in two distinct areas. First, it proposes the application of Chekhov's technique to the training of what I call the 'actor-dramaturg', a performer who is equipped to engage in collaborative writing processes. Second, it theorizes what MacDonald calls 'the inner flow of a dynamic system' represented by new dramaturgy on the basis of Chekhov's concept of atmosphere, proposing 'atmospheric dramaturgy' as a way of conceptualizing dramaturgical form for the interdisciplinary and intercultural context of twenty-first-century performance.

## 3 A neo-Chekhovian training for the actor-dramaturg

### 3.1 Dramaturgical training at the Chekhov Theatre Studio

It is axiomatic to this publication that Chekhov's work as an actor, director, teacher and theorist of the theatre went far beyond the corpus of his exercises that feature regularly in twenty-first-century actor training and theatre-making. Indeed, the outline of the programme of training provided in the Chekhov Theatre Studio's prospectus notably proposes a far broader approach than Chekhov would subsequently detail in Anglophone publications. Chekhov divided the Studio's proposed training into nine sections. The first of these, 'Exercises', is separated into 'concentration', 'imagination', 'speech-formation', 'eurythmy' and the use of the body in 'fencing, acrobatics, tumbling, etc. [. . .] as well as special training in gesture as a means of expression conveying the most delicate of emotions and meanings' (1936: 20). In other words, this section contains, but is not limited to, the majority of the material in the English-language version of Chekhov's *To the Actor* (first published in 1953 and still the mainstay of Chekhov's legacy in Anglophone contexts today). Of the remaining eight sections, one, 'Laws of Composition, Harmony and Rhythm', is also covered by a chapter in *To the Actor*, and another, 'Dramatic Studies, Improvisations, and Extracts from Plays' is touched upon in an appendix to Chekhov's book, which offers examples of subjects for **improvisation** (2002: 93–122, 162–82).

The remaining six sections of Chekhov's proposed training, however, fall outside the scope of *To the Actor*, and offer an enlightening perspective on some significant aspects of Chekhov's work that are at risk of being excluded from a consideration of Chekhov's significance if it is constrained by a narrow conception of the purpose and function of actor training. Two of these six remaining sections relate to the students performing in public: 'Appearances Before a Selected Audience' and 'Public Appearances'. These public performances were not, however, conceived merely as opportunities to demonstrate students' achievements by presenting 'selected passages from plays' (though those did form part of the programme). Chekhov also describes public 'demonstrations of studio exercises', which attests to his unusual (indeed, at the time, almost unique) commitment to sharing creative processes with the public. Such public appearances were also explicitly described not as demonstrations of attainment but as learning opportunities in themselves: 'they will further serve the purpose of developing in students a proper relationship to spectators', as the brochure explains (Chekhov Theatre Studio 1936: 25).

Students would have been prepared for such a consideration of their 'relationship to spectators' by other sections of their training: 'Lectures on the History and Development of the Theatre and Playwriting' and 'Stage Design, Lighting, Make-Up', as well as by classes in 'Production' (meaning 'the preparation of an entire play'). In these classes, the brochure tells us that '[s]tudents will learn the technique of studying whole productions with special reference to the methods necessary for a thorough approach to the main idea of the play' (1936: 22). We can therefore see that (other perspectives offered in this volume notwithstanding) Chekhov's process of training as described in the Studio brochure was intensely dramaturgical. From students learning 'Laws of Composition, Harmony and Rhythm', through their consideration of a performance's 'relationship to spectators' and of the histories of theatre and playwriting, to their development of 'a thorough approach to the main idea of the play', Chekhov conceived the study of acting as imbricated at all stages with the discipline of dramaturgy. This is nowhere more visible than in the only section of the Studio's training plan that I have not yet mentioned: 'Co-ordinated Experimental Work', which was intended to 'bring together in practical form all the elements of instruction in the Studio' and thus enable students 'to express original artistic ideas, whether as actors, producers, playwrights, scene painters or costume designers' (1936: 24).

Chekhov's plan for training in his Studio therefore offers a practical, historical precedent for Hana Worthen's proposal that '[a]s part of an educational mission, dramaturgy should not be side-tracked alongside the visibly materialized functions – acting, directing, design – but should engage in a mutually sustaining dialogue with them, one that alters the rationalized consensus by which theatre is taught, created and reproduced' (2014: 176). This 'mutually sustaining dialogue' between dramaturgy and other creative practices promises to create theatre artists equipped to embrace and extend the distribution of dramaturgical functions among collaborative companies. I term performers working in this context 'actor-dramaturgs' to denote the dissolving of dramaturgical functions into their practice. These performers require a combined performative and dramaturgical training, and Chekhov's technique provides a model for this and for generating an embodied vocabulary for Worthen's 'mutually sustaining dialogue' between dramaturgy and theatre's other creative processes.

## 3.2 A neo-Chekhovian dramaturgical technique

My own practice research, undertaken with Hannah Davies and our collaborators in Common Ground Theatre from 2014 to 2016, explored numerous ways of using Chekhov's technique to generate such an embodied dramaturgical vocabulary. We were both trained in Chekhov's technique as performers and used Chekhovian principles to generate dramaturgical structures to underpin the making processes both for original works and adaptations. These included *Kitty Bridges' Pocket Book of Tunes* (Regional Tour 2015), a gig theatre performance for a solo actor and musicians based on a collection of eighteenth-century dance tunes, and *The Lumberjills* (Dalby Forest 2016), a site-specific performance about the women who worked in Britain's forests during the Second World War, as well as adaptations of Shakespeare's *The Winter's Tale* (Regional Tour 2014), and of Dostoyevsky's *Demons* (2015), created with a student company and professional creative team at the University of York. During the process of creating these productions, we used Chekhov's techniques as a dramaturgical vocabulary. These included the compositional principles of **polarity** and **triplicity**; the **archetypal centres** of thought, feeling and will; the archetypal **directions in space** of forwards, backwards, upwards, downwards, expanding and contracting, and the archetypal **movement qualities** of **moulding, flowing, flying** and **radiating**.

Our performances were always scored in advance of their scripting, sometimes dividing them into three parts with the first and last polarized as Chekhov proposes (2002: 94), sometimes in other forms whose possible relations to each other could be explored by asking where polarities were to be found – between which scenes, characters, events or locations, for example. We also used other archetypal structures to consider how such dramaturgical elements might relate to each other. We grouped characters, for example, into those who might be dominated by thought, feeling or will. We asked if a particular scene might expand or contract, or rise or fall. We asked what dominant movement quality a sequence of action should have. We also used the **four brothers** of **entirety, form, ease** and **beauty** to analyse performances as they were developed to ensure that we did not, for example, overemphasize form at the expense of ease or lose the sense of a performance's entirety as we developed its details. This process of embodied exploration of a performance in advance of its writing offered us an unusually coherent and integrated system for dramaturgical development. It drew our attention to the various layers of signification to be found within the texture of a production, and Chekhov's insistence on a spiritual plane at which level a play or production can be experienced in its entirety forced us to focus on the guiding idea of the work that we were creating.

The following paragraphs explore the range of techniques that we encountered in the archive and subsequently explored through practice. We also found, however, that

Chekhov's dramaturgical assertions tend towards universalism, encoding certain culturally and historically specific assumptions as though they were applicable regardless of context. I therefore go on to analyse here some of the limitations of Chekhov's approach to dramaturgy. In the light of these shortcomings, I propose some adaptations of Chekhov's technique and ways of blending its application to dramaturgy and collaborative playwriting with other approaches, particularly Viewpoints and Composition, as developed by Anne Bogart, Tina Landau and the SITI Company from the work of choreographer Mary Overlie (Bogart and Landau 2005: 5–6).

Chekhov's student and assistant Deirdre Hurst du Prey remembered that the creation of new plays was an essential part of the training undertaken by performers in the Chekhov Theatre Studio. She recalled that 'we had to write plays or scenes, design costumes, sets and lighting, create music and sound effects and direct', adding that '[t]his began as early as our second term' (1980: 14). A study of Hurst du Prey's own transcripts of Chekhov's first classes at Dartington shows, however, that Chekhov's teaching began to engage with the exploration of dramaturgy in the students' first month at Dartington. Chekhov taught his students from the outset that the actor's *'ability to delve with his intellect into the play'* was his *'enemy'* (TAITT: 22 October 1936, my emphasis). Nonetheless, the exploration of play forms was always central to Chekhov's training: *'Our rehearsals will be for the purpose of finding one line, one path, for the whole group, and for the play'*, he said (TAITT: 27 October 1936). Chekhov went on to explain the distinction between this approach and intellectual analysis: *'We must not allow our intellects to function but must [. . .] call upon our imagination and capture and create images. We must write and re-write the play, creating new atmospheres and images all the time'* (TAITT: 27 October 1936). In this process of dramaturgical exploration, as in all aspects of Chekhov's technique, imagination is partnered with embodiment; Chekhov continues by saying that *'[w]e must penetrate into the atmosphere with our hands, legs, bodies, voices, etc.'* (TAITT: 27 October 1936). Chekhov was insistent that achieving this partnership of imagination and incorporation is only possible *'by excluding the intellect, and by doing things'*, and was also dependent upon *'a spiritual ability to see the spiritual really everywhere'* (TAITT: 17 February 1938).

Chekhov gave this active, spiritual conception of dramaturgical form the name 'rhythm':

> *[W]e must start by doing the thing again, and by doing it all the lines and forms will be joined together in quite a new manner. [. . .] We must create the thing afresh, then we will get the rhythm of it. [. . .] With will, and feeling and thinking it.* (TAITT: 17 February 1938)

It is important to note that, although Chekhov was implacably opposed to what he described as intellectual approaches to dramaturgical analysis, by which he meant a kind of cold, dry analysis of a text, he was not anti-intellectual in the sense that he was opposed to thinking. Instead, his approach attempts to blend thinking with will and feeling so that analysis is never merely thought but also felt and enacted, and therefore is able to embrace all of the three ways in which Chekhov thought that human beings interact with their environment. Chekhov's approach is therefore holistic both in the sense that it attempts to embrace the entirety of a human being's interactive capacity and in the sense that he seeks not to break down a play analytically into its various constituent parts but to join its elements together. Chekhov's approach is also anthropocentric: it is modelled on the form of the human body so that, for Chekhov, *'there is no difference'* between rhythm and gesture

(TAITT: 17 February 1938). The technique commonly known as **psychological gesture**, therefore, by which the entirety of a character's psychology is expressed and experienced in a movement of the whole body, can be applied equally to a play: *'We have called it the psychological gesture'*, Chekhov said, *'but it is actually a rhythmical gesture'* (TAITT: 17 February 1938). The anthropocentrism of Chekhov's approach leads to some political problems with Chekhov's understanding of dramaturgy, to which I will return, but when combined with the holism of his approach, it also creates clear opportunities for the collaborative development of dramaturgy.

## 3.3 Rhythm

The principal opportunity of Chekhov's approach is that it enables the actor-dramaturg to explore a play in its entirety, in advance of its writing, as a rhythmical form which can only be experienced by the conscious action of the human body, by which Chekhov means movements that engage *'the whole being'* (TAITT: 17 March 1938):

> *Each scene has its own rhythmical gesture, and this is a very very complicated thing, this rhythmical pattern of the play. The rhythm of the play is the highest spiritual movement of the play. When you begin to feel this, you will speak your words with much more understanding.*
>
> *Find what gesture there is in your words. First find the gesture before you speak, then you will find the right speech.* (TAITT: 5 November 1936)

By 'rhythmical', Chekhov does not simply mean that the gesture has a **rhythm**. Chekhov's conception of rhythm is closely related to his notion of the feeling of entirety or wholeness, one of the fundamental principles of his technique:

> *Every rhythmical movement consists of a beginning, a middle part and an end in each case. When we have a feeling for the beginning, the middle and the end, we will be able to feel the whole movement. When we start at the beginning, we must feel the future of the middle and the end. When we are in the middle, we must feel the past and the future; and when we are at the end, we must feel the middle and the beginning. When you have finished and are out of this pattern, then you have the feeling of the whole which has happened.* (TAITT: 27 November 1936)

Rhythm, Chekhov said, is *'something which is accomplished'*, *'started and finished'* (TAITT: 15 February 1938). As we can see here, rhythm therefore encompasses polarity, Chekhov's term for a dialectical condition of inextricably connected opposition. When the beginning and the end [of a play] are not opposite, Chekhov said, *'that means that the event is not rhythmical'*, though he added the caveat that *'in certain cases'* this rule can be broken *'to underline [. . .] rhythmical contradiction'* (TAITT: 16 March 1938). Chekhov also notes that polarity necessitates the further structural principle of triplicity, since it is impossible to have a polarized *'beginning'* and *'end'* without a *'middle part which binds the beginning and the end'* (TAITT: 16 March 1938), thereby creating a pattern of three phases. Chekhov asserted that in all dramaturgical forms, *'[t]here must be a definite beginning, middle part and end although it seems to be continuous movement and endlessness'* (TAITT: 21 February 1938). Gestures, in Chekhov's sense, also have three phases, beginning in one position, travelling through a transitional phase, and reaching their completion in a position that is, in some way, polar in relation to their beginning. Thus, Chekhov asserted that '*[t]hrough your feeling of the gesture, through your feeling for the rhythmical whole, every moment in the play must be organized. [. . .] Then you will be working in the right way*' (TAITT: 8 November 1936).

## 3.4 Gesture

In the case of Chekhov and his collaborator George Shdanoff's adaptation of Dostoyevsky's *The Possessed*, Chekhov describes the structure of the play in the following gesture:

> *[T]he play begins from underneath. Verkhovenski appears from somewhere, from darkness, abroad, unknown, etc., and he develops his activities more and more [. . .] at the meeting he opens himself entirely – then revolution and downfall. [. . .] Then the line divides – Stavrgoin goes upwards [. . .] and Verkhovenski goes down, from the point of the meeting and the revolution. From this point there are two lines. Mr Dobujinsky [the designer] tries each day to find how to incorporate in the settings this big gesture which divides, and which gestures are in each scene, because each scene has its gesture.* (TAITT: 11 July 1938)

Chekhov said that to be an artist is '*[t]o make cosmos ["which has form"] out of chaos ["which is not yet created"]*' (TAITT: 7 February 1938) and '*to create things behind things*' (TAITT: 28 March 1938). Rhythm, he said, '*lies behind everything*' and is therefore fundamental to any artistic endeavour (TAITT: 17 February 1938). In the case of *The Possessed*, Chekhov articulated the process of finding the gesture described in the quote above as an uncovering of the play's rhythm: '*from that which is behind the psychology we will find a certain rhythmical pattern which embraces this scene, or that character, or the whole play*' (TAITT: 17 February 1938). Crucially, for Chekhov, a rhythmical gesture relates to a play's narrative but is not limited to it. It attempts, he said, to encompass '*the idea of the play*' rather than its '*plot*', which is the focus of the '*naturalistic theatre*' (TAITT: 18 July 1937); without rhythm, '*art falls down into naturalism*' (TAITT: 15 February 1938). The gesture Chekhov describes, however, is not intended to be fixed, rather, '*by changing certain conditions in the rhythmical pattern, diminuendo, crescendo, etc., we change really the content of the thing – [. . .] what we call interpretation becomes different*' (TAITT: 16 March 1938). In the rhythmical gesture, therefore, plot and idea meet, generating interpretation.

## 3.5 Entirety

Chekhov proposes that we do not, however, merely explore a play's rhythmical pattern through the use of gesture. He also developed a technique known as '*flying over the play*' in order '*to give the cast the opportunity, even before the play is ready, to experience the whole construction of it*' (TAITT: 8 December 1938). This exercise, in which participants walk across a space, imagining the form of a play like a landscape laid out beneath them, literalizes Chekhov's idea that '*[w]e must be above the thing we are going to do or improvise, and as artists we must get a feeling for the beginning and end*' (TAITT: 8 October 1937):

> *The method to fly over the whole play keeps the group more alive, and with our imagination we are able to envision the beginning and the end. You can start with something which*

*seems to be the climax, and then when you discover the real climax you can discard the old one. All this gives much freedom – you are not compelled to keep to your first vision.* (TAITT: 28 October 1937)

This technique therefore exposes both what is clear and what is not yet clear about the structure of the play and allows actor-dramaturgs to begin to fill in the gaps or adjust the form of a play as new details emerge.

As well as zooming out from the detail of individual scenes or characters, flying over the play allows actor-dramaturgs to zoom in on particular details in the context of their perception of the whole. Chekhov gave an example to his students while working on Jan Rainis's play *The Golden Steed*: '*The good group has three gestures: 1. Toward the mountain. 2. To protect the good people. 3. To gently push the evil forces away. The whole scene is a composition of these movements. This is the scaffolding*' (TAITT: 8 November 1936). Chekhov acknowledged that '*at first this work on rhythm may seem to us quite mechanical and not really rhythmical, this is only the form. It is a staircase on which we can climb to the next level, which is the real rhythm based on this form*' (TAITT: 15 February 1938). Dorothy Elmhirst's script for *The Golden Steed* exemplifies this movement from the scaffolding of these gestures to a fully performed scene in the process noted in the margin: '*Gesture alone / Gesture and Words / Words alone*' (MC/S6/4/B). In this process, the actors can be seen to have used gesture as a 'staircase', to borrow Chekhov's analogy, on which they could climb to the pre-existing text, and Chekhov took the same approach to the collaborative creation of text. His main technique in this process is usually referred to as the 'sketch'.

## 3.6 Sketches

For Chekhov, sketches are short improvisations, usually '*no longer than one minute, perhaps even less*', which '*must be full of meaning*' and '*contain a few short sentences*'. They must also '*have a very strong atmosphere, very clear objectives for each person, and all the other means which we have learned through our exercises must be incorporated into these sketches*' (TAITT: 27 September 1937). Sketches therefore served simultaneously as pedagogical means of enabling student actors to apply their technique to work on a scene and as exercises in collaborative writing that enabled scenes to be created from a dramaturgical scaffolding. Sketches were invariably preceded by Chekhov's description of '*the content of [. . .] particular moments*' (TAITT: 18 March 1938). He requested that rather than asking why these events happen, the actors would '*[t]ake [the description] as a picture drawn by some painter*', and then '*imagine in waves what can be done, and on the basis of this you will partially incorporate the moment itself*' (TAITT: 18 March 1938). Having partially embodied the given moment through this process of active listening, the actors would proceed to improvise it. Chekhov repeatedly stresses two aspects of improvisation that are essential to this process: the director's responsibility to give '*a real ground on which to improvise*' (TAITT: 29 September 1937), and the actors' responsibility to add something '*to the given scaffolding*' (TAITT: 27 September 1937). He argued that '*improvisation means that on a certain given ground, and with certain conditions, you have to fill each moment as full as possible with your creative psychology*' (TAITT: 15 November 1937).

Often, Chekhov will describe the events of a sketch in terms of their atmosphere and give this as a ground for improvisation; sometimes he will focus on objectives or on the characters' psychology and sometimes on a play's intended style. Whichever of these he chooses, however, Chekhov stresses the requirement that the actors incorporate them fully. For Chekhov, to play an objective means *'taking the activity with the whole body'* (27 September 1937); atmospheres, likewise, must *'permeate your whole body'*, as must a character, though he stressed that, in all of these cases, the imagination remains crucial: *'don't allow your images to be embodied only with the body'* (TAITT: 5 November 1936), he instructed.

These aspects of Chekhov's approach to acting are well known, but there are two particularly significant aspects of this process for the dramaturg or collaborative playwright. The first of these is Chekhov's iterative use of improvisation to enable a text to *'give action and atmosphere'* (TAITT: 4 December 1937). Chekhov insisted that words must always be *'the outcome of thought-out action'* (TAITT: 1 February 1938) based upon *'a certain fight or conflict'* or *'action and counter-action'*, so that there is a *'line in the play which expresses this fight, without which everything is static'* (TAITT: 29 November 1937). He also argued that *'it is absolutely necessary for the playwright to write his text having always the feeling of atmosphere in which the text is to be acted'* because *'[t]he sound of the words creates an atmosphere'* and so does *'the structure or composition of the sentences and words'* (TAITT: 29 November 1937). He therefore created a process of repeated improvisations in which a scene is changed *'again and again'* by the use of different grounds and the gradual addition of details, enabling an author (in this case, Shdanoff) *'to re-compose the thoughts so that they are all there but with the minimum of words'* (TAITT: 11 July 1938).

The second noteworthy aspect of Chekhov's technique for application to dramaturgy is the crucial role of style in this process. Again, style is treated as an embodied phenomenon, and Chekhov uses, for example, music to enable actors to incorporate it into a performance. In the case of *A Spanish Evening*, during rehearsal *'a light, capricious theme was played on the piano – the task was to take this light frothy quality and to keep it inside while pretending [. . .] to be sad, then to be angry'* so that the play's chosen style (which Chekhov described as being like a *'butterfly'* (TAITT: 24 January 1938) and later like a *'juggler'*: *'childlike [. . .], open, concentrated (outward), ease'* (TAITT: 17 January 1939)) would be sustained throughout. In the case of 'The Fishers' Scene', the chosen style was *'"storm". [. . .] Everything is urgent. [. . .] There are no objectives which are not urgent'* (TAITT: 15 March 1938). For *The Possessed*, *'the style is shown in the dimension of the gesture – large gestures. The play is in the style of drama near to tragedy – not in the style of Ibsen and Chekhov – the difference is in the dimension of gesture'* (TAITT: 22 March 1939).

## 3.7 Characters

After actor-dramaturgs have explored the whole form of a play through gesture and by 'flying over' it, and its constituent parts have been iteratively developed through improvised 'sketches', Chekhov returns to the play in its entirety by exploring what he calls *'the composition of characters'* (TAITT: 3 November 1938). This technique emphasizes that although each character can be considered as a whole and developed using, for example, the psychological gesture or **imaginary body**, they are also part of a greater whole. By exploring the composition of characters, Chekhov told his students, *'you will see how important it is that Ophelia and Hamlet are creating something which is above them – plus*

*Claudius – a new world*' (TAITT: 3 November 1938). By working on the composition of characters as a whole, Chekhov argued, we are able to '*create one play*', in which '*each character must be in harmony with the other*' (TAITT: 5 November 1936). This technique is the basis of Chekhov's description in *To the Actor* of the way in which the characters of Cornwall, Edmund, Goneril and Regan combine to create a complex, multi-layered portrait of evil in *King Lear*, which is a sophisticated dramaturgical analysis (2002: 120–1). However, it also returns us to some problematic political consequences of Chekhov's holistic anthropocentrism.

If, as Chekhov, believed, '*[i]n the human gesture lives the human soul*' (TAITT: 11 July 1938), and the rhythm and form of a play can therefore be considered to be modelled upon the human body and its gestures, we are compelled to ask upon whose body/ies they are modelled. We might take the example of *Hamlet*, and the composition created by the characters of Hamlet and Ophelia '*which is above them*'. What is this form? In rehearsals for his 1924 production of *Hamlet*, Chekhov had described Ophelia as 'the part of Hamlet's soul which is in the hands of the earth' and hinders him 'with earthly love' and must, therefore, be rejected as 'the first step along Hamlet's thorny path'. Thus, he interpreted Hamlet's cruel rejection of Ophelia as an act of 'victorious wisdom' (Kirillov and Chamberlain 2013: 247). The form, both of *Hamlet* and Hamlet, that underpins this reading of the play is a 'visible embodiment of the victory of the spirit of light over the spirit of darkness' (Law 1983: 35). It is modelled, in short, upon a heroic (explicitly male and implicitly White) body.

Chekhov was openly committed to heroism as a dramaturgical ideal. In the Studio's prospectus he argued that '[i]t should be the function of the theatre [. . .] to reveal the heroic in preference to the defeated and to recall the greatness of the human spirit in its age-long struggle with adversity' (1936: 17). This aim was exemplified by Chekhov's exploration of the Latvian writer Jan Rainis's 1909 play *The Golden Steed* early in his students' training. Rainis's play is an adaptation of an Estonian myth in which a peasant boy, Antin, scales a glass mountain to rescue a princess, symbolizing Latvia's fight for independence from the Russian empire (which it achieved with the end of the First World War in 1918). Chekhov, however, fastened upon the requirement that Antin must relinquish 'earthly desires' in order to complete his quest (Šmidchens 2007: 498): '*Antin is coming from the world of passion and trying to rise above it, while all the powers are trying to push him back to their level. This is the rhythmical dynamic,*' he said (TAITT: 8 November 1936). In other words, instead of a political reading of this aspect of the narrative (emphasizing Latvia's requirement to free itself from the wealth brought by Russian imperial rule), Chekhov understands Antin's quest spiritually, as a requirement to forego earthly attachments in order to achieve spiritual insight. Unlike Chekhov's reading of *Hamlet*, here those earthly attachments are not represented by female characters, but the play's female characters do only exist in relation to (male) heroism. The sleeping princess who is finally awakened, for example, 'cannot live' if Antin does not wear her ring (Straumanis 1979: 99). The play also uses the gender binary to represent the opposition of death (in the character of the 'mother of night') and life (the 'father of light'), which reinforces racialized depictions of enlightenment and benightedness (Straumanis 1979: 59).

In short, Chekhov's conception of heroism (like many others) both explicitly and implicitly marginalizes and denies subjectivity to anyone who does not fit within its model of White masculinity. It also repeatedly reinscribes the wave-shaped curve of a dramaturgical form that traces an archetypally Christian trajectory of struggle, temporary defeat and ultimate victory. Characters that do not fit this pattern are inevitably sidelined by such a dramaturgical schema, and it is easy to see how it can therefore be co-opted to individualism and nationalism, such as in the image of choral movements in *The Golden Steed* that echo those of the lone rider climbing the mountain (MC/S6/4/B). These problems are also visible in the play *Troublemaker-Doublemaker*, developed collaboratively in Chekhov's Studio and scripted by Henry Lyon Young. It features an Indian chief and his helper who are versions of Oberon and Puck in *A Midsummer Night's Dream*, an idea reinforced by the character Biff who complains: 'If we was only Indians, we could call on a spirit to help us. Spirits is always helpin' Indians they say [sic]' (Young 1941: 6). Female characters are similarly stereotyped. A female servant tries to get the attention of a male servant by telling him 'If you'll sneak into the kitchen I got a little surprise for you', to which he responds: 'Oh, get back into the kitchen you dish-washin', pot-wipin' lemon-puss' (5). Likewise, a young, upper-class woman called 'Bunny' responds to the news of the imminent arrival of a young man by saying, 'Oh, Mama, is he really coming! Quick, pretty me up! Make me beautiful! Oh, Biff!' (3). Needless to say, the White, male characters, positioned more centrally in Chekhov's compositions, are afforded greater complexity and agency than this.

## 3.8 Chekhov's technique and Viewpoints

It is, of course, possible to use Chekhov's technique without uncritically accepting some of these assumptions, but it is also possible to blend his work with other approaches, and one solution that Davies and I have developed for this, and for expanding the range of compositional possibilities in our work, is to use Chekhov's work in dialogue with Viewpoints and Composition, as developed and taught principally by Anne Bogart and Tina Landau. Viewpoints, like Chekhov's technique, is deeply process-conscious. It is also more explicitly committed to addressing the challenges of intercultural and politically conscious practice than Chekhov was. Viewpoints sees dramaturgy and acting as inseparable, and, like Chekhov, is committed to developing new, post-mimetic forms for performance that are perfectly adapted to the ideas and questions they wish to explore.

Two particular examples will serve to illustrate ways in which the approaches may be blended. The first is Bogart and Landau's method of encapsulating a performance by asking three questions of it: what is its central *question*, to whom or what is that question *anchored* and through what *structure* is that question explored (2005: 154)? The technique of Question-Anchor-Structure is allied to the commitment of Chekhov's technique to develop a performance in its entirety, but does not assume, for example, a linear structure with a polarized beginning and ending that is so easily aligned with individualism and White, male supremacy. It also offers more freedom in the process of adaptation to appropriate a text or narrative by, for example, anchoring its central question to a character who may not occupy an obviously central position in the narrative that is being adapted. Whereas Chekhov's approach, in other words, tends to favour and reproduce the heroic patterns of *Hamlet* or *King Lear*, and to view the eponymous hero as a microcosm of a play's dramaturgical pattern, Bogart and Landau's technique creates multiple possibilities for the dramaturgy of these narratives. *Hamlet* might, for example, be anchored to Rosencrantz and Guildenstern (as in Tom Stoppard's 1966 play *Rosencrantz and Guildenstern Are Dead*), Ophelia (as in Alice Birch's 2016 adaptation, *Ophelias Zimmer*) or to the location of Elsinore (as in dreamthinkspeak's 2012 site-specific performance *The Rest Is Silence*), all of which would yield different questions that would find their expression in different structures. Thus, rather than reinscribing the hierarchical patterns of colonial power, as Chekhov's dramaturgy may justifiably be considered to do, Bogart and Landau's plural approach creates, to borrow the slogan of the Zapatista movement, 'a world where many worlds fit'.[1] Chekhov's technique should not, however, be considered redundant. The concept of polarity, for example, can be applied to any given question or structure, as can the techniques of, for example, gesture and atmosphere: what are the polarities that are engaged by a particular question, for example, and how might these be expressed in gesture? Likewise, what atmospheres are suggested by a given structure, and how might these be made manifest in a performance? By blending Chekhov's technique with Viewpoints in this way, we can make use of his embodied concepts in contexts that reach beyond his own applications of them.

Once the structure of a project has been decided, there are further ways in which Chekhov's approach and Viewpoints may be blended. For example, Davies and I developed an approach to working with atmospheres that we referred to as 'landscaping'. Having chosen the atmosphere for a particular scene or section of a performance, we asked the actors to create, sustain and explore a given atmosphere through long-form improvisations, usually without text (though speech can be included). This is an approach Chekhov used himself, but we found (as Roanna Mitchell also discusses elsewhere in this volume) that actors would often be resistant to improvising large, abstract movements and would require some prompting and direction. We drew upon the technique of Open Viewpoints (Bogart and Landau 2005: 71–3) to address this problem, using the practice of side-coaching to draw the performers' attention to any of the Viewpoints during an improvisation in order to remind them of possibilities they may be neglecting or to encourage them to develop an exploration that seems to be emerging. We also began to use the vocabulary of the Viewpoints of time (tempo, duration, repetition, kinaesthetic response) and space (shape, gesture, spatial relationship, topography and architecture) to articulate the 'landscapes' that we had generated from each atmosphere in these explorations. These landscapes are not exactly the same as atmospheres and are not intended to replace discussion of the atmosphere. Instead, they represent concrete, choreographic notations upon which to base all elements of a performance's development: text, scenography, movement, music and so on. Thus, a given atmosphere can be translated into more concrete features of a performance, such as a fast, irregular tempo, long durations, curving topography, narrow shapes, spiky gestures and so on.

This physical exploration of atmosphere is certainly not beyond the realms of Chekhov's own practice, but using the vocabulary of Viewpoints enables a very specific and concrete exploration of the ways in which atmosphere may underpin all aspects of a performance, from the quality and form of its language to the patterns of its performances and scenography. The objectivity for which Viewpoints strives also stands in stark contrast to Chekhov's deeply subjective tendency to ascribe associations to, for example, colours. His association of the colour 'white' with goodness and spiritual radiance, and 'black' with evil and spiritual poverty (Chekhov 1937), is a view that reproduces the racist narratives of European colonialism (Sinéad Rushe explores this in detail in her chapter of this book). There are, however, close connections between the two approaches. Bogart and Landau assert, for example, that Viewpoints is designed to generate in performers a positive awareness of themselves in the moment of performance because, although '[s]elf-consciousness is a kind of prison, consciousness is freedom' (2005: 61). Likewise, Chekhov advocated a close compositional awareness in his actors so that they would be able to create a dramaturgical form with the feeling of entirety:

> *This use of a rhythmical law makes the scene much stronger. [. . .] when [the latter scene] is done in this immovable way, the previous scene comes to the mind of the audience, [. . .] there are rhythmical means to preserve the scenes which are [. . .] passed [. . .] they can be brought back. And this is one of the most important laws of rhythm. We want to preserve everything which has been done before in this scene. [. . .] If we are able, by means of rhythm, to keep everything which has already passed, and to bring it somehow back, we give the audience the opportunity to experience the feeling of the whole – [. . .] the whole thing which has already passed – in one instant all is present here.* (TAITT: 21 August 1939)

This idea, that by tracing back from a speech or an image, audiences should be able to discern the wider patterns that shape a performance, and thus experience its parts in relation with each other as it unfolds, is essential to the practice of dramaturgy. Combining Chekhov's approaches with those of Viewpoints in the ways I have proposed offers opportunities for dramaturgs and collaborative creators of a performance to develop processes that expand Chekhov's techniques by offering practical ways of engaging with their political biases and decolonizing the aesthetic forms to which they are suited.

We must also, however, consider the blending of Chekhov's approaches with Viewpoints from the opposite direction, and ask what Chekhov's technique brings to the practice of dramaturgy as theorized by Viewpoints. Viewpoints has, for example, no equivalent to Chekhov's concept of 'radiation', in which the actor consciously imagines 'that invisible rays stream from [their] movements into space, in the direction of the movement itself' (1991: 46–7), or to the intimate connections, in Chekhov's technique, between physical activity, the imagination and the '[f]eelings within us that are the essence of our art' (1991: 31). This entangling of 'inner' and 'outer' experience, which is crucial to Chekhov's dramaturgical practice (and somewhat absent from Viewpoints) is fundamental to a concept that is effectively unique to Chekhov, the notion of atmosphere. Chekhov argues that what we take from a performance, which he calls elsewhere its *'main idea'*, is *'the spirit of the performance'*, whereas *'[a]ll that we can see and hear is not the spirit of the performance, but the body'* (TAITT: 16 October 1936). The play text, its staging and scenography, in other words, represent a performance's body, and what Viewpoints terms its Question, Chekhov calls its spirit: that elusive but essential experiential element that can live on beyond the performance's end (the death of its body). But Chekhov adds that we must also consider *'that which is between the spirit and the body of the performance – the atmosphere, or soul of the performance'*. This, he explained, is *'what we, as the audience, have to feel'* (emphasis in original) in order to grasp a performance's spirit. Chekhov went on to assert that *'[o]ur theatre will be very responsible for the soul of the performance'* (TAITT: 16 October 1936). In negotiating the blurry space between a performance's material forms and that which it seeks to communicate, dramaturgs must likewise be 'very responsible for the soul of the performance'. In the final section of this chapter, I will therefore argue that the most significant contribution that can be drawn from Chekhov's practice for the study and practice of dramaturgy is to be found in his theory of atmospheres.

## 4  A neo-Chekhovian atmospheric dramaturgy

Chekhov told his students on their first day in the Studio that it was their shared aim '*to be actors and more than actors – artists*' (TAITT: 5 October 1936). He elaborated on this statement three days later, defining an artist as someone who will not only '*create something*' but '*live with it*':

> your creation influences you, its creator, and the soul of the creator changes under the influence of his own creation. This is really the ability of an artist – to be changed because of his own creation. (TAITT: 8 October 1936)

Chekhov's reference here to the two-way ability to change and 'to be changed' articulates the concept of 'affect', first elaborated by Spinoza as the extent to which a 'human body is affected by external bodies', and is 'capable of affecting external bodies' (Spinoza 2020: 130, 255). Chekhov's practice, both in training students and developing productions, of '*cross[ing] over [a play or story] many times*' so that '*we [. . .] realize what we have understood through our movements, words, and positions*' (TAITT: 24 November 1936), frames the dynamic forms of a performance's dramaturgy as a measure of its capacity to affect and be affected by its performers and audiences. I want, therefore, to propose, in this concluding section, first, that we consider dramaturgy as a register of the affective dimension of a performance, and second, that Chekhov's most significant contribution to such a conception of dramaturgy is his elaboration of the concept of atmosphere as the primary condition of any performative encounter. Chekhov's technique enables us, in other words, to consider atmosphere as the substrate of dramaturgy: 'the material on or from which [it] lives, grows or obtains its nourishment' (*OED*).

Brian Massumi has proposed that affect is both transversal (in Deleuze and Guattari's sense of cutting across conventional categories) and polyvalent:

> Thinking the transversality of affect requires [. . .] honing concepts for mutual inclusion in the event of elements usually separated out from it, and from each other. [. . .] Although affect positively concerns relations in encounter, it is at the same time positively productive of the individualities in relation. (2015: x)

Like Massumi, Chekhov was concerned that the dialectical pair of 'individuality' and 'relation' should be sustained, with neither concept being allowed to overwhelm or escape from the other. For example, in his response to a holiday task to write about 'The Function of Theatre in Regard to the Social Life of our Times', Chekhov's then student, the actor Paul Rogers, wrote that an '*individual who can be a member of this group [. . .] realizes the beauty of individualism operating in harmony with and for the benefit of the group*' (MC/S4/14/S). Rogers's conception of 'the group' answers (or rather foreshadows) Massumi's call for the development of 'concepts for mutual inclusion in the event of elements usually separated out from it', as does Chekhov's notion of '*contact*': '*a special feeling [. . .] that no-one is alone on the stage, and is never alone, even if he or she speaks a soliloquy'* (TAITT: 2 October 1937). For Chekhov, '[t]he actor must get the ability to be in contact not only with everybody around him on the stage, but with everything' (TAITT: 2 October 1937).

In Chekhov's technique, **contact** is a necessary precondition for the generation of dramaturgical forms, as he told his student actors:

> We must develop this feeling of contact not only with the other persons, but with the structures, with the space around, with the chairs, etc. [. . .] Each setting is a special world in which we have to create our actor's activity. [. . .] The problem is to find and establish contact with each other and with the setting, and to find the moments of climax in the play. (TAITT: 27 October 1937)

For Chekhov, then, the exploration of dramaturgy is a process which is continually reabsorbed into the contact which gave rise to it, engendering an ongoing reimagining of both the possibilities of encounter and the potentialities of dramaturgical form. The crucial function of contact in Chekhov's vision of the development of dramaturgy might remind us of Chekhov's insistence that '*the author of the new theatre*' must work 'with *and* among' a play's cast, and take their impulse *from* '*the actors and directors*' who are '*the heart of the theatre*'. The prepositions – words that articulate relation – in these phrases (which I have emphasized here) are striking. Furthermore, if the heart of a theatre is the collective identity of '*actors and directors*', then perhaps its heart's core is neither the directors nor the actors but their conjunction: '*and*'. Chekhov's exploration of dramaturgy begins, then, in the middle, with the contact signalled by '*with*', '*among*', '*from*' and '*and*'. It is also notable that Chekhov conceives of 'contact' affectively: it is a space in which he asks his actors to 'find' (or be affected by) a form they must also 'create' (or affect).

Chekhov developed his students' sensitivities to the affective process of creating by taking them into the grounds of Dartington Hall and asking them to find/create gestures to express the forms of the trees:

> a cypress streams upward (Gesture), and has a quiet, positive, concentrated character (Quality); whereas, the old, many-branched oak, rising upward and sideways (Gesture), will speak to us of a violent, uncontrolled, broad character (Quality). (1991: 39)

Chekhov described this exercise as a way of developing his students' understanding of '*what it means to live in a world of form – psychological or physical form*' (TAITT: 22 October 1937). Chekhov's affective account of perception anticipated Merleau-Ponty's phenomenological approach that describes the process of perceiving as an 'inspiration and expiration of Being': a breathing in and out of the world through which mutual process of discovery, as he writes, 'things become things' and 'worlds become worlds' (Ingold 2015: 84). Anthropologist Tim Ingold borrows the phrase 'coiling over' from Merleau-Ponty to describe the process of looking at a tree in terms that strikingly recall Chekhov's practice: 'my being with the tree and the tree's being with me' (2015: 86). We can therefore say that when Chekhov asks his students to develop their '*feeling of contact [. . .] not only with the other persons, but with the structures, with the space around*', he is creating a space of 'coiling over', in which subject-object distinctions blur and double, and in which we encounter a relational experience of and interaction with an objective, external reality that is also fundamentally unstable and continually co-created with and among us.

Chekhov's term for such an affective space is 'atmosphere': 'a feeling which does not belong to anybody [. . .] which lives in the space in the room', as he defined it (TAITT: 16 October 1936). Since they do not belong to anybody but are experienced by everyone, atmospheres both alter the actions that take place within them and are capable of being altered by those actions. Therefore, an atmosphere is both the feeling of the space within which the action of a play takes places and the feeling that shapes that action. As Chekhov reminded his students: '[I]f we take the text and try to interpret it first from the words, it is mechanical. We must find the atmosphere of the play, and it must inspire us' (16 October 1936, emphasis in original). He said: 'You must be in the music of the play. [. . .] You must always consider the atmosphere so that the gesture will be born out of the atmosphere. You must start with the atmosphere and then you will find the right way to produce the gesture and be full of feeling' (TAITT: 8 November 1936). As we have seen, however, Chekhov's dramaturgical training focused particularly on those moments in a play when the atmosphere changes, and we are therefore faced by a second paradox: not only are atmospheres both produced by and productive of a play's action; they are also both constant and constantly in flux. This is because an atmosphere is the feeling not only of a space but of an *event-space*. Atmospheres are therefore spatio-temporal phenomena, experienced simultaneously and capable of being changed by all of the participants in an event-space.

While rehearsing the Chekhov Theatre Studio's adaptation of Charles Dickens's *Pickwick Papers*, Chekhov gave his actors the following instruction:

> *Imagine the air around you filled with atmosphere – filled with this raging thing around you. Don't try to squeeze anything out of yourselves – that would be wrong. Everything is in tremendous movement, in you and around you. If you will imagine this raging atmosphere truly, you will become either as small as a mouse or as big as King Lear. You will merge with it. Rachel will become like a mouse and Jingle like King Lear. Stiggins takes the atmosphere as inspiration. He is always involved in it, throughout the whole scene. The thunder storm is his inspiration. It forms a cloud around him.* (TAITT: 21 August 1939)

This instruction is particularly significant in qualifying Chekhov's commitment to the objectivity of atmosphere. The '*raging atmosphere*' of this scene is objectively experienced by all of the participants in the action, but, crucially, it does not affect them all in the same way. It overwhelms the character of Rachel, making her '*become like a mouse*', while the character of Stiggins is inspired by it: it '*forms a cloud around him*'. Far from being mystical, this conception of atmosphere draws upon the simple fact that all living things require a medium – air or water – within which to exist. Tim Ingold observes:

> The air is not an interactant so much as the very condition of interaction. It is only because of their suspension in the currents of the medium that things can interact. Without it, birds would plummet from the sky, plants would wither and we humans would suffocate. Even as we breathe in and out, the air mingles with our bodily tissues, filling the lungs and oxygenating the blood. (2015: 70)

Ingold goes on to argue that 'if the medium is a condition of interaction, then it follows that the quality of that interaction will be tempered by what is going on in that medium, that is, by the weather', and that we therefore live in a 'weather-world' (2015: 70). This weather-world of atmosphere is therefore a necessary condition of all affective relations and, thus, a necessary condition of dramaturgy.

Like Ingold's weather-world, Chekhov told his students (as we have already seen) that the atmospheres of a play must be explored physically: '*We must penetrate into the atmosphere with our [. . .] hands, legs, bodies, voices*' (TAITT: 27 October 1936), he said, applying the technique of finding-creating the gestural forms of trees to the process of finding-creating – to borrow from Ingold – the ways in which the 'qualit[ies] of [. . .] interaction' that constitute a play 'will be tempered by what is going on in [the] medium' of the play-world. Chekhov's most significant contribution to dramaturgy is therefore the development of what he called a '*score of atmospheres*' (TAITT: 9 October 1937): a processual, embodied articulation of the changing qualities of the 'weather-world' of a play. The score of atmospheres is the crucial step whereby Chekhov's dramaturgical practice moves from contact (the processual generation of a collective form of identity) to the creation of dramaturgical form, about which Chekhov has the following advice:

> *First find the atmosphere, and then try to find the dialogues and soliloquies in the music of the atmosphere. First, very simply, try to find what is the music of the words. Each scene has its own rhythmical gesture, and this is a very very complicated thing, this rhythmical pattern of the play. The rhythm of the play is the highest spiritual movement of the play.* (TAITT: 5 November 1936)

In this rhythmical conception of dramaturgy, Chekhov implicitly proposes that dramaturgical time is not chronological (a sequence of events), but *kairological*. *Kairos* is both the modern Greek word for weather and the ancient Greek word for a significant time, the moment when something needs to happen; it is therefore doubly atmospheric. It is also always relational and always patterned: it charts the constantly evolving yet structurally perceptible conditions of relation. Thus, Chekhov's affective, atmospheric conception of dramaturgy takes us beyond the familiar notion that dramaturgy maps a set series of actions or a fixed structure of relationships and allows us to contemplate dramaturgy ecologically: as a dynamic, processual becoming that is always complex and yet retains what Brian Massumi, drawing on Gilles Deleuze, calls 'the dynamic unity of an event' (2017: 87).

Considering dramaturgy as an ongoing, dynamic process of becoming goes considerably beyond the Aristotelian assumptions of Chekhov's own dramaturgical analyses, which repeatedly return to, for example, the notion of linear progression. In a twenty-first-century context, however, it returns us to the core components of 'new dramaturgy' as outlined by Trencsényi and Cochrane. The 'dynamic unity' of such a becoming (that arises from a number of autonomous-yet-related processes) demonstrates the extent to which atmospheric dramaturgy is always 'process-conscious' and embraces the entirety of the performance-making process. Atmospheres are created collectively by all aspects of a performance, and therefore atmospheric dramaturgy underpins all of the processes and specialisms that a performance involves. Secondly, atmospheres are not mimetic. This is partly because atmosphere seeks to communicate not the surface appearance of an event but the feeling(s) of its occurrence. Atmospheres are also not created but captured and worked with; they cannot be fully mastered but always exist, in part at least, beyond the reach of human intervention. An atmospheric conception of dramaturgy, therefore, exceeds the reach of any particular aesthetic form.

In addition to being both rooted in process and formally expansive, atmospheric dramaturgy has a further advantage, which again takes us beyond the scope of Chekhov's published writings on the subject: it can enable us to overcome the assumptions of bourgeois individualism in the study and practice of dramaturgy. The first of these assumptions, that of individualism, seeks to analyse a play text or performance at the level of character. It proposes that relationships and events are generated by the actions and intentions of individual characters. By contrast, atmospheric dramaturgy proposes that we consider the relations *between*, rather than the intentions *of*, characters as the sources of action. Secondly, this relational conception of dramaturgy counters the bourgeois assumption that individuals can be considered to exist outside of political and cultural contexts. This is to take up an important critique of some instances of the deployment of affect, in which it becomes a purely embodied relation between bodies that are assumed to float somehow free of social context. Feminist, queer and critical race theorists have pointed out that the power to affect and be affected is not equally distributed across populations or the globe and therefore argued that, in the words of Sianne Ngai, 'far from being merely private or idiosyncratic phenomena, [. . .] feelings are as fundamentally "social" as the institutions and collective practices that have been the more traditional objects of historicist criticism [. . .], and as "material" as the linguistic signs and significations that have been the more traditional objects of literary formalism' (2005: 25). Sara Ahmed has also analysed in detail the ways that discourses of bodily freedom assume and rely upon a normative (e.g. heterosexual and White) 'orientation' to the world (2006: 85), and its cultural forces.

In spite of his political distance from such arguments, Chekhov did pay particular attention to the cultural forces at play in dramaturgy:

*The first step is to research the various atmospheres [. . .]. The next step is to study the play – its historical values, background, costumes, etc. In this study we must discover the 'world' in which the play has to be acted. Each play must have a special world around and about it. Hamlet is a special world. Faust is another world. We must develop each play as a world; therefore, we need special study for each play.* (TAITT: 27 October 1936)

We can see the consequences of the connection between atmosphere and a play-world in Chekhov's direction (quoted above) of the characters of Rachel and Stiggins' in the *Pickwick Papers*. As I have observed, whereas Rachel is overwhelmed and diminished by the atmosphere of the scene that Chekhov describes, Stiggins is empowered and expanded by it. Although Chekhov does not make the point himself, the atmosphere he is seeking to generate is clearly gendered in its effect upon these characters. Atmosphere, then, can be seen to recognize and work upon and through categories such as gender, race and sexuality, and therefore enables us to give experiential form to the development of '*each play as a world*', or, in other words, to the ways in which the forces of culture operate at an embodied level within it. To think of culture as an atmosphere is, unavoidably, to ask what kinds of lives and relations it supports and nurtures and what kinds it punishes or poisons. This approach establishes, therefore, the conditions for the kinds of intercultural encounter that are crucial to new dramaturgy. Intercultural performances depend upon the possibility of horizontal relations between cultural contexts and, therefore, of affective spaces for cultural encounter that are capable of resisting the reproduction of hierarchical relations, such as those that we have noted in some of Chekhov's own work. In short, atmospheric dramaturgy offers to twenty-first-century theatre-makers a theoretical and experiential model that is extremely well suited both to the tasks of interdisciplinary, collaborative performance-making and to the complex political and intercultural contexts of their practice.

## 5 Conclusion

This chapter has pursued a threefold argument in relation to Chekhov's technique, collaborative playwriting and dramaturgy. First, I have proposed that Chekhov's technique should be understood as an approach to performance in which acting and dramaturgy are always imbricated with each other: its development at the Chekhov Theatre Studio specifically for the purposes of collaborative playwriting created a thread of embodied dramaturgy that can be seen to connect its various practices. On this basis, I have argued that a neo-Chekhovian training is well suited to the development of actor-dramaturgs and that the reinvention or sublation of Chekhov's technique for this purpose – and its blending with other approaches, notably Viewpoints – offers an ideal embodied vocabulary for artists who engage in new dramaturgy, a practice which, as Claire MacDonald observes,

> does not proceed from text as a known set of procedures, but instead explores what those procedures might be. It allows for the possibility that writing may 'materialize' on stage in different ways, understanding that the legible page of a pre-scriptive text may invite the performer to work on it, or with it, as co-author, creating a performance text from its instructive prompts rather than directly performing words that have already been written. In the new dramaturgy, text moves closer to texture, and to the notion of fabrication as a material practice. We seem thus to be moving towards an idea (or even a definition) of dramaturgy as a kinetic and time-based practice, a material process in movement, that both frames and takes place in the moment of performance, located in the space/place of production, attending to the many dimensions of making and making sense – complex but nevertheless generative. (2010: 94–5)

MacDonald's provisional definition of new dramaturgy here as a 'kinetic and time-based practice' both underpins the work of the actor-dramaturg for whom I propose a neo-Chekhovian training, and frames my development – in the final section of the chapter – of a theory of atmospheric dramaturgy, founded in Chekhov's practice.

This atmospheric conception of dramaturgy, like the neo-Chekhovian dramaturgical training proposed before it, does not discriminate between forms of performance and can be used equally to analyse the dramaturgy of a play, a dance or a piece of music. This is because atmospheres, like Heidegger's 'Stimmungen' (moods), pre-exist subjectivity: 'the possibilities of disclosure which belong to cognition reach far too short a way compared with the primordial disclosure belonging to moods' (1962: 173). Atmospheric dramaturgy, then – to bring MacDonald, Chekhov and Heidegger together – is a material process in movement, in which context artistry is constituted by our capacity collectively to attune ourselves to and come into a fully embodied dialogue with possibilities of disclosure that will always exceed our capacity to capture and manipulate them.

This neo-Chekhovian conception presents two challenges to the practice of dramaturgy. The first is philosophical: grounding dramaturgy in collective attunement to emergent, transversal forms challenges, as I have shown, the individualist assumptions of conventional dramaturgy. When Felix Guattari argues that 'we must learn to think transversally' (2000: 28), he emphasizes that '[w]hile the logic of the discursive' [which serves as the basis of dramaturgy] sets endeavours to completely de-limit its objects', and is grounded in system and structure, 'the logic of intensities', by contrast, 'strives to capture existence in the very act of its constitution, definition and deterritorialization' (2000: 29). The aleatoric forms of new dramaturgy, therefore, require a theory that is likewise concerned with processes of ongoing formation and not locked into definitive discursive systems. The second challenge is political: the concept of tranversality was developed by Guattari with the intent to challenge hierarchical organization, and therefore had, as Gary Genosko observes, 'practical tasks to perform in specific institutional settings' (Guattari 2000: 51), in which '[t]he Master must allow himself to be displaced' (57).

Both of these challenges to dramaturgy will inevitably tend to displace the traditional playwright, whose function is grounded both in delimited discursive structures and hierarchical authority. Both also underscore the significance of theory and practice for dramaturgy, such as I have proposed, that are fundamentally attuned to collectivity and the relations and interstices to which it gives rise. As my analysis has shown, however, Chekhov's relation to both of these challenges to dramaturgical practice is somewhat ambivalent and paradoxical. On the one hand, the processes of collective training and collaborative playwriting, and the pre-subjective nature of atmosphere, are all drawn directly from his practice. On the other hand, Chekhov's conception of training remains rooted in the exploration of subjectivity (which positions the individual as a microcosm of wider being), and dedicated to the achievement of 'mastery' (conceived as a form of heroism), both of which contradict the existential and political values of the collective and aleatoric practices of new dramaturgy. Thus, even where Chekhov was willing to displace his own authority, the significance for his technique of mastery as a model of creative practice remained intact, and therefore the possibilities of collaborative playwriting that were initiated by Chekhov's technique always exist to some extent in tension with its investment in the actors' mastery over their art, the teacher's over their students, and the director's over the play and/or collaborative process. It is impossible to ascertain, from the brief life of the Chekhov Theatre Studio, the extent to which Chekhov and his technique would have been able or willing to accommodate and adapt themselves in response to these tensions. It has not been my concern here to solve these paradoxes, or to force Chekhov's ambivalence into a single argument in relation to my subject. Rather than disentangling his practice, I have sought to reappropriate it by positioning myself within its tangles, and thereby to generate an account of its significance for dramaturgical training and practice in the twenty-first century. I hope that the neo-Chekhovian approach that I have developed, which includes Chekhov even as it surpasses his practice, will prove to be a foundation for new dramaturgies that reach further still beyond the anticipated uses of both Chekhov's technique and my reappropriation of it.

## Note

1. The slogan of the Zapatistas, adopted as the aim of the armed insurrection they began in Chiapas, Mexico on 1 January 1994, was 'Un Mundo Donde Quepan Muchos Mundos', 'a world where many worlds fit'.

# Section Two  Chekhov technique: Beyond acting

# 3 The expressive voice in performance

## Chekhov's techniques for voice and singing

### DARON ORAM

In this chapter, I examine archival evidence of voice practice during, and since, the time of Chekhov's Dartington Studio. The results of this examination suggest a lack of integration between approaches to voice and Chekhov's techniques during his lifetime and point the way towards an interdisciplinary model for the ongoing development of new pathways in this area. I will discuss two examples of interdisciplinary approaches to voice and Chekhov that have emerged in the early part of the twenty-first century and show how these approaches offer a model for further interdisciplinary exploration of Chekhov for Voice and Singing.

Chekhov wishes the actor to 'anatomize the body, emotions, and voice' (Hurst du Prey 1985: 25), and he regularly writes about the expressive qualities of the voice in performance. However, he rarely discusses the technical aspects of training the voice. In Mala Powers' preface to *On the Technique of Acting*, she shares Chekhov's 'Chart for Inspired Acting' and describes how Chekhov instructed her 'to imagine that all of the various techniques mentioned on the chart—Atmosphere, Characterization, Qualities, etc.—were like light bulbs [. . .] when inspiration "strikes," all the light bulbs are instantly turned on, illuminated' (Chekhov 1991: xxxvi). In Chekhov's chart, neither voice nor speech appears as one of the light bulbs to be illuminated. In the absence of any in-depth discussion of voice practice in his published writings, the transcripts of Chekhov's teaching, collected in the Michael Chekhov Theatre Studio Deirdre Hurst du Prey Archive, offer an insight into how voice and speech were approached at the time when 'nearly the entire pantheon of Chekhov's Method was set' (Hurst du Prey 1985: 16). However, despite the comprehensive nature of Hurst du Prey's records and the advanced state of Chekhov's techniques at the time, there are notable gaps in the archive. The approach used in the speech classes is not directly described, and it is only the outcomes of this work that are discussed and noted. Further, a written archive cannot provide aural evidence, so any discussions of vocal tone, accent or rhythmic qualities are open to interpretation. Caroline Steedman notes that 'historians read for what is not there: the silences and the absences of the documents always speak to us' (2001: 1165). In archival voice research, those silences must be filled, not only by conceptual data but by sound. Thomas Osbourne (1999: 52) defines the archive as a '*centre of interpretation*' (emphasis in original) which is 'orientated, one is tempted to say dialogically – towards some or other kind of recipient, the future' (1999: 56). In this discussion of voice and Michael Chekhov, the du Prey archive has been listened to dialogically, in the hope that this dialogue might reveal something of use for future pathways for voice and Chekhov's techniques.

## 1 Voice and Chekhov at Dartington: Listening to the archives

As part of Michael Chekhov's plan for a 'theatre of the future' (Hurst du Prey 1985: 27), the training methods that he began to systematize at the Chekhov Theatre Studio at Dartington Hall included an approach to voice using Rudolf Steiner's Eurythmy and Speech Formation exercises. Steiner's influence on the overall approach to training developed by Michael Chekhov is well documented. In his introduction to *Lessons for the Professional Actor,* Mel Gordon states that 'marrying the inner truth and emotional depth of Stanislavsky's system with the beauty and spiritual impact of Steiner's work became Chekhov's obsession' (Hurst du Prey 1985: 15). Steiner's ideas of the higher ego, the use of gesture, moods, wholeness and so on (see Steiner 1959) are intimately woven into Chekhov's approach to acting; however, when it came to approaching voice work in his Studio, Chekhov was clear that the methods developed by Steiner himself were to be taught.

> The voice is a special thing and a very interesting one. I cannot speak about the voice here because it is not my special field, but the method which we use in our school, that of Dr Rudolf Steiner, is a very interesting and profound one. (Hurst du Prey 1985: 23–4)

Alice Crowther worked alongside Chekhov at Dartington. Crowther had trained in Eurythmy and Speech Formation at the Steiner training centre in Dornach, Switzerland, and was invited by Chekhov to teach this work at the Chekhov Studio. As the archives do not describe the content of her 45-minute daily speech classes, the technical aspects of her approach must be inferred from other sources. To do this, I take a dialogical approach that engages with the archival references to actors' performances at the Studio and publications discussing the Steiner approach made at the time Crowther was working – Steiner's own *Speech and Drama* (1959), a collection of his 1924 lectures, is a valuable resource in this respect.[1] Alongside these written sources, I engage with an examination of the work of contemporary practitioners who have a connection back to the original Steiner work – such as Sarah Kane, who trained in the Steiner method in Germany and teaches Chekhov's techniques, and Graham Dixon, who was trained by Alice Crowther after she returned to her native Australia.[2]

Rudolf Steiner (1861–1925) was an Austrian philosopher. He founded the esoteric movement of Anthroposophy and wrote about science, agriculture, architecture and the performing arts. His theories on education form the basis of the curriculum at Steiner Waldorf schools across the globe. The Steiner approach to speech work is based on the principle that the body and voice will be trained by working with speech, rather than focusing on the anatomy of the voice and the physiology of vocal production. It was an approach that Chekhov believed in wholeheartedly:

> The approach to mastering the spoken word (through articulation, voice training, etc.) is wrong mainly because this approach leads the actor from anatomy and physiology [. . .] to the living word. [. . .] No outward methods can teach the actor to speak truly artistically and expressively if he has not first penetrated into the deep and rich content of every individual letter, each syllable. (Chekhov 2005: 79)

Steiner says that 'speech originates in the artistic side of man's nature – not the intellectual' (Steiner 1959: 29) and, by rejecting the thought behind the word, the speaker is enabled to embody the sounds and express 'something that belongs to the very essence of man's being' (Steiner 1959: 32). Breathing is not trained as a conscious activity within the Steiner work, but it is trained via the work on speech formation:

> To live consciously in the breath, to give form to the breath, to use the breath as a chisel and with it give plastic form to the air, to feel the quivering, subtle vibrations of air and ether, to experience the overtones and the undertones, the delicate intervals within the diphthongs, through which filters the stream of the spirit – here is an artistic activity indeed, working creatively in the finest of substances. (Steiner 1926)

Outside Dartington, the dominant English voice and speech training methods of the time, at schools such as Elsie Fogarty's Central School of Speech and Drama (Central), focused on rib-reserve breathing and the anatomical and phonetic principles of voice and speech production. Chekhov demonstrates a strong desire to have a voice method that eschewed this pure mechanics and acoustics approach to vocal production and speech as part of a more radical move away from post-industrial rationalism and towards a future theatre where the 'primary aim' was to 'penetrate all of the parts of the body with fine psychological vibrations' (Chekhov 1991: 43) in order to 'rediscover' the 'spirit of the human being' (Hurst du Prey 1985: 141). In this way, actors were to develop 'an understanding of language not only as an intellectual medium (as in the contemporary theatre) but also as an artistic medium' (Chekhov Theatre Studio 1936: 21).

One element of the Steiner work taught by Crowther in Dartington was Eurythmy, where every speech sound has an accompanying gesture. 'For Steiner, language is not only a human quality, but it is a feeling of the cosmos itself' (Anderson 2011: 162). 'In speaking for a Eurythmy performance of poetry, the speaker needs to attempt to create macrocosmic gestures in their speech so that the Eurythmist can move in harmony with it' (Anderson 2011: 163). Chekhov, himself, describes the consonants as 'imitating the outer world, whereas the vowels express primarily human feelings' (Chekhov 1991: 75). In his 2006 *Michael Chekhov, Voice and Text Summer School*,[3] Graham Dixon taught gestures for the 'ah' and 'oo' vowels based on Steiner's teaching. The first involved opening the arms wide above the shoulders as if feeling warm sunshine and the second involved drawing the arms together and down in front of the torso as if cold and contracting.

The second element of the Steiner approach was speech formation, which included the use of **archetypal gestures** for Lyric, Epic and Dramatic styles, along with six speech gestures relating to specific vocal tones. Dixon teaches the lyric gesture to be like an overflowing jug with the hands rising up and spilling over in front of the body. The dramatic gesture relates to the throwing of a spear and is strong and direct, while the epic gesture draws the energy up from behind the body and over the head. These physical gestures would be invisible in performance but were intended to be alive in the voices of the actors as they spoke. This was not simply about putting movement to speech; the intention was to awaken 'sensitive feelings' in the 'actor's soul' so that 'harmony and natural beauty will permeate the speech and whole being of the actor and will lift him into the realm of art' (Chekhov 1991: 77).

In this way, Chekhov is seeking a unified approach to performance. By developing an approach to acting which drew heavily on principles drawn from Steiner and by coupling it with the speech training developed by Steiner himself, he would seem to have gone some way in realizing his objective. The pictorial depiction (Figure 3.1) of how '*all qualities come together in the actor*' (TAITT: 2 November 1936) found in the archives gives an idea of how Chekhov perceived the unity of his approach. In this diagram, which predates the 'Chart for Inspired Acting' mentioned earlier in this chapter, speech takes its place alongside the other qualities relating to the actor's body, feelings and thought. However, other evidence from the archive indicates that the approach was, in practice, less than unified. One of Chekhov's actors, known as 'Woodie', explains:

> *I find that in rehearsing for speech and going through everything as for a proper rehearsal, I start out working fully but I have to drop the acting because I cannot concentrate on the speech method and the inner life of the character at the same time.* (MC/S1/9/A)

In a draft of her 1977 PhD thesis, 'Theatre of Inspiration', which is held in the archive, Nancy Kindelan says, '*Both Beatrice Straight and Deidre Hurst du Prey signify that the Steiner method of speech lacks the definition that is so predominant throughout Chekhov's methodology*' (MC/S4/27/A: 182). In an interview with Kindelan, Beatrice Straight elaborates:

> *I think one of the weakest aspects of training was the speech. He applied a lot of the Steiner method to speech, and the idea was that in doing something bigger than life it provided a wonderful training for feeling, for sound, for each word and content. [. . .] And it took a long time to overcome that. You could tell a Chekhov student by the way he rather intoned [. . .] it was all talking from the emotion, and the form, rather than the idea.* (MC/S4/27/A: 182)

Kindelan goes on to say that Chekhov never visited a Steiner speech class and '*consequently, it is unclear to them how Chekhov wished to apply this technique*'. Hurst du Prey herself suggests '*Had we had a teacher who was trained by Michael Chekhov or trained as an*

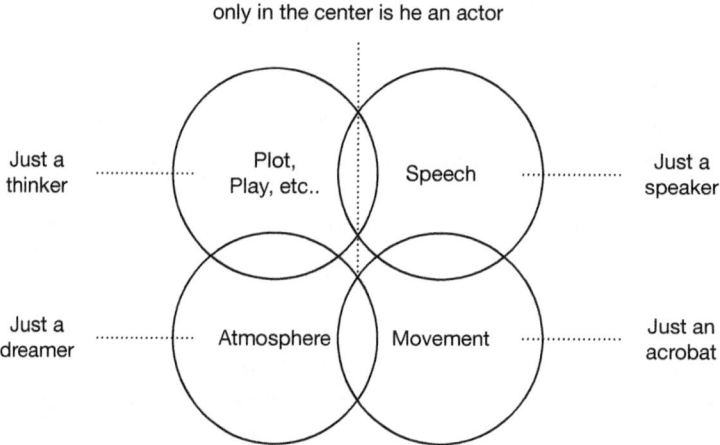

Fig. 3.1 'All qualities come together in the actor', diagram. TAITT: 2 November 1936, CTS-DHDPA.

*actress and also in speech, I think it would have been different. But they [the teachers] were just trained for speech*' (MC/S4/27/A: 183).

It is only possible to speculate as to why Chekhov took this hands-off approach to the speech work. It could be that he believed that the unifying philosophy and esoteric principles at the heart of his and Steiner's work would be enough to ensure compatibility of the practices without further efforts. Perhaps it was a personal debt he felt to Steiner or that this area of the work was, indeed, not his 'special field' and should be respectfully left alone. Conceivably, it might have been Chekhov's speaking of English as a second language that held him back from engaging directly with the specifics of speech. However, what is clear is that there was a disparity between the aims of the acting work and that of the speech work. Graham Dixon[4] described this as the 'archetypal problem' with the Steiner speech work, arguing that Steiner teachers always want the speech to be placed in 'objective space' without allowing the subjective response of the speaker to come through, a problem that is exacerbated because they themselves 'are not actors'.

## 2 Voice and Chekhov: Post-Dartington

In response to the impending Second World War, Chekhov moved his Studio to Ridgefield, Connecticut, where they remained from 1938 until 1942. The Studio closed in 1942 when the United States joined the war, and Chekhov moved to Los Angeles in 1943. There he pursued his own film acting career and continued to teach actors. While in Ridgefield, the speech work continued to be taught by Steiner practitioners. Neil Anderson notes that, as Chekhov had not trained in the work himself, 'when he was working alone in Hollywood [. . .] the speech aspect was neglected' (Anderson 2011: 171).

Jerri Daboo notes that since Chekhov went to the United States 'there has been no direct or continual thread of transmission within Britain itself from the time of the Dartington Studio' (2012: 62). When the Chekhov work did begin to return to the UK, Sarah Kane and Graham Dixon were two of the core practitioners, both of whom have had training in the Steiner voice work. They both embody a synthesis of the acting techniques of Chekhov and the Steiner speech work and in their individual approaches have managed to bridge the divide evident during the Dartington Studio years. Kane states that '[w]hat I have done is transform [Steiner's] voice and speech work that I learnt. I teach it now not out of the vocabulary in which I had learnt it but out of the Chekhov vocabulary' (Ashperger 2008: 143). One example of this is Kane's development of ball-throwing as a basis for exercises on voice and speech (Ashperger 2008: 143). These exercises draw on Chekhov's own use of ball-throwing, exemplified by the rehearsal protocols for *Hamlet* (Kirillov and Chamberlain 2013: 252–79). Both Kane and Dixon maintain a connection to the esoteric aspects of the Steiner work, Dixon regularly referred to the 'higher creative self' in his 2006 summer school and discusses this further in his interview for the *Theatre, Dance and Performance Training* themed issue on Chekhov (Cornford et al. 2013: 317). Kane teaches that understanding syllables . . . elevates speaking to an art done on a high level of consciousness of one's inner life and likens this to 'the Higher Ego activity within the Soul' (Cornford et al. 2013: 218).

In New Zealand, Jane Gilmer also teaches Steiner and Chekhov work. She trained in Australia with Mechthild Harkness, wife of Alan Harkness, who taught with Chekhov in Dartington and the United States. Gilmer notes that very few Chekhov practitioners 'go there', in terms of Steiner's ideas. Gilmer advocates for a reincorporation of Steiner's esoteric ideas. In a 2013 article, she asks the question as to 'whether an actor can become conversant with Steiner's spiritual philosophy without adhering to it, in order to do the exercises and, importantly, be able to find the substance behind the creative word' (Gilmer 2013: 208). Answering in the negative, Gilmer proposes an integrated technique that embraces Steiner's esoteric views:

> The less tangible issue of working with the sounds together with the Technique as a meditative practice may demand a Copernican-like shift in consciousness to include self-reflection, self-reflexivity, and not only open-mindedness to a 'spiritual' world but the courage to map it for oneself. (Gilmer 2013: 217)

For many, this demand to embrace a specific spiritual philosophy is problematic. Indeed, as Anderson points out, 'Chekhov only reached a mass public in America when much of his spiritual explanations and references to Steiner were removed' (Anderson 2011: 171). Franc Chamberlain (2003) argues that the removal of Eurythmy from Chekhov's approach was deliberate and sees Chekhov's 1953 publication of *To the Actor* as the 'summary of his life's work' (Chamberlain 2003). Daboo further suggests that this connection to 'the esoteric may well have contributed to the fifty-year gap of knowledge and practice of Chekhov's work in Britain' (Daboo 2012: 72).

In Britain, Australia and the United States, Chekhov's work is being incorporated into higher education and acting conservatoire curricula, such as on courses at Central and the London Academy of Music and Dramatic Art (LAMDA), the Victorian College of the Arts in Melbourne, Australia, and Point Park University, Northern Colorado and Rider University in Lawrenceville, New Jersey, in the United States. These educational settings are increasingly culturally diverse and are seeking to develop inclusive approaches to training.[5] In this context, it is necessary to question the ethics of an imposed spiritual ideology within curricula that seek to celebrate plurality and a multiplicity of belief systems. Chamberlain talks of how he teaches the techniques without specific reference to esoteric principles and that he does not teach any of the Eurythmy or speech work – only returning to Steiner when he's 'wanting to reflect on the roots of an idea in Chekhov' (Chamberlain 2003). The ethical questions that arise out of the spiritual aspects of the Steiner work, coupled with archival examples of the conflict between the speech and acting approaches, provide compelling reasons to explore alternative future pathways for voice and Chekhov's techniques.

## 3 Future pathways: Voice and Chekhov in the twenty-first century

Daboo notes that, in the case of the Chekhov's techniques, 'what is being taught in Britain now is adapted and translated through different teachers and practices in order to be useful for actors working in the contemporary theatre world' (2012: 79). The pluralistic perspective of contemporary theatre is far removed from the universalizing ideologies of Chekhov and Steiner's liberal humanist approaches. Beyond the ethical issues of Steiner's esoteric rhetoric, the search for a unified approach to acting is also problematic, as it fails to recognize that the work is culturally bound and that Chekhovian principles cannot be expected entirely to transcend the cultural and historical contexts in which they have been developed. Chekhov himself said *after some time you have the right to re-create the exercises'* (LTT: 23 May 1936) and, the interdisciplinary model offered here, similarly allows a freedom to adapt and translate the techniques.

My own engagement with the Chekhov work began when, as part of research for my MA in Voice Studies at Central, in July 2006, I attended the Chekhov, Voice and Text Summer School led by Graham Dixon. Since then, I have continued to explore Chekhov's techniques and voice work, by synthesizing it with my concurrent training to become a designated Linklater voice teacher in 2011 and, through an ongoing practice-based research project with my colleague Sinéad Rushe, who teaches Chekhov's techniques to trainee actors alongside my own work at Central. I shared some of this work with participants of the New Pathways Voice Symposium in September 2016. This symposium took participants through a practical exploration of some of the recent developments in voice and Michael Chekhov work. Alongside my work, participants were invited to participate in, and reflect on, the work of Christina Gutekunst and John Gillett. Gutekunst is also a graduate of the Voice Studies course at Central. Her work with John Gillett seeks to synthesize the psychophysical work of Stanislavsky and Michael Chekhov with voice-training approaches. The interdisciplinary approach exemplified by my research and the work of Gutekunst and Gillett not only suggests specific practices for future pathways but also offers a model for the development of further alternative pathways for Michael Chekhov's techniques, voice and singing.

The first area of voice work to be considered here has a lineage from Elsie Fogarty's Central School. Cicely Berry trained at the school in the 1940s and went on to develop her work on voice and text at the Royal Shakespeare Company. Berry is significant in that she moved away from the technique of rib-reserve breathing, which was common at the time. Berry began to focus on a connection of breath into the diaphragm and the abdomen, 'touching down into your centre you are finding the 'I' of your voice' (Berry 1973: 22). She encouraged actors to work 'technically and imaginatively' (Berry 1973: 15) and claims that actors had 'to be continually balancing [their] need to be truthful with a way of presenting that truth to an audience through the style of the language' (Berry 2000: 31).[6] This tension between an authentic connection to the inner life of the character and the effective delivery of language on stage is a recurring theme within Western-language-based theatre of the twentieth century and is echoed by Berry's successor at the Royal Shakespeare Company, Andrew Wade: 'When the psychological approach is given sole prominence, there is often – in the best cases – a comfortable sound but lack of verbal presence to define it. Speech is indeed more than sound' (1997: 139). Within the Central/Royal Shakespeare Company approach to voice training, there is focus on 'breath and thought as one' (Berry 1987: 26). When the actor moves on to working with the text, they are trained to see 'breath . . . as the physical life of the thought' (Berry 1987: 26). Berry does acknowledge that by thought she means 'the utterance of a character charged with whatever feelings he may have' (Berry 1987); however, the focus within the training is the connection of breath to language. While this has value in deepening a sensory/emotional connection in the delivery of the spoken word, any work on the feeling life of the character in relation to the imagined world of the play is left to the acting class or the rehearsal room. This separation of the imaginative world of the character from the actor's work on language has the danger of reinforcing a divide similar to that experienced by the actors within Chekhov's Studio.

Gutekunst and Gillett recognize the danger of separating language and imagination when they say:

> If we train voice separately from acting process, the stimuli of the organic acting experience may always be missing from the voice. The danger is that we have a separate and mechanical vocal response rather than a seamless interplay between receiving and communicating. (2014: 176)

In their workshop at the New Pathways Symposium on Voice and Chekhov, Gutekunst and Gillett took participants through an exploration of Chekhov's principle of **receiving** and connected this to an awareness of breath (Figure 3.2). This foundation principle of receiving is one that is often neglected in voice work; however, Gutekunst and Gillet demonstrated that by engaging Chekhov's principle of receiving, with an awareness of breath, and 'by placing ourselves into imaginary circumstances as if they are real, we can receive stimuli that will create an inner life and prompt believable action' (2014: 175).

In Berry's work, she does connect a deeply rooted breath to thought, and this can help the actor to avoid the purely intellectual approach to language that Chekhov wished to move away from; however, little attention is given as to *how* the breath comes into the body. For Berry, the exercising of the in-breath is achieved solely through technical and mechanical means, focusing on the engagement of the muscles of the ribs and abdomen and extending the count over which the breath is taken in and held before being released (see Berry 1973, Chapter 2). Gutekunst and Gillett's incorporation of breath with the principle of receiving addresses this issue. Gutekunst and Gillett draw on several of Chekhov's other principles to develop an interdisciplinary approach to voice and acting. In their 2014 book *Voice into Acting,* they explore how using Chekhov's work on **atmosphere** can change the onset, resonance, range and rhythm of the speaker (236–7), and they work with **psychological gesture** while sounding out the 'essence' of the character to help the actor 'become more vocally defined' (2014: 247). Gutekunst and Gillett are not alone in pursuing a pathway that adopts Chekhovian principles to bridge the divide between technical work on voice and the imaginative world of acting. Max Haffler's 2016 publication *Teaching Voice* uses a similar tactic to engage young performers with voice work. Similarly, Leslie Bennet's article on singing and Chekhov 'seeks to help the actor work from an inspired state' and 'balance naturalistic spontaneity within a discipline that is at once heightened and highly polished' (2013: 146). These examples show how, rather than rejecting an anatomical understanding of the voice, as advocated by Chekhov and Steiner, an interdisciplinary approach can help to bridge any perceived divide between acting and a more traditional approach to voice work.

The second interdisciplinary pathway explored here engages the Chekhov work with an approach to voice that already uses psychophysical principles. *Freeing the Natural Voice* (Linklater 2006) is an approach to voice work developed by Kristin Linklater over the past half-century and has many parallels with the development of Chekhov's work. The training has its roots in the work of Iris Warren, who was teaching voice at the Royal Academy of Dramatic Art when Chekhov was in Dartington. After this, Warren moved to LAMDA, where in the 1950s she taught Kristin Linklater, who subsequently became her apprentice. Unlike the work being taught at Central, Warren's work focused on 'the physical and mental tensions caused by blocked emotions' with the aim of 'shifting the controls from external physical muscles to internal, psychological impulses' (Linklater 2006: 5–6). Linklater continued to develop Warren's work and then moved to the United States, where her psychophysical approach to voice met the emotional and psychological needs of the American theatre of the 1960s, and, over time, became strongly established.

Linklater has not had any direct influence from the Chekhov work, but the parallels between the approaches are clear. Linklater talks about the 'Actor's Quartet', which is 'made up of Body, Voice, Emotion and Intellect – played (conducted, led, inspired) by Creative Imagination' (Linklater 2016: 59). This quartet can be directly mapped onto Chekhov's diagram from the Dartington archives, where he links the circles of atmosphere, plot, movement and speech. In his diagram, Chekhov indicates how an overbalance of one of these elements can lead to an actor who is just a dreamer, thinker, speaker or acrobat. In her teaching, Linklater also takes her students through a lively demonstration of the possible imbalances in the quartet. In this humorous demonstration, she gives practical examples of how an imbalance in one of the four areas can lead to an overly emotional, cognitive, physical or rhetorical actor.[7]

Both Chekhov and Linklater seek to awaken human feelings through the imagination. In the Linklater approach, breath is never approached from a purely mechanical perspective and always enters the body connected to a thought/feeling impulse in response to imaginative circumstances. The actor is encouraged to develop sensitivity to feeling in their body and to feel the vibrations of their voice rather than listen to the resultant sound. Compare this to Chekhov, who says, '*The more our body is full of feeling, the more you awaken this natural desire to act. [. . .] The human being is able to recreate his body and voice only from the inside. What a great power it is – our feelings – if we can manage them consciously*' (TAITT: 16 January 1938).

Unlike the Central/Royal Shakespeare Company model earlier, there is no perceptible divide between the work on voice and speech and approaches to acting, as both come from a place of imagination and psychophysical connection. In this pathway, the interdisciplinary nature of the work is not a matter of one approach filling the gaps left by another, rather, it is experienced at an embodied level, where the two approaches overlap, deepening the actor's psychophysical experience. In my own practice, I have noted how blending Chekhov and Linklater 'seems to be giving my work on the voice more purpose' as well as giving some of the imaginative principles of the Chekhov work 'a more physical, flesh and blood existence'.[8] The simplest example of this is the experience of working with Chekhov's 'Objective Atmosphere' (Chekhov 1991: 26) and an awareness of breath and receiving, whereby an awareness of the sensory and anatomical principles involved in breathing led to an experience of the imagined atmosphere 'at a deep cellular level'.[9]

At the level of fundamental technique, this overlapping and deepening of experience as the two approaches blend together has been one of the core findings of mine and Sinéad Rushe's practice-based research, and we have been able to develop a coherent progression through this foundational work. Linklater's exploration of physical awareness is deepened by working with Chekhov's principle of *ease* and together they enable the actor to access receiving more effectively. Receiving itself enables the actor to engage more deeply with the core Linklater exercise of the 'sigh of relief', which uses a pleasurable thought/feeling impulse of relief to stimulate the breathing musculature (Linklater 2006: 50–1). As the actor moves on to vocalization, Chekhov's principle of **radiating**, a psychophysical exercise imagining rays of energy emanating from the body, is effective in giving the actor's voice clarity of intention. Linklater's freeing vibrations work then enables the actor to find even more ease and greater volume. The freeing vibrations exercises involve loosening and vibrating the voice from the lips, through the head and neck, and into the whole body. At this point, the actor's whole body is experiencing a connection to vibration, and when Chekhov's archetypal gesture of expansion is added, the voice begins to carry even further. As with Gutekunst and Gillett's work, the awareness of breath and receiving in this process is a vital component, and the actor can experience a direct link between their inner feelings and sensory life and the imaginative space around them.

At the end of this fundamental exploration of voice and the Chekhov work, the actor has a strong sense of their own psychophysical presence and connection to the space around them. In our research, Sinéad Rushe and I have used this foundation to explore a continuing present-state awareness as the actor begins to work with language and an active engagement with the audience. To begin the work on language we have drawn on Kristin Linklater's practice of sound and movement. In this work, the actor receives individual sounds of language aurally as they simultaneously receive breath into their solar plexus, as if the sounds were *dropping in* to their body with the breath. This activates a feeling/sensory response in the actor, who then radiates out the feeling through their voice while making a full-body gesture. It is possible to draw links between this work and Steiner's Eurythmy; however, there is a fundamental difference between the two approaches. In the Steiner work, the sounds of language are considered to have an objective existence and the gestures attached to them are prescribed. Steiner explains that 'wherever, for example, an a appears in a word, we shall ultimately find, hidden away within the word, the inner experience of wonder' (Steiner 1959: 136). The 'a' sound is therefore accompanied by a gesture of 'opening out wide' (Steiner 1959: 38). Steiner insists that these experiences of sound have the status of universal truths that apply to 'all languages'. This universalizing rhetoric is, again, problematic for a contemporary pluralistic setting and becomes even more unpalatable when the supposedly correct formation of sounds is applied to accents. For example, we see in the archival records of Alice Crowther's feedback about Chekhov's actor-students: '*Hurd has a naturally good quality of voice, but he has a very bad accent, and he has yet no control over his vowels and consonants, and is not able to get any form into his speech*' (TAITT: 31 January 1938). Here again, the separation between the subjective experience of the actor in response to imaginative stimuli and the technical precision of speech is reinforced.

In the Linklater sound and movement work, the actor is able have their own subjective response to a range of speech sounds, which they can express freely, without the need to adhere to a speech standard. Over time, the *dropping in* of sounds extends to words and phrases so that language emerges from a visceral psychophysical experience, rather than a cognitive idea attached to the meanings of words. This goes some way towards Chekhov's aim to initially 'anatomize the body, emotions, and voice and have nothing to do with the intellect', after which process, the 'intellect is allowed to come and serve' (Hurst du Prey 1985: 25). In other words, the actor's analytical thinking comes in at a later stage to reflect on the psychophysical experience of the language.

In my research and practice, the aim has been to allow the actor's embodied cultural and social knowledge to respond psychophysically prior to any rational response to the written text. This approach does not value one type of response – rational or psychophysical – above another. It merely asks the actor to hold off from making narrative sense of the text before experiencing it through the body. To achieve this, I have explored the actor's ability to connect to voice and language while maintaining a present-tense awareness of self. Chekhov's own reflections on the impact of the audience partly stimulated my research, which has sought to examine the psychophysical experiences of the actor and the audience in these present-tense situations.

As part of this progression of work, the actors build towards playing a scene while holding direct eye contact with the audience. After a set of preparatory exercises, the actors attempt to receive the audience by paying visual attention to them at the same time as staying in dialogue with the other character in the scene. During this process, the actors continue to work with the fundamental principles of receiving, breath, impulse, feeling and vibration, as explored in the preparatory Linklater/Chekhov progression. When the actors return to playing the scene conventionally, they report an experience of 'ongoing connection to the audience' and the audience members have described a 'transparency or immediacy in the performance'.[10] As this interaction of the voice work and Chekhov's techniques has developed it has become increasingly difficult to find a language to adequately convey the embodied knowledge and experiences that arise. Mladen Dolar recognizes a similar issue when he says, '[W]ords fail us when we are faced with the infinite shades of the voice, which infinitely exceed meaning' (Dolar 2006: 13). Faced with a similar challenge, Chekhov adopted Steiner's esoteric frame of reference, imbued with the liberal humanist ideologies of the time, to try to communicate the subtle shifts of awareness and physical transformation within his work. The potential problems of this frame of reference for contemporary practice have already been explored. In response to this challenge, Chamberlain encourages the contemporary actor to experience the work and analyse it 'in any way they deem appropriate' and perhaps 'come to explanations . . . that are profoundly different from Chekhov' (Chamberlain 2003).

Many contemporary theatre practitioners have taken to neuroscience to analyse complex psychophysical experiences, and theoretical approaches have increasingly been influenced by this, as discussed in McConachie and Hart's 2006 book *Performance and Cognition: Theatre Studies and the Cognitive Turn*. In my own research into Chekov's techniques and voice, I, too, have begun to explore whether the use of a cognitive framework is helpful for talking about experiences that previously might have been framed in more esoteric language.

To help with this, I have turned to the research of Dr Norman Farb et al. (2007) into mindfulness and neuroscience. This cognitive model gives an insight into what happens in the brain during this type of psychophysical work. The research of Farb et al. identifies two neurological modes of self-reference, 'narrative focus (NF)' and 'experiential focus (EF)' (Farb et al. 2007: 314). 'EF was characterised as engaging present-centred self-reference, sensing what is occurring in one's thoughts, feelings and body state', whereas 'NF was characterised as judging what is occurring . . . and allowing oneself to be caught up in a given train of thought' (Farb et al. 2007: 314). Essentially, there are two processes at play in the brain: one that deals with the ability to stay in the present moment and have an awareness of feelings and sensations in the body and another that thinks *about* the experience and processes thoughts about the past or the future. The most striking finding of this research is that these two functions are 'inversely related' (Chaskalson 2014: 136). Seen from the perspective of voice and acting, it can be implied that an actor who is having to focus on the narrative function of the technical production of speech and language will not have the cognitive capacity to have an experiential awareness of their feelings and inner-life responses to the imagined circumstances at the same time. In the du Prey archives, the actor Woodie's assertion that he must *'drop the acting because [he] cannot concentrate on the speech method and the inner life of the character at the same time'* correlates with this. This research describes the narrative mode as the default setting,[11] and Chekhov knew this instinctively when he said that *'this is a long work, and you must be very patient. You must not lose the idea that we must awaken our feelings'* (TAITT: 29 September 1937).

## 4 Conclusion

This chapter has shown how Steiner's speech work and Chekhov's acting approach share the same liberal humanist and esoteric philosophy. However, at the Dartington Studio there was a lack of integration of the embodied practice of both techniques, and this caused problems for the actors. It has been recognized that where these two disciplines have since been further integrated, as exemplified in the psychophysical practices of Graham Dixon and Sarah Kane, the work has become more effective. Where this integration has taken place, the esoteric perspectives that come from Steiner have been maintained, and this can present problems when applied to contemporary pluralistic training settings.

This chapter has proposed that, rather than seeking a unified approach to voice and acting, it is beneficial to explore multiple interdisciplinary explorations of Chekhov's techniques and voice, from which numerous new pathways might emerge. Within the interdisciplinary model proposed here, the dialogue and connection between practices is not assumed at a theoretical level, as it was in the Dartington Studio. Rather, the dialogue happens within the psychophysical experiences of the actors themselves. The actor is then free to respond to the interplay of voice and acting approaches within their own bodies and to frame this from their own cultural perspectives. As Chamberlain suggests, each individual is allowed to experience the work and analyse it 'in any way they deem appropriate' (Chamberlain 2003). In the examples explored here, Gutekunst and Gillett frame their exploration of Chekhov's techniques and voice in relation to the psychophysical approaches of Stanislavsky; whereas, in my own research into Chekhov's techniques and Linklater voice work, I have framed the experiences in relation to neuroscience and the cognitive turn in theatre studies.

Both my approach and that of Gutekunst and Gillett find significant benefits in exploring the solar plexus as an emotional centre in connection to breathing and Chekhov's principles of receiving. This is slightly at odds with Chekhov's ideal centre in the chest, and it is tempting to draw out this emergent anatomical connection between breath and emotion in the solar plexus as a new universal principle to be adopted in future voice and Chekhov pathways.

However, I am mindful that both my explorations and those of Gutekunst and Gillett are sited within the culturally embedded practices of English-language-based psychological realism and Western views of the body. The experience of Chekhov's principle of receiving might take on significantly different resonances when engaged, for example, from an embodied knowledge of breath and the Hindu Chakra system, the Chinese Dāntián or the broader Japanese area of the Hara.

Breath awareness is common to many contemporary voice practices but does not feature in the Steiner work, where it is developed indirectly through work on text. Breath can be understood from multiple intercultural perspectives, such as its relation to prana in the yogic traditions; however, I would suggest that the use of breath awareness to deepen psychophysical experience might well be a key factor in numerous future pathways of voice and Chekhov. I propose that some aspect of breath awareness might usefully join the other 'qualities that come together in an actor' as described in the revised diagram (Figure 3.2).

By opening a dialogue between the Dartington archive and contemporary practice, much of the liberal humanist universalizing at the heart of Chekhov's work becomes unstable. Concepts such as the ideal centre in the chest start to break down when alternative perspectives on the body come into play – such as the work incorporating the solar plexus in both pathways explored here – and universal principles become even harder to sustain when those perspectives expand to incorporate differently abled bodies or bodies from outside of Western cultures. However, it is through this process of fragmentation that an interdisciplinary approach, which can engage with a plurality of experience, becomes possible. This in turn allows Chekhov's techniques to engage with voice practices far beyond the limitations of twentieth-century psychological realism and opens the way for multiple future pathways in the twenty-first century.

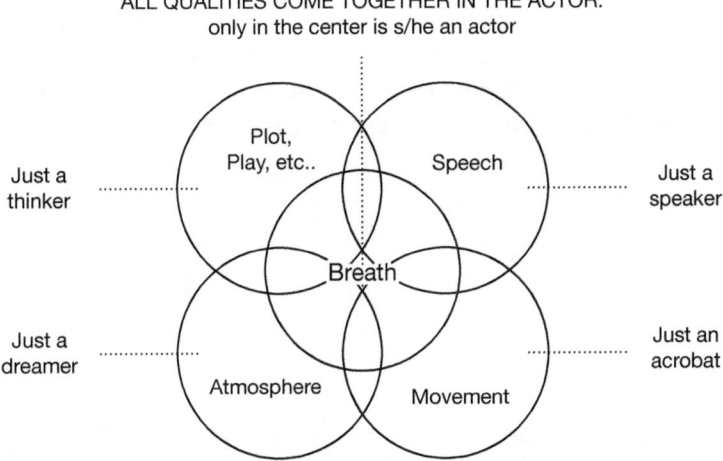

Fig. 3.2 'All qualities come together in the actor', revised by Daron Oram. TAITT: 2 November 1936, CTS-DHDPA.

## Notes

1. A more contemporary publication that explores Steiner's speech work is Dawn Langman's *The Art of Speech: Body – Soul – Spirit – Word, A Practical and Spiritual Guide* (Langman 2014).
2. Kane and Dixon went on to study with some of the original students of Michael Chekov, such as Joanna Merlin and Deidre Hurst du Prey. Kane is a founding member of Michael Chekhov UK, which Dixon joined when he moved to the UK.
3. Dixon runs regular workshops and annual summer schools through his training studio (www.michaelchekhovstudio.org.uk, last accessed 14 August 2019). The 2006 summer school took place at Rudolf Steiner House, London. Sarah Kane has recently established a new school to teach her work in the UK, Performing Arts International.
4. Author's interview with Dixon (2006).
5. LAMDA's website discusses an active approach to inclusivity and shares positive diversity statistics (https://www.lamda.org.uk/access-and-diversity-at-lamda, last accessed 14 August 2019). At Central, the BA Acting CDT course 'embraces a multicultural and multidisciplinary methodology' (http://www.cssd.ac.uk/course/acting-cdt-ba, last accessed 14 August 2019) and regularly produces work that places marginalized narratives centre stage.
6. In her book, *Text in Action,* Berry discusses attending a Steiner workshop and offers an exercise of embodying the feeling of vowels through gesture (Berry and Noble 2010). This exercise is more free form than Steiner's prescribed vowel gestures, and actors are able to find any gesture that comes to them in relation to the sound.
7. While I have seen Kristin demonstrate these distinctions a number of times since, I first witnessed this demonstration during my Linklater Teacher Designation training at the Royal Central School of Speech and Drama, London, in 2010.
8. Notes from the author's reflective journal 9 November 2014.
9. Reflective Journal 9 November 2014.
10. Reflective Journal 9 November 2014.
11. While the research of Farb et al. defines the narrative mode as the default setting, this can only be assumed to represent the default setting for the population of their study in North America. They do not explore the cultural background of their participants. The danger of following the cognitive turn in performance studies is that we try to create another essentializing paradigm. Neuroscience itself is culturally bound and it is offered here, not as a universal truth, but as one of many potential perspectives as part of an interdisciplinary approach.

# 4 'The moment you are not inwardly moving and inwardly participating, you are dead'

## Chekhov technique in actor-movement and dance

ROANNA MITCHELL

This chapter is concerned with the ways in which Chekhov technique is currently used in actor-movement, dance and the crossover between them, both in terms of training and making. Discussion of Chekhov's techniques in any context will make mention of movement, as it is woven into all aspects of his work; however, to date there is little scholarly investigation of the use of his technique in the fields of actor-movement and dance, specifically. Cass Fleming (2013) includes some discussion of these areas in her analysis of embodied play as a central aspect of Chekhov's approach, drawing parallels with play-enabling practices in Suzanne Bing's work and genealogies of the French tradition. Historical reviews of the pedagogic practices at Chekhov's Theatre Studio at Dartington touch upon the role of both integrated movement work and separate movement classes, including dance classes taught by Lisa Ullmann and Eurythmy lessons, both of which will be discussed later (Chamberlain 2004; Cornford 2012; Autant-Mathieu and Meerzon 2015), and Jerri Daboo (2012) makes important links from Chekhov's work to contemporary lineages of physical theatre practice, specifically in the UK. More recently, Lenka Pichlikova (2017) examines Chekhov's technique in the context of teaching mask work, *Commedia dell'Arte* and mime, while Suzanne Bennett (2013) provides the only published discussion to date on use of the technique in institutional dance training.

This chapter will refer and respond to these existing contributions and the archives of Chekhov's work at Dartington, as well as discussing current experiments with the technique. Examples of the latter are drawn from practitioner interviews, my own practice as a movement pedagogue and performance-maker, as well as discussions at the New Pathways praxis symposium session in 2016 on Chekhov Technique in Actor-Movement and Dance. This session was attended by dancers, somatic practitioners and teacher-practitioners in the areas of actor-movement, physical theatre, embodied theatre and dance-theatre. It was led by myself and Juliet Chambers, Laban Movement Analyst and Lecturer in Actor-Movement and Dance, who gave a practical taste of the dialogue between Laban's and Chekhov's approach in her own teaching and contextualized this through a paper on the two practitioners' shared interest in spirituality. This was followed by discussion of archival materials relating to the role of movement in Chekhov's techniques, with participants focusing particularly on how the technique might help to navigate the meeting point between dance and acting as well as the relationship between inner life and the form of outer expression.

The notion of crossover, of blends and bridges, forms a key theme in this discussion, as there is no 'pure' application of Chekhov's technique in actor-movement and dance. I therefore take a selectively genealogical approach to help us understand the web of overlaps and influences in contemporary practice. This means not only investigating Deirdre Hurst du Prey's archive to develop a clearer picture of Chekhov's own practice but also branching out to examine the embodied dance and mime practices of Hurst du Prey herself, as well as the affinities between Chekhov's work and that of his contemporaries. Such genealogy enables a non-linear dialogue between past, present and future projections, and thus constitutes a form of feminist historiography. It acknowledges that the emergence of physical practices – both in Chekhov's time and now – can rarely be ascribed to one 'original' source but instead 'occurs in the interstices' of collaboration, cross-fertilization and silent transfer of embodied knowledge (Foucault 1977: 150).

The first part of this chapter focuses on actor-movement. It examines Chekhov's thinking about movement and the aspects of his technique that cause it to be integrated in contemporary actor-movement settings. Then it provides three examples of contemporary blends between Chekhov's techniques and other embodied practices in the classroom. The actor's ownership of their embodied experience and the emphasis on **creative individuality** are key here, as well as the fact that Chekhov's technique does not distinguish between 'acting' and 'movement', which raises critical questions for our contemporary conceptions of holistic actor training and the role of movement within it.

The second part of this chapter focuses on applications of Chekhov's technique in dance and dance-theatre crossovers. I begin by examining the embodied history of Chekhov's female collaborators and the affinities between Chekhov's practice and dance practices of the early twentieth century in order to illustrate their common languages and shared roots. Against this backdrop, I discuss contemporary experiments with Chekhov's technique as an acting technique for dance, a technique to develop the inner life and expressivity of the dancer and an approach to dance-theatre dramaturgy. These examples highlight ways in which Chekhov's technique can provide a shared language among actors and dancers, empower dancers' creative agency, and facilitate their exploration of acting tools without asking them to abandon familiar technique or form.

The process of examining these areas of movement practice in relation to Chekhov's approach allows us to reflect on the role of movement in the contemporary moment, against the backdrop of past practice. In doing so, it invites the reader to consider potential future applications of Chekhov's technique in movement and dance, and to rethink current training- and rehearsal-room structures in order to facilitate such changes.

## 1 Chekhov technique for actor-movement

Chekhov's technique was not designed specifically as a movement practice, and in fact must be read as a manifesto for the holistic training of the actor, as Chekhov emphasizes from the early stages of his work at Dartington Hall:

> *All our exercises are built as an organic whole – they are organically related – and cannot be separated. It is necessary to find the 'spine' of each exercise, but it is not possible to divide them any more than it is possible to divide the hand from the body.* (TAITT: 26 May 1936)

Nonetheless, Chekhov's technique has much to offer for the contemporary movement practitioner and pedagogue, as movement is woven into all its aspects. A spirit of embodied enquiry extends all the way from Chekhov's first simple exercises on concentration and rediscovery of the body through to the complexity of a full performance. The process of enquiry through movement that he developed means that understanding of self, character/persona and performance score are all developed through embodied experience, both in training and in the rehearsal process. Embodied enquiry acts as a means for the actor both to develop what Chekhov terms their creative individuality and to recognize their individual work as part of a larger, more complex and relational organic whole. Resisting the separation between individual and ensemble, the idea of a psychophysical **whole** in this view of training and performance encompasses not only the individual actor's expression but the whole *'complicated rhythmical body of our theatre'* (LTT: 4 June 1936).

As a consequence, we find that information concerning actor-movement can be found in each of Chekhov's exercises, including **atmosphere, psychological gesture, movement qualities, imaginary centre, imaginary body, the four brothers** and so on – always with a key emphasis on the imagination, which for Chekhov was an integral aspect of the actor's embodied work. The examples of imaginary centre, atmosphere and gesture may serve to illustrate this. Imaginary centre explores the place from which an individual's movements originate and the effect this area of origin has on direction, rhythm, quality of movement and inner sensations. More than just a question of leading with a physical body part, this work requires an engaged and nuanced imagination to make the **centre** as specific as possible: the actor chooses not only where it is but also its size, texture, temperature, colour, and so on, such as a sharp, pointed metallic centre of 10cm length that hovers just outside the forehead. This in turn develops a very specific movement language. When used to develop characterization, the imaginary centre is an expression of the character's 'psychological makeup', with imaginative engagement and attention to inner sensation forming 'the link between the psychology and outer means of expression of the actor' (Chekhov 1991: 104).

The example of atmosphere, meanwhile, allows the movement practitioner to also consider the movement of the intangible, the dynamics of the 'feeling dimension which links everything together' (Chamberlain 2004: 53). Chekhov's exercises in this regard remind us that movement and words are 'born out of' the dynamics of an atmosphere, and in turn intensify it, so that atmosphere becomes a 'catalytic power . . . which awakens [the actor's] activity' (1991: 35). It inspires certain qualities of movement, rhythms and relationship with space and can enable the driving objective of a scene to be recognized and then shaped into a specific psychological gesture (Chekhov 1991: 33–4).

Chekhov's notion of gesture is perhaps the key reason why movement can be found at the heart of all parts of his technique. Similar to Jacques Lecoq's understanding of the 'mimodynamics' of nature and life (2002: 47–8), for Chekhov gesture encompasses the dynamic expression in space of everything in the world including 'a plant, a tree, a chair . . . different flights of stairs' (Hurst du Prey 1985: 85) and, of course, a character's psychology. While his exercises on psychological gesture for character development have been noted as one of his 'most original' contributions to the actor's craft (Chamberlain 2004: 81), the notion of gesture permeates his pedagogy more broadly too. As Fleming (2013), Kirillov (2005) and others have argued, it ties together the various different aspects of his technique, presenting 'a kind of "urform" for the whole of his acting system' (Pitches 2006: 162). Kirillov describes gesture as 'the common denominator on which various aspects of acting such as speech, movement, psychology, etc. can be integrated and unified into the "whole" picture' (2005: 227), while Chekhov himself notes that '[w]e can take any point in the method and turn it into a gesture' (Chekhov and Hurst du Prey, 1985: 108). Deirdre Hurst du Prey, meanwhile, reminds us that for Chekhov gesture was also closely linked to his interest in rhythm: 'Up to the very end of his work, rhythm was all important to him. The rhythm of an idea, the rhythm of a concept, the rhythm of the whole . . . gesture and rhythm, so close. The living force' (1978: 14–15).

The fact that this pedagogy of rhythm and gesture does not easily distinguish between 'acting' and 'movement' can make Chekhov's approach an uneasy bedfellow for contemporary structures of actor training where the two are often taught as separate subjects. At present, in most UK conservatoire training, movement for the actor is a subject which is taught by movement specialists and focuses on the body as the actor's expressive 'instrument' (Dennis 2002: 8). The movement studio becomes a space of preparation, and the discoveries and developments of the body made here can then be applied within acting classes. This specific focus on movement is useful in many ways: it allows for focused engagement with the body and embodied habits through movement fundamentals and somatic practice, such as in Litz Pisk's pure movement work (2017), Bonnie Bainbridge Cohen's Body-Mind-Centering (2012) or Alexander Technique (Alexander 1955; McEvenue 2001). It also encourages exploration of the body's ability to communicate and transform through classes focused on movement expression, which might include approaches based in the work of Rudolf Laban (2011), Jacques Lecoq (2002, 2006) or animal study. Insisting on the distinct existence of movement classes might be seen as an act of 'strategic essentialism' (Heddon 2008: 28) on the part of movement practitioners. In clearly defining and naming actor-movement as a subject of study in its own right, it becomes a place from which to speak, to insist that the practitioners' specific expertise is legitimized. This is important in view of the fact that the emergence of this subject over the last century is significantly shaped by female practitioners, whose impact on actor training practices is only gradually being acknowledged in historiographies of actor training that have previously accepted the work of male performer trainers as canonical (Clarke 2009; Fleming 2013).

However, this separation also presents a number of challenges. One of these is that it may reinforce an often implicitly gendered hierarchy of subject areas in the training that undermines the perception of movement as an integral aspect of the actor's craft. We see this illustrated in Gaunt's preface to Jackie Snow's *Movement Training for Actors* (2012), in which he sees it necessary to convince the reader of the relevance of movement work by underlining its usefulness for the actor's employability. 'What use is movement or dance to an actor? How can it be employed to enrich and support an actor's training?' he asks, and then answers in part by noting that '[a]ctors need to be fit and agile and a sound introduction to movement and how it supports characterization will be of benefit to them throughout their professional lives' (Snow 2012: ix–x). Although surely well intentioned in making the case for actor-movement, his choice of words also implies a hierarchy in which movement plays a supporting role, to 'enrich' actor training and 'support' intellectual and text-based analysis rather than being assumed as integral to training and an active catalyst for character creation. A division between concerns of the body and concerns of the mind is implied, constituting a type of institutionalized mind-body split.

This leads us to another, more practical challenge, which is the question of how the explorations and discoveries made in movement classes then become reintegrated with other parts of the training. Although staff with responsibility for movement, voice and acting will 'work together to plan a syllabus . . . that supports the holistic and progressive development of their students' (Snow 2012: ix), the way in which individual students then make connections between these subjects may be less clear. Snow, for example, suggests that whether a student is able to do so successfully is 'a mystery to everyone who trains actors' (2012: xvi).

Chekhov's techniques offer contemporary practitioners an opportunity to engage with both of the challenges described here, albeit within the constraints of the existing curriculum. By considering movement within the training as crucial not only to the actor's *means of expression* but also as a tool for the actor to *understand* text, composition and dramaturgy, Chekhov's approach subverts the hierarchy of subject areas by tackling them simultaneously. As practitioner and pedagogue Sinéad Rushe notes, for instance, Chekhov's technique can provide a link between Lecoq-based movement training and the staging of an Anton Chekhov play. For her, the technique reminds the students that '[t]he body in movement and internal and external expressivity and motivation *is* acting', which helps actors understand and harness what was previously deemed 'movement' work as an integral aspect of work on a play text (Rushe 2017). Consequently, in many drama schools Chekhov's technique is used as an integration tool: it is taught in acting classes, but also by movement teachers, and frequently used as a bridge between the two disciplines.

The New Pathways Symposium and the interviews conducted for this chapter have also shown that in actor-movement Chekhov's technique is frequently used in blends with other practices, sitting in nuanced dialogue with practitioners such as Rudolf Laban, Jacques Lecoq and Vsevolod Meyerhold, and often drawing on Chekhov's principles rather than necessarily employing a pure form of his technique. These blends make use of the fact that movement in Chekhov's technique has various pedagogic functions that, I would argue, are shared with most other approaches to actor-movement and might broadly be described as developing awareness of inner sensation in relation to outer form, developing an understanding of rhythmic and spatial dynamics within and between individuals and the world, and developing the capacity for transformation into other beings and characters. In addition to these, the examples of blends examined in this chapter show that the technique introduces three key interconnected principles into movement work that are distinctively Chekhovian: a heightened focus on the imagination, an emphasis on the actor's creative individuality and an embodied understanding of the fact that movement is already 'acting'. Before discussing the blends, I will first examine these three principles in more detail.

## 1.1 Heightened focus on the imagination

In *To the Actor,* Chekhov begins by emphasizing how important it is for the actor to achieve complete harmony between body and mind. The very first sentence of this volume states: 'It is a known fact that the human body and psychology influence each other and are in constant interplay' (2002: 1), a statement that, as Rick Kemp notes, prefigures cognitive science's later understanding of 'the way in which physical experience in the material world shapes conceptual thought' (2012: 48). However, for

Chekhov the notion of the psychophysical is incomplete without attunement to the dimension of the imagination. In his training, influenced by Stanislavsky and Vakhtangov (Gordon 1987: 103 and 136), the first step towards achieving this is by concentration on inner sensation. In an approach that resonates with somatic movement practices that frequently form part of contemporary actor training, such as the Feldenkrais Method (1980) or Alexander Technique (1955), Chekhov asks the actor to re-encounter their body by attending to sensations stirred by movement. This allows them to practice discovering '*the great possibilities within their bodies of which they have previously been absolutely unaware*' (LTT: 15 May 1936):

> *We must know what our bodies are capable of. [. . .] In order to 'know', the pupils must discover possibilities in their own bodies – must explore these possibilities as if for the first time and must be aware every time they discover a new sensation or reaction during the movement exercises.* (LTT: 15 May 1936)

Once the actor is trained to become sensitive to this psychophysical connection, they can progress from experiencing inner movement as a consequence of outer movement to consciously creating inner movement by imagining it: 'As concentration develops we can then begin to imagine these inner movements as happening. We make them happen' (Petit 2010: 15). Additionally, the actor is tasked with the responsibility to 'enrich the quality of his own imagination in order to enhance his creative approach to the stage', and so the technique is infused with exercises that encourage free association of images, often stimulated by movement (Cristini 2015: 72).

In his emphasis on the dimension of the imagination, Chekhov is profoundly influenced by Rudolf Steiner's anthroposophy, a spiritual movement to which Chekhov turned in what he termed a 'spiritual crisis' and which shaped many aspects of his technique and wider philosophy about art and life (Chamberlain 2004: 14). The spiritual dimension of Chekhov's work and its relationship with Steiner's anthroposophy has been discussed in detail elsewhere (see, for example, Chamberlain 2004; Langman 2014; Cristini 2015). For the purpose of this discussion, it will suffice to explain that Chekhov held a belief in the '(hidden) spiritual dimension in man', following Steiner's concept of the tripartite nature of the human being as composed of body, soul and spirit (Cristini 2015: 70).

Chekhov uses Steiner's ideas to argue that in trusting the unpredictable stimuli provided by the imagination, the actor is connecting with the spiritual dimension, a 'higher-level I' which 'enriches and expands the consciousness' (Chekhov 2002: 87). Many of his exercises thus reflect his belief that the realm of the imagination is 'an objective world where images have their own life beyond the control of the actor, a dimension that Rudolf Steiner considers part of the spirituality of the actor himself' (Cristini 2015: 71). The degree to which anthroposophical ideas are taught as part of Chekhov's technique varies between practitioners. The spiritual interpretation of his work may not appeal to all actors and pedagogues, and indeed, for some, such romantic ideals of creativity as the gateway to a spiritual plane may be mystifying, or even alienating. Chekhov was perhaps aware of this, and as Dawn Langman reminds us, is recorded as saying 'I will never impose on our students anything of Anthroposophy' (Langman 2014: 9). Along with Chamberlain (2003) and Pitches (2006: 155), I would therefore argue that the central idea here – of being led by inner sensation and being surprised by imagination – can be usefully adopted without necessarily requiring the practitioner to subscribe to an anthroposophical belief system. The following two principles will further illustrate this.

## 1.2 An emphasis on the actor's creative individuality

Chekhov aims for the actor to have a strong sense of creative agency in every aspect of their work and to develop their 'creative individuality' (1991: 16). Thus, even in the simplest exercises to develop sensory awareness, he emphasizes the autonomy of the actor: attentiveness to the ways in which inner sensations relate to movement offers a way of *'giving to the body wisdom'* that comes *'from the actor themselves'* and directs their individual route of enquiry (LTT: 23 May 1936). This aim also leads him to distinguish between the use of 'acrobatics' and his own movement exercises:

> *The difference between acrobatic movements and our kind of movement is that acrobatics are purely for training the body, while our exercises in movement are for sending out the soul, the feelings, through the body.* (TAITT: 5 October 1936)

Movement in the technique should therefore not be understood as gymnastic but rather 'psychological in that it affords us the experience of states and conditions of being' (Petit 2010: 15). In this we can again observe Steiner's influence, in connection with his movement practice of Eurythmy, which Chekhov embedded in his curriculum at Dartington.

The purpose of Eurythmy was to improve the actors' speech and sense of musicality by awakening 'the deep, synesthetic connection of movement with words on the one hand and emotions on the other, which could be expressed through qualities' (Whyman 2015: 278). In Steiner's lectures on the principles of Eurythmy we can locate the root of Chekhov's eagerness to distinguish between acrobatics and the kind of movement he sought from his actors:

> Gymnastics is an art of movement that contains no soul or spiritual element whatever. By contrast, you will see here an art of movement that lets the soul-spiritual element shine directly into the movements of the human limbs, letting the eurythmist feel himself as a soul-and-spiritual being. (Steiner 1984: Stuttgart, 6 May 1919)

Recognizing the risk that purely training the body, without attention to inner life, may lead to automatized movement, Chekhov insists that his own movement exercises – which, as we have seen, are difficult to identify as separate from what we might call 'acting' exercises – must always be undertaken in the spirit of creativity:

> *If we grow to considering our simple exercises as wonders, we will get from them much more than if we consider them something dull and ordinary. We rob ourselves of a certain power. We reject something which is very necessary for our creative work. We must do our simplest exercises with love and care.* (TAITT: 16 December 1937)

Cass Fleming has identified Chekhov's emphasis on the actor's creative individuality as an aspect of the 'very specific type of embodied playful awareness' required in his training, constituting a radical proposal for the actor's creative agency in the process of training and making (2013: 75). This requires a willingness from the pedagogue (or indeed the director) to 'create spaces for discoveries . . . which do not always centre on reason and rationality, and that are based in the body' (Fleming 2013: 155).

The movement teacher using Chekhov's technique may thus empower the actor's creative agency even within fundamental movement work – work which focuses on aspects such as alignment, flexibility, weight, breath or release – by foregrounding the principle of 'exercising with creativity' and encouraging the imaginative engagement discussed here. There are myriad ways in which this might take place, and the principle of exercising with creativity is, of course, not the provenance of Chekhov's technique alone. Specific to Chekhov's approach, however, is its integrative nature: the very same language and principles that are applied in the macrocosm of a full production can also be applied in the microcosm of a movement fundamentals exercise and vice versa. This leads us to the third principle to be discussed here, which connects to both imagination and creative individuality, and which I examine by giving some examples of practical application.

## 1.3 An embodied understanding of the fact that movement is already 'acting'

Rather than a linear progression through his exercises, Chekhov's approach forms a non-hierarchical 'web' of interdependent skills, 'organized holistically with each element of the system contributing as a whole to a harmonious outcome for the actor' (Pitches 2006: 162). In this, as Pitches notes, Chekhov was influenced by Goethe's romanticism and his belief that 'you must learn to discover the whole in the smallest part' (Goethe 1996: 59; Pitches 2006: 162). There is thus no need to find a way to 'bridge' between preparation of the body and creative work, or between movement and 'acting', as each part of the technique is a synthesis of the whole in the process of embodied inquiry (a concept we will revisit below in relation to Rudolf Laban's approach).

For the movement practitioner, this means that, in practice, improvements in movement fundamentals may be achieved as part of engaging in an imaginative and creative task – helpfully blurring the boundaries between what is a movement exercise and what is already creative 'acting' work. The actor may, for instance, investigate Chekhov's technique of *radiating* from the primary imaginary centre, known as the 'ideal' centre, and simultaneously improve alignment. While other teachers of the technique have since experimented with the effects of locating the primary working centre variously in the area of the solar plexus (see Oram in this volume), or abdomen (see Zinder 2002: 120), Chekhov locates the 'ideal' centre in the chest, and invites the actor to discover this as 'the source of inner activity and *power*' within their body (Chekhov 2002: 7). This working centre may be imagined as the point in the chest where the vertical and two horizontal axes through the body intersect. In radiating – energetically extending – along these axes the actor is engaging with the experience of giving and receiving energy, while simultaneously finding an easefully adjusted alignment through ankles, knees and spine without having to think about each of these as discrete components.

Selecting and focusing on a certain **ground** (discussed in Chapter 1) can be another way in which to achieve physical development while nurturing creative individuality (TAITT: 16 December 1937). Each chosen ground – in other words, the chosen focus every time an exercise, improvisation or scene is practised – can be selected in response to the actors' needs on that particular occasion, in the knowledge that alongside this main focus many other aspects of work will be taking place simultaneously. For instance, the four brothers may be used as grounds in a yoga sequence. While the sequence of movements themselves helps with flexibility and engagement with the breath, it can be done with attention to a **feeling of form**, or a **feeling of ease** – each ground allowing for new discoveries about the exercise, as it would for a scene or play. It might also be done while imagining a surrounding colour, or with attention to every gesture of opening, closing, pushing, pulling or wringing it entails.[1]

While the technique enables the teacher to scaffold, guide and develop the actor's physical work creatively in this way, it also, however, requires the teacher to relinquish a level of control. Using a ground to provide a working focus, rather than concentrating on a desired outcome, creates space for what a participant at the 2016 symposium termed the 'anarchy of creativity' – the unpredictability of how students will play within, explore, interpret and break the rules of the game as they follow the guidance of their imagination. To be able to facilitate such work, Chekhov recommends in his *Lessons to Teachers* (2018) that teachers themselves adopt the technique to guide their pedagogic practice. Weaving the three principles into movement practice thus involves radically rethinking pedagogy in actor training: reconsidering current hierarchies of subjects, accepting and developing the actor's creative individuality and abandoning any notion of the actor's body as a servant of the craft. Instead, Chekhov's approach requires teachers of movement and acting to subtly but significantly adjust terminology to acknowledge the body – which includes imagination – as the very heart and source of creativity and understanding.

## 2 Chekhov technique in dialogue with other actor-movement practices

As mentioned earlier, elements of Chekhov's techniques are often introduced into contemporary movement classes through dialogue with other movement practices. In the section that follows I will examine three examples of such blends, which relate to the approaches of Rudolf Laban, Vsevolod Meyerhold and Jacques Lecoq.

### 2.1 Chekhov in dialogue with Laban

Rudolf Laban was Chekhov's contemporary, and Chekhov encountered his practices, mainly through Laban's students and collaborators, at Dartington Hall.[2] Laban's work and Chekhov's technique lend themselves to blending by virtue of the fact that there are extensive points of convergence between them (as discussed by Chamberlain 2004; McCaw 2005), as well as differences in approach that mean they are sometimes employed to supplement each other. In a series of practice laboratories, initiated by the New Pathways Symposium in 2016, I have been exploring these crossovers with Juliet Chambers, Laban Movement Analyst and Lecturer in Actor-Movement and Dance in the UK.

Chambers, whose research seeks to rehabilitate the spiritual aspects that have, to a great extent, been edited out of Laban's published work, reminds us that the synergies between Laban and Chekhov are linked to their shared attraction to certain spiritual beliefs involving a non-Cartesian conception of the human and the artist, many of which can be traced back to the ideas of Rudolf Steiner. As she argues, both practitioners were 'deeply influenced by . . . the rise of "alternative" esoteric/spiritual views of Anthroposophy and Rosicrucianism which sought the Arts as a physical/material manifestation of their beliefs' (Chambers 2017), and as a consequence both were 'concerned with the question of spirituality and harmony in the work of the actor and mover' (Chambers 2016).

Coloured by these spiritual beliefs, in practice the dialogue between the two approaches appears to centre on the correlations, and subtle distinctions, between how these practitioners engage with and expand the idea of the psychophysical. Chekhov, as discussed earlier, takes as a given the constant feedback loop between physical experience, thoughts and creative imagination. Laban also searches for a non-dualist conception of both body and mind, human and artist, and Chambers emphasizes, in particular, his exhortation to 'movement thinking':

> Movement thinking could be considered as a gathering of impressions of happenings in one's own mind, for which nomenclature is lacking. This thinking does not, as thinking in words does, serve orientation in the external world, but rather it perfects man's orientation in his inner world in which impulses continually surge and seek an outlet in doing, acting and dancing. (Laban 2011: 15)

In some ways, this 'movement thinking' can be compared to Chekhov's call for embodied inquiry. However, their approaches to such enquiry differ in certain respects. Chekhov 'was opposed to the notion of materialist analysis' through dissection (Fleming 2013: 121) and instead, as discussed above, preferred romantic theories of interconnectedness and synthesis (Pitches 2006: 165), discovered through attending to inner sensation awakened by outer form and vice versa.

Laban was similarly resistant to a purely materialistic approach to creativity and consciousness (McCaw 2005) and also emphasized notions of harmonious integration and the connection of the individual to a bigger universal whole (Chambers 2016). However, his aim was to develop an approach for movement analysis – including a taxonomy for describing and understanding human movement and a system of movement notation – and, as Chambers notes, the legacy of these aspects of his work 'somewhat overshadow the spiritual foundation on which they were built' (Chambers 2016). Much of what is commonly communicated about his work thus bears the hallmark of a more mechanistic world view, with an emphasis on breaking movement down into its constituent parts in order to analyse and systematize. For instance, most actors will be introduced to Laban's dissection of movement into the motion factors of Weight, Time, Space and Flow, which produce a complex mathematics of the various combinations between them. Each of these combinations form what Laban calls an Effort (Laban 2011: 67–81). These Efforts are also to be understood psychophysically, as each Effort involves a certain inner attitude towards the various motion factors. The motion factor of Time, for example, involves 'an effort attitude towards time, in which either the struggling against or the indulging in time is prevailing' (McCaw 2011: 225).

Even in explaining just this one element of Laban's work, it becomes evident that to understand these concepts requires the performer to learn a complex terminology. Looking to Chekhov's ideas of how we engage with the world through the **centres** of the head (thinking), the heart (feeling), and the pelvis and legs (willing) (1991: 52–3), one might argue that to achieve an embodied understanding of Laban's terminology requires, first of all, a great deal of engagement with the head centre and intellectual analysis, potentially diverting attention away from the psychophysical whole. As the terminology becomes familiar, the actor can then inhabit exercises more fully, bringing to awareness the activities of the feeling- and will-centre, and gradually arriving at an understanding of how 'the inner and outer domains of human activity harmoniously integrate, revealing the whole person' (Chambers 2016). The difference between this approach and Chekhov's can be illustrated by examining the case of the Efforts in more detail.

In exploring Laban's Efforts, acting students discover the dramatic potential of various attitudes towards weight, time, space and flow. This can also be described as work that 'deals with different qualities of movement' (McCaw 2011: 198), suggesting a parallel with Chekhov's movement qualities. The latter will indeed also lead the actor to discover attitudes towards weight, time, space and flow. Chekhov, however, true to his subscription to interconnectedness, begins with the movement quality itself, with the whole, rather than with the various components that give rise to it. In his work, four archetypal movement qualities of '**moulding, floating, flying and radiating**' are discovered through an imaginative encounter with the four elements and their recognizable dynamic characteristics (Chekhov 2002: 13). The encounter with each element and its quality of movement is fully incorporated in 'wide, broad movements', for instance, by imagining 'the air around you as instigating your flying movements', importantly also revealing shifts in the inner life (Chekhov 2002: 11). In this way, for Chekhov, the four elements act as embodied metaphors that make 'one thing out of a multitude of things' (Petit 2010: 16). Each one gives access to a plethora of movement possibilities and concomitant sensations. As Lenard Petit notes: 'Earth is much more than wet clay; it is also sand, or gravel or heavy stone. Each image delivers a new yet related movement experience' (2010: 44).

Through this work, which heightens the focus on the imagination, the actor will begin to understand organically that every movement quality necessarily entails a specific relationship with, and attitude towards, weight, time, space and flow, and consequently certain possibilities of relating to the world. Petit's description of the movement quality of **flowing** – also referred to as '**floating**' (Chekhov 2002: 13) – illustrates this:

> Flowing movements (water) are not at all restricted by space, but are led along by the space. The space is flowing like a river. [. . .] It can be fast or slow, heavy or light. Moving like this you will find ease and charm, pleasure, joy, conviction. Moving in this way, one can also experience helplessness. (2010: 44–5)

The example of movement qualities shows why Chekhov's approach may be seen as more 'intuitive' than Laban's analytical 'movement thinking'. His approach – dependent as always on the delivery of the teacher – may allow the actor to maintain an experiential focus in their initial exploration, which in turn may lead to reflection and analysis informed by that experience. It is in the interface between intuition/imagination and analysis that many movement practitioners find the potential to bring the two into productive dialogue. For example, Chambers states,

> I find that I often 'blend' some of Chekhov's approaches to movement which excites 'interior' movement thinking with Laban's vocabulary for effort qualities, which I find gives the actors I work with some clear landmarks for their imaginary work and helps them 'fill' from the inside into form (outside) expressively. (Chambers 2017)

Other movement practitioners make similar connections. Jennifer Mizenko, Laban Movement Analyst and Professor of Movement for the Actor and Dancer in the United States, states, for example, that she uses Chekhov work in her actor-movement classes – specifically psychological gesture, imaginary body and movement qualities – and notes, 'I make links from these concepts to [Laban's] Effort' (Mizenko 2017). She gives another example of such links in *The Laban Workbook for Actors*, describing the use of the Still Shapes of 'Wall, Ball, Pin, Screw and Pyramid' in Laban Movement Analysis 'in support of Chekhov's concept of Psychological Gesture' (Mizenko et al. 2018: 167).

It is worth noting that just as Chambers argues that Laban's spirituality needs reconsidering, we need to remember that Chekhov's work with the intangible and intuition is always wedded to the rigour of careful observation, and requires disciplined imagination and great specificity in its embodiment: '*Form in every sense – physical and mental and psychological*' (TAITT: 25 July 1939). In this way, he is seeking to marry precision and rigour with intuitive and creative modes of response, always rooting the one in the other: 'Organic sensibility yes, but a sensibility which is focused by reflective thought. Feelings yes, but feelings which are in a dynamic and creative tension with the intellect' (Pitches 2006: 131, 135).[3]

Chekhov's and Laban's techniques thus offer different points of access, through different approaches to imagination and analysis, to the same principle of embodied inquiry. Each approach can provide challenges for the actor, with Chekhov's techniques having the potential to be read as too intangible, and Laban's as too mathematical and head-centred. These proclivities within each approach are not necessarily inevitable – it is possible to teach Chekhov with an emphasis on clarity of form and structure, while Laban's approach can be taught with greater awareness of the imaginative and intuitive possibilities in his work. However, the tendency to relate the two perhaps indicates that, in the contemporary context, a dialogue between both approaches can provide the movement pedagogue with a broader set of tools through which to respond to the needs of individuals and make the work accessible to student actors.

## 2.2 Chekhov in dialogue with Meyerhold

For all Chekhov's emphasis on movement as integral to acting, we must also acknowledge the fact that he was not a movement specialist in the sense in which we understand this term today. Some of the work that he desires from the actor, and which he did intuitively, may need a preparation of the body that many practitioners find easiest to source from other practices. Further, as shown in the discussion of the Laban-Chekhov dialogue, some practitioners feel that in contemporary context it is useful to introduce language from other techniques, in order to make the more intangible aspects of Chekhov's approach more accessible. This leads to a vibrant, and arguably very healthy, dialogue between various movement practices and Chekhov's approach, which in turn feeds back into the importance of integrating elements of training to form a coherent whole.

Sinéad Rushe, a lecturer in Acting and Movement in the UK, for instance, teaches both Vsevolod Meyerhold's Biomechanics as part of voice and movement fundamentals, and Chekhov's technique in acting fundamentals, and states that she tries 'to cross-reference between the two' (Rushe 2017).

In the dialogue between Meyerhold and Chekhov in the contemporary context, we can again recognize a drive to activate the materialist and romantic/spiritual elements of both approaches. Meyerhold's Biomechanics, like Laban's work, follow the early twentieth-century impulse to systematize, and take inspiration from the idea of the machine. Meyerhold does not envision the actor themselves as a machine but proposes that 'by adopting machine-like behaviour, the actor's expressivity is increased tenfold' (Pitches 2006: 84). Suspicious of the uncontrollable inner psyche, for Meyerhold '"Theatrical" form precedes emotional content' (Pitches 2006: 69), and thus form is seen as the key to shaping emotion: 'A theatre which relies on physical elements is at the very least assured of clarity' (Meyerhold 1999: 199).

Rushe picks up on this theme by noting that the Biomechanics work can be a helpful way for students in the early stages of training to avoid overemphasizing introspection, allowing them to focus on full-body movement without feeling pressured to think about feeling and sensation (Rushe 2017). Although in some ways contrary to Chekhov's insistence that inner sensation must always be attended to, this observation does chime with Chekhov's idea that a confident understanding of the body is a prerequisite for further development:

> *You must establish this feeling of confidence in your body so that no matter what you are called upon to do, your body will respond with complete confidence. For instance, the Meyerhold actors are trained in a special way to achieve this thing, and everything they do on stage has this feeling of complete confidence.* (LTT: 12 October 1936)

While Meyerhold's materialist approach runs counter to much of Chekhov's thinking, there is an underlying complementarity here in their emphasis on clarity of form as a means for full expression. Cornford argues that in fact Chekhov's work engages deeply with the material form, understanding it as the key access point to the spiritual and insisting that 'the artist can only achieve freedom through the discipline of concrete study' (Cornford 2013: 191). This complementarity is also evident in the connection Rushe makes between the two approaches. She highlights especially the way in which they can come together to help actors develop 'forms of style that are more than naturalism', something she is concerned we have perhaps lost touch with:

> It's a constant work in training actors to fully embrace the possibilities of full three-dimensional expressivity in a play or as a character. . . . Actors really can take much more responsibility for composition of the work at large if they are more sensitive to this. (Rushe 2017)

For her, then, the two techniques can productively cross-fertilize to help the actor to 'craft more boldly' and develop a real sensitivity to how 'inner life can really manifest in space' (2017). Through this, and in concert with Chekhov's appeal for a movement that lies in between acting and dance (see below in this chapter), Rushe hopes to facilitate an understanding that '[a]n actor's performance can be as expressive, as visually and aesthetically engaging as a dance, without actually needing to be dance' (2017).

## 2.3 Chekhov in dialogue with Lecoq

Another frequently cited example of blending is the fruitful dialogue Chekhov's technique can have with pedagogies of the French tradition. As Fleming has argued, the actor training practices of Suzanne Bing and Jacques Copeau in the early twentieth century reveal close affinities with Chekhov's work in the emphasis on embodied play and gesture (Fleming 2013). Pichlikova, building on Fleming, also notes the way in which their 'common point of view regarding gestural art' extends, via Charles Dullin and Etienne Decroux, to Marcel Marceau's illusionistic mime, and discovers 'astonishing parallels' between his work and Chekhov's ideas (Pichlikova 2017). This genealogy of a training based in play-based practice and gesture extends to the contemporary moment through the work of Jacques Lecoq, where the synergies with Chekhov's technique are revealed by the ways in which practitioners have blended them.

Anna Tringham, a Lecturer in Movement for Acting in the UK, notes, for example, that she finds it useful to allow students to bring their work on Chekhov's psychological gesture from acting classes into their movement sessions, where she facilitates its dialogue with Lecoq's approach. Psychological gesture requires that the actor is able to experience themselves fully and dynamically in three-dimensional space, and Tringham observes, like Rushe, that among student actors, '[q]uite often there is a reluctance to '"be bigger" than one's own space' (Tringham 2017). Chekhov's response to this (as Fleming discusses in Chapter 1) was to introduce experimentation with fairy tales, mythical creatures, animals and natural forms as a means to find expression that could be 'bigger' than the everyday self. Tringham's approach meanwhile takes its route through Lecoq's movement technique, where '[w]e always begin by expanding the movement to its maximum in order to find its spatial limits' (Lecoq 2002: 78).

By moving through the dynamics of undulation, eclosion (contraction and expansion) and push and pull – which, for Lecoq, encapsulate the basic principles of human movement – she finds that the students achieve a 'fuller experience of their bodies', which allows them to 'use these new bodies in other classes that focus on Chekhov Technique' (Tringham 2017). Conversely, while Lecoq suggests that 'everything in life can be reduced to two essential actions: "to pull" and "to push"' (Lecoq 2002: 86), students can take this principle and expand it through Chekhov's more varied catalogue of gestures that engage all spatial axes and may, for instance, include 'to wring', 'to lift', or 'to embrace'.[4]

Tringham observes that the students 'invariably make the connection before I bring it up' – a sign that here the 'acting' and 'movement' classes are working together organically, riding on the shared principles between the techniques (Tringham 2017). Lecoq's exercises are based in the notion that '[p]sychological acting ought to be the result of a performance that has been through maximum expansion in space' (Lecoq 2006), complementing Chekhov's idea that '[p]sychological gesture can be done inwardly, without making the physical gesture, but it must first be experienced as a physical movement' (Hurst du Prey 1978: 4).

Another instance of blending, this time from my own teaching practice, illustrates the importance of nuances in language and their impact on the quality of the actor's work. This example pertains both to the correlations and differences between Lecoq's work on the dynamics of nature and Chekhov's movement qualities. In Lecoq's approach, 'the body is trained to represent life, and transform it into poetry', and what Chekhov would call the gestures of the natural world are used by the actor to feed their understanding of rhythm and space: 'For example, the rhythm of the sea is different from the rhythm of fire. Fire will strive toward the vertical . . . the sea has this amazing ritual, going back and forth forever. If we embody these contrasting elements we can find our way of dealing with the vertical and horizontal – with space' (Fusetti and Willson 2002: 94). When analysing the dynamics of nature, Lecoq asks his students to observe and interact with, but then also to incorporate, the four elements. Where Chekhov's movement qualities typically invite the actor to imagine themselves moving through and being moved by each element, in Lecoq's approach the actor eventually *becomes* the element: 'Starting from the earth, which I manipulate, I gradually turn into the manipulated clay' (2002: 88). Contemporary Chekhov practitioners also include this element of incorporation, highlighting an awareness that each approach produces subtly different qualities in performance and that it is useful for the actor to recognize this and to be able to make conscious choices between them. Once fully understood separately, it is also possible to play between the two approaches: imagining the quality of moulding to involve the movement of breath, heartbeat, gaze and thought might transition into imagining the whole body and inner life to be solidifying into clay, with its concomitant weight, definitive character and lack of rebound in movement.

## 2.4 Chekhov technique and actor-movement: Looking to the future

The examples presented illustrate how crucial terminology is to pedagogy, and perhaps particularly so in teaching actor-movement. The words that teachers use to guide students through exercises not only are processed by the students' conscious thinking but also elicit responses in the whole neural system (Kemp 2012). The language of any given technique will bring with it certain 'conceptual metaphors' of the body (Lakoff and Johnson 1999, 2003) – for example, the Body as Container, as a consequence of being asked to be 'in the body' – as well as playing an active part in focusing the actor's attention towards particular aspects of an (inner) action. All actor-trainers use language in this way, but Chekhov was perhaps especially sensitive to the crucial clues that terminology provides for the actor, and this aspect of his work may prove one of the key elements to inform the future place of his work in actor-movement. As Gordon notes, Chekhov 'invented a vocabulary that spoke more directly to the performer's thought-process and imagination' by dealing 'primarily with images, especially visceral ones, that short-circuited complicated and secondary mental processes' (Gordon 1987: 126).[5] Hurst du Prey also highlights Chekhov's attention to linguistic detail when she discusses how he might invite an actor to perform an action with a certain quality:

> If you command yourself to be angry, no-one will believe you – it will not be true. . . . But if you do a simple action with the *quality* of anger, it works. I think this is where Chekhov's genius lay – with such subtle and beautiful nuances. (1978: 6, emphasis in original)

We cannot, of course, forget that the language of acting techniques is always rooted in certain belief systems, as discussed by Joseph Roach (1993) and holds certain sociopolitical assumptions (Evans 2009, 2014; Mitchell 2014). Thus, in the choice to bring different practitioners' vocabularies together, teachers are often responding to the needs of their students as they arise in our contemporary training structures as well as to the growing diversity of the student body in terms of, for example, ethnicity and religion, socio-economic background, sexuality, gender identity, disability and neurodiversity. Recent discussions regarding neurodiverse learning (Oram 2018), for example, raise questions around when and how certain techniques require adaptation to ensure accessibility – as in the condition of aphantasia, in which an individual cannot consciously visualize images (Keogh and Pearson 2018) and which requires a significant rethinking of Chekhov's techniques or a blending with other approaches. Expanding the emphasis on visual imagination to include aural imagination may be one way in which some of Chekhov's exercises could be adapted, but much more research is needed in this area.

Thus, in the quest for inclusion and accessibility, teachers are constantly re-discovering and re-thinking their practice. While considering acting techniques in the 'pure' form in which they were originally developed has its own merits, we must also acknowledge that every technique is already in itself a blend, and emerges from the interstice of exchange and collaboration. The notion of a 'pure' form of any technique is thus perhaps more ideological than historical, and the ability for teachers to blend and bring into dialogue various approaches is vital as part of a living and constantly evolving practice, or as part of what Ben Spatz calls 'research *in* acting' where 'like any other form of knowledge, acting technique is sustained by the ongoing and dynamic *interaction of training and research*' (2015: 118, 121). The increasing degree to which Chekhov's technique is integrated into various programmes of actor training across the globe perhaps signifies a readiness to rethink the reign of rationalization and taxonomy over intuition and imagination. The examples presented suggest, however, that this next phase of our work does not involve discarding one for the other – instead, actors and their teachers are blending and adapting, looking to find those vocabularies and routes of access that best respond to the contemporary moment. As Jerri Daboo notes, 'Lineage, in this sense, is about being inspired by a practitioner's work, and feeling an affinity with it that informs and expands what the actor is doing' (2012: 80). While we do not know where this embodied enquiry will eventually lead us, it is evident that in the meantime Chekhov's approach plays an important part in interweaving 'acting' and 'movement' work, thereby facilitating an experience of actor training that 'makes sense' as a whole.

## 3 Chekhov technique in the context of dance and dance-theatre crossovers

Applications of Chekhov's technique within dance training are still in their infancy and include the work of Suzanne Bennett in Canada, Kim Chen in Taiwan and Margot Fenley in Australia, discussed later; meanwhile, experiments in using Chekhov's work in the context of dance-making, and especially in the dance-theatre crossover, are proliferating. In the UK, these include the work of choreographer and dancer Julie Cunningham, director-choreographer Sinéad Rushe and the collaboration between choreographer Katie Green and Tom Cornford as dramaturg. It is these teachers and practitioners, who are working with dancers specifically, whom I have chosen to focus on here. It is worth acknowledging, however, that in the broad field of performances that emphasize the 'physical *in* theatre' (Murray and Keefe 2016: 8), the technique has also been employed extensively, as discussed by Daboo (2012) and Fleming (see Chapter 1).

In this section, the particular focus on dance allows me to examine contemporary applications of the technique against the backdrop of Chekhov's own connections with the world of dance during his time at Dartington. This includes looking to his female collaborators there, who were also responsible for much of the teaching of his practice in the United States after his death. This dialogue between past and present serves to illuminate the ways in which Chekhov's technique can be a useful tool for the dancer. As we will see, his thinking about movement has close affinities with dance practices of the early twentieth century, and these shared roots mean that his technique, rather than being an add-on for the dancer, already contains the seeds of dance practice.

## 3.1 Chekhov technique and dance: Dialogues and shared roots

Chekhov describes movement in his technique as neither dance nor acting:

> *There are two different things on the stage – acting and dance, and what we are doing lies in between. It is not dance, it is not acting, it is pure use of the qualities of our bodies – qualities which penetrate the whole body. We can fill our whole bodies with the quality of heaviness, or floating, or radiating, etc., just by standing still.* (TAITT: 19 October 1937)

This statement implies that rather than being neither acting nor dance, his approach finds principles that can be shared by both, even while acknowledging that they are distinct practices. Indeed, some of the exchanges between Chekhov and dance practitioners at Dartington are fairly well known: Jerri Daboo, for example, discusses the important dialogue between Chekhov and Indian dancer Uday Shankar, whose performance at the opening of the Dartington Studio left a deep impression on Chekhov (Daboo, 2015: 282). Notes from his first lesson show him referring to this performance, using it as an example to emphasize to his actors the importance of musicality: '*We don't have to dance, but we have to be full of music*' – and the fact that '*art must be based on technique*' (TAITT: 5 October 1936).

Further encounters with dancers took place through the immediate proximity to the Jooss-Leeder School of Dance at Dartington, where Kurt Jooss, Sigurd Leeder and Lisa Ullmann taught and created works with significant influence from their teacher and collaborator, Rudolf Laban. Students from both schools mingled in the medieval courtyard at Dartington Hall (Nicholas 2007: 97), Chekhov's students were taught by Ullmann (Cornford 2012: 98) and Ullmann and Leeder attended Chekhov's classes (Autant-Mathieu and Meerzon 2015: 16). While some points of convergence between Laban's and Chekhov's working principles have been discussed earlier, unfortunately there are no records of what exactly Ullmann taught in her classes to Chekhov's students. However, we do know that she worked closely with Jooss on developing physical expressivity in a way that connected inner feeling and movement – an ethos that one assumes would have given Chekhov confidence that his students would find an embodied connection between her dance classes and his own work. Indeed, Cornford suggests that 'Ullmann's classes would have been instrumental in developing the physical freedom and expressiveness of Chekhov's students and therefore vital to the process of 'bind[ing] together our feeling with our body' that he described' (2012: 99).

In addition to these explicit exchanges with dancers, a further underlying cross-fertilization with dance can be found when we trace the embodied practices of those women who worked closely with Chekhov at Dartington. They include Deirdre Hurst du Prey, Beatrice Straight and Dorothy Elmhirst (see Introduction). While the influence of Chekhov's time in Russia and his work there with practitioners such as Meyerhold, Vakhtangov and Stanislavsky is eloquently documented elsewhere (Gordon 1987; Chamberlain 2004; Autant-Mathieu and Meerzon 2015), and his collaboration with Georgette Boner has recently been considered by Mittelsteiner (2015), the influence of these women merits further consideration. It is Hurst du Prey in particular that this section will address, as the archive we are investigating is, in many ways, her archive.

Hurst du Prey, nicknamed 'The Pencil', is best known for her work of transcribing Chekhov's lessons and rehearsals at Dartington and at Ridgefield, Connecticut, and for helping him compile his materials for publication. Chekhov's trust in her ability to translate and formulate his ideas in writing indicate that she should be remembered not only for her job title as his 'personal secretary' (Cornford 2012: 62) but also as an experienced practitioner and pedagogue, with a deep understanding of Chekhov's aims and their broader context in the field of theatre.[6] Further, she was trained as a teacher by Chekhov, along with Straight, and continued to teach his technique in the United States after his death, as well as being among the teachers whose workshop in 1986 led to the revival of Chekhov's technique in the UK (Daboo 2012: 78). Consequently a great deal of the legacy we now hold of Chekhov's work was filtered through Hurst du Prey, crucially in terms of their writings, but also in terms of bodily transmission of the technique.

A reflection on the embodied knowledge that Hurst du Prey brought to her work with Chekhov, and the resonance his technique had for her, is particularly revealing of the extent to which his approach resonated with dance practices of the time. Archive notes on her own trajectory are helpful in bringing this to the fore. Hurst du Prey began her performance training thinking she would become a dancer, following *'a desire . . . from the time when I first walked'* (Hurst du Prey in Kindelan, MC/S4/27/A 1977: 2). However, during her training at the Cornish School in Seattle in the early 1930s, which included classes in *'drama'* and puppetry alongside various forms of dance, she was advised that her talents *'really were more dramatic than dance'* (Hurst du Prey in Kindelan, MC/S4/27/A 1977: 4).[7] For Hurst du Prey, heeding this advice did not mean abandoning dance; instead, she began a search for a training that would allow her to use what her body already knew from her dance training, *'a style of my own'*, but apply it in dramatic settings (Hurst du Prey in Cariaccolo, MC/S4/36/H 1999: 4). The potential she saw for Chekhov's work to enable this is reflected in her account of first seeing him perform, leading her to describe him as a kind of dancing actor:

> *What was so remarkable was his performance as Khlestakov, the Inspector General – an unbelievable performance. Truly tremendous experience of an actor who moved, a dancer who was everywhere on the stage with scintillating ease and brilliance and bringing such vitality and life with every movement, everything that he did . . . he had performed like a ballet dancer in this rather grotesque performance.* (Hurst du Prey in Kindelan, MC/S4/27/A 1977: 5)

It seems significant, then, that Chekhov's right-hand woman was someone who approached theatre with an acute sensibility to movement, whose dance training remained ingrained in her thinking about dramatic performance and who continued to seek approaches that united the two.

Hurst du Prey's personal archive materials reveal synergies between Chekhov's technique and Mary Wigman's expressionist dance and pedagogical principles[8] as well as Martha Graham's and Isadora Duncan's notions of gesture.[9] Duncan's influence on Chekhov's use of gesture is explicitly mentioned by Hurst du Prey (1978: 4). Some of Duncan's writings on gesture precede Chekhov's, and emphasize that the dancer should look to nature to find an understanding of how will, or desire, are expressed in movement dynamic and quality: 'to seek the human movement from the rhythm of water in motion, from the blowing of the winds on the world, in all the earth's movements' (Duncan in Cheney, 1969: 78).[10] This is, of course, echoed in Chekhov's belief that any aspect of the world can be captured by discovering its essential gesture and quality (Chekhov 1991: 40).

It is also worth noting the important cross-disciplinary experiments that Margaret Barr was undertaking at Dartington's School for Dance-Mime, which Hurst du Prey attended before Chekhov's arrival. For Barr, the dramatic idea was central, and the material of the work could cross between dance, rhythmic mime and scripted dialogue. The performances she created were praised for their strength of atmosphere and as 'a model of ensemble playing', laying key foundations in the students for Chekhov's future experiments (Nicholas 2007: 79). Such resonances serve to remind us that the ground for applying Chekhov's technique in dance and dance-theatre crossovers was already prepared a century ago.

## 3.2 Chekhov technique in dance: Contemporary investigations

Shifting now to the contemporary context, experiments with Chekhov's technique in dance show a rediscovery of this common ground. Practitioners interviewed for this chapter employ his approaches for various purposes, examined in the next three sections. These approaches include generating movement material and developing movement dramaturgy, developing an acting technique for dance and developing the presence, imaginative engagement and performative quality of the individual dancer. Furthermore, and within all these areas, practitioners note that the technique emphasizes both creative individuality/agency and collaboration in ways that are important for a form in which top-down hierarchical structures still prevail in many training and making environments.

### 3.2.1 AN ACTING TECHNIQUE FOR DANCE

As cross-disciplinary work continues to proliferate on UK stages and internationally (Radosavljević 2013a; Mermikides and Smart 2010; Murray and Keefe 2016), practitioners are searching for corresponding interdisciplinary training approaches. In 2008, choreographer and director Jasmin Vardimon, searching for dancers who can also deliver text and become a character, observed that there is a 'big gap in education in the UK, because there are good dance schools and there are good drama schools but there is no school that trains for the "in-between"' (Nisbet 2007). Participants at the 2016 New Pathways session on Chekhov in Movement and Dance also raised the key question of how they might enable dancers to work confidently and to their full potential alongside actors in such an intersection of disciplines.

Whereas the field of movement for actors is fairly well established, the question of what acting for dance might entail is still being explored. Chekhov's technique, as a pedagogy of gesture and rhythm that can facilitate a range of styles, is central to a number of these explorations internationally, as the following examples show.

In Taiwan, Chekhov teacher and actor Kim Chen notes that dancers are especially interested in finding ways to use their voice, not least because dance-theatre is a highly popular form in the current Taiwanese context. Chen's work with Chekhov's tools brings together acting and dance training by emphasizing the fact that voice and speech, like dance, have to be trained and perceived with clear form and movement. Consequently, she leads a progression, first of all emphasizing imagination as a central aspect of movement by exploring imaginary centres, images and atmosphere. From here, she works with **directions in space** and psychological gesture, articulated first in broad movements of the body and then shifted into the movement of voice through the body and into space. In doing this, for Chen Chekhov's technique bridges the perceived distinction between acting and dance; additionally, she notes that it has the potential to bring crucial 'light, hope and warmth' into otherwise mainly disciplinarian dance training (Chen 2018).

Margot Fenley, meanwhile, teaches acting through dance as part of a Music Theatre programme in Melbourne, Australia, and observes that Chekhov's technique is unique in providing her with the means to construct a holistic pedagogic process that aligns music, text and movement. Which aspects of the technique are foregrounded depends on the function of a dance within a given production: dance that replaces dialogue and develops narrative might involve discovering the driving action and psychological gesture, whereas ensemble numbers that set the tone for a scene require an understanding of the objective atmosphere. Related principles are also applied in acting through song, creating a coherent process by applying the same components across the whole form. It is evident from this discussion that both Chen and Fenley use Chekhov's techniques to reveal and harness the shared principles between acting and dance.

### 3.2.2 A TECHNIQUE TO DEVELOP THE INNER LIFE AND EXPRESSIVITY OF THE DANCER

Often experiments with Chekhov's technique in dance appear to arise from a need of the dancer, teacher or choreographer to discover, or facilitate, a greater engagement with what Chekhov would term our 'inner life': a constant engagement with imagination and inner sensation that simultaneously radiates outward and is shared and exchanged with other performers and the audience. Although it is neither possible nor desirable to generalize across dance forms, the consensus among the dancers and dance-makers interviewed is that this engagement with inner life is often neglected, or alternatively is overemphasized in a solipsistic manner at the expense of the relational. Dancer-choreographer Julie Cunningham observes, for instance, that at times dancers 'forget to be people and just become dancers and do the steps. A formality of what you do when you dance doesn't allow you to be human or have a human response' (Cunningham 2016). Artistic Director of Ballet Jörgen Canada, Bengt Jörgen, makes a similar observation, noting the 'stilted acting quality of otherwise technically gifted dance artists' when his corps dancers are asked to 'move naturally on stage in simple choreographic scene work' (Bennett 2013: 162).

Suzanne Bennett, invited by Jörgen to teach 'Acting for Dance' at Toronto's George Brown College Dance department, consequently developed a course in which she applied and adapted Chekhov's technique for dancers. Here, the technique was employed not with the aim of interdisciplinary performance but to achieve greater expressivity in the field of dance itself (2013: 163). Her account of this work is the only scholarly discussion to date that investigates the application of Chekhov's technique in dance training. Bennett's experience illustrates that introducing Chekhov's technique into this environment is not without its challenges. Both she and other teachers interviewed highlight, in particular, dancers' reluctance to engage with intangibles such as their inner life and their fear of the freedom of creative individuality in improvisation, with one dancer feeding back: 'I don't get what I am supposed to be "sensing". Just tell me what to do and I'll do it!' (2013: 164). For Bennett, the key to enabling her students to trust the intangible lies in diverting attention away from 'form-driven technique' without removing the security of what the dancer already knows well. Moving through various exercises such as concentration exercises, ball work and movement qualities, Bennett gradually introduces and firms up Chekhov's notion of a *'life force'*, a kind of inner, energetic version of the outer body. Bennett terms this 'inner-getic material', and teaches how that energy can be transformed, through the use of imagery, senses and the will, into outer movement and shape:

> Sensations and images move through the body and are released. They fill not only the larger dance elements, but also the spaces between. . . . This single concept, that the possibility and power of energetic transformation is in their bodies, changes their perception of why they are taking acting and how it relates to dance performance. (2013: 170)

Bennett is tapping into the heart of Chekhov's work, here, as a pedagogy of gesture, 'a new kind of movement' which he understands as 'not only a movement of the body' but 'movement *and* feeling *and* will and other elements' (Hurst du Prey 1978: 4). By emphasizing that the engagement with inner life fills not only the movements but also 'the spaces between' (2013: 170), she introduces the important element of the relational and touches upon a key problem for both the actor and the dancer: 'The moment you are not inwardly moving and inwardly participating, you are dead. For the audience you die' (Hurst du Prey 1978: 7).

Investigating similar problems, Julie Cunningham invited me to work with Julie Cunningham & Company to explore the ability for Chekhov's 'tools' to facilitate an engaged imagination and real connection between the dancers. Having excelled in form-driven and non-narrative areas of dance practice through their work with Merce Cunningham and Michael Clark, Cunningham was now seeking new approaches, 'different ways of being alive', that could prioritize creative agency and imagination, while at the same time wanting to maintain clarity of form and the discipline of their technique (Cunningham 2017). Working with the company in the studio, we progressed from ball work and discovering energetic connections between dancers in a playful manner through movement qualities, as a means to reveal emotional textures, to atmosphere work that opened the possibility of creative agency within a set choreographic structure. Reflecting on how our experiments have affected their working process, Cunningham observes that the idea of movement quality, 'not just asking people what movements to do but also asking for certain qualities, which then also creates rhythm', has become a staple of their process: 'Generally I am asking people a lot more to imagine, which I guess is always there but I am being more explicit about that' (2017). Further, in generating material, Cunningham reflects that using atmosphere as a choreographic stimulus has become an important supplement to teaching choreography through demonstration and imitation. This work from atmosphere, which for Cunningham is about 'maintaining a now-ness' and awareness of 'how we are attending to ourselves, each other, and the space around us' (2017), introduces the relational element they have been seeking. By emphasizing 'now-ness' in performance, Cunningham's approach echoes what Hurst du Prey articulates so clearly: that by 'inwardly moving the entire time . . . the inner gesture, the inner rhythm involves your whole being, and that's contact, that's feeling of the whole, that's the ensemble – the whole mystery and magic lies in that' (1978: 7).

However, the notion that the dancer can be *led* by the engaged imagination, and that dance, like acting, can be imaginative and process-driven, is potentially as much a destabilizing as a revelatory experience. A Canadian dancer describing her encounter with Chekhov's technique as both delightful and 'just so opposite to dancing' (Cook 2017) highlights the fact that such work is still often seen as a transgression beyond what the dancer conceives 'dance' to be – not so much in terms of the form it takes, but rather in terms of the processes involved to reach the form. In pursuing Chekhov's work in this context, it is therefore important to show the dancer that the work can support their virtuosity and does not ask them to abandon their technique. It must, of course, be acknowledged that the above discussion refers to dancers trained in specific dance practices, with Cunningham's dancers trained at three key UK contemporary dance schools, and Bennett's students engaged in 'a medley of . . . modern, jazz, composition, and vocal, with hip hop and chorus repertoire for the commercial program' supported by 'a strong and enduring discipline in ballet' (2013: 164). Other forms of dance might thus present a different set of opportunities and challenges when investigated through Chekhov's technique, making this a fruitful area for further future investigation. What is already clear from these examples is that Chekhov's approach can provide a shorthand in the quest for the inner engagement that many dance practitioners seek to achieve or facilitate. In Cunningham's case, introduction to the technique allowed the choreographer to develop a vocabulary through which they are able to clearly communicate to their company the imaginative work that they themselves do intuitively. In doing so Cunningham is bringing the specificity of their movement language into dialogue with the dancers' inner life, inadvertently proving the technique's stylistic flexibility. As Bennett similarly concludes from her teaching experience, by centralizing the imagination, 'through powerful gestures, sustained atmosphere, embodied qualities, and radiating presence', Chekhov's technique brings content into dialogue with form, and 'ignites the potential for individual creativity, while supporting expectations of traditional dance training' (2013: 174).

### 3.2.3 AN APPROACH TO DANCE DRAMATURGY

A final example of the use of Chekhov's technique in dance pertains to the ways in which it can influence dramaturgical thinking in dance creation, in this instance especially in relation to character. The notion of Chekhov's dramaturgy as essentially somatic, choreographic and atmospheric is discussed extensively by Tom Cornford (see Chapter 2). Reflecting on his own dramaturgical work with choreographer Katie Green, Cornford notes that Chekhov provides 'a language that can easily span the choreographic and dramatic, that is both expressive and psychological' (Green and Cornford 2016). While Cornford and Green's collaboration makes use of Chekhov's more well-known compositional principles, such as polarity and discovering the overarching gesture for a piece, they also make innovative adaptations.

One of these is a shared, collective approach to the imaginary centre, which illustrates that aspects of the technique conceived for the development of character can become useful even in the context of postmodern fragmentation. Green often begins her process with a collective exploration through which her dancers together discover the imaginary centre and movement qualities of one specific character. She then makes an adaptation of the technique in accordance with her performance medium: having reached a collective embodied understanding of the character, this one character is then able to be 'shared' between dancers: any dancer can slip into this character, whose psychophysical specificities provide an anchor that can be recognized by the audience regardless of who performs them. This in turn allows the dramaturgical structure to 'loosen away from needing to have a linear narrative' (Green and Cornford 2016). Such a process can reveal various facets of a character, as it would reveal various facets of a mask if it was passed between performers: 'We can see the character in a different way, and they can, for example, become detached from the gender of the dancer' (Green and Cornford 2016).

Similarly, my own efforts to encourage experimentation with dramaturgical approaches among students on the MA Physical Acting at the University of Kent resulted in interesting blends between Chekhov's imaginary centre and William Forsythe's nine-point system of relating the body to surrounding space. In the latter, any body part, 'even inner body-parts' can be the initiator of movement, thereby creating a new point of orientation, with the result that 'there is no fixed center, because the center is shifting all the time' (Lampert 2015: 240). In a free and flexible approach to Chekhov's original ideas, students creating solo performances worked with multiple imaginary centres, thus shifting away from discovering the essence of a character and instead developing a psychophysical colour palette for their performance.

It seems likely that Chekhov would appreciate these adaptations and experiments as well as the new possibilities which they open up. After all, he reminds us that 'we have the freedom to make the most of the best in all techniques. . . . All it takes is a little wisdom, imagination and courageous experimentation' (Chekhov and Leonard 1963: 48).

## 4 Conclusion

Throughout this chapter, I have highlighted ways in which Chekhov's technique may be fruitfully adapted along the whole spectrum of crossover between acting and dance. It offers a shared language where elements of the technique, such as atmosphere, gesture, rhythm, a feeling of form or of wholeness, can be engaged with fully and equally by all involved, without having to make concessions or defend territories. In doing so, it also invites a disruption of all kinds of notional hierarchies in the theatre and especially puts into question the idea of the movement practitioner as 'merely' the facilitator of a specialist aspect of performance work.

Deirdre Hurst du Prey, when asked if she found any one aspect of Chekhov's technique more illuminating than others, answers that to reply to this would be too difficult, as 'at one point they all become one' (1978: 11). Arguably something similar can be said for different roles in the making process when working with this technique. Conceptualizing movement as a crucial part of any deep and rigorous engagement with text and dramaturgy blurs the boundaries between what a movement director does, what a director does, what a writer and an actor do. This does not mean a de-specialization of those professions but rather a more intense and open-hearted listening between them 'in which each member of the theatre – actor, director, designer, or author – will each be responsible for everyone . . . in a real, true and deep sense of the word, a collaboration' (TAITT: 14 January 1937). It does not expect the utopia of an automatic shared understanding but rather a commitment to 'listening for a mutual future possibility' (Meyer-Horsch 2017). As Chekhov's technique becomes a familiar sight in the curricula of actor training courses, as dancers begin to adopt, adapt and develop it and take it into their own training institutions, as directors and movement directors become increasingly keen to engage with Chekhov's language, we may be approaching a future in which the space between acting and dance is occupied with confidence, led by Chekhov's emphasis on imaginative embodied enquiry as a means to discover what moves us.

## Notes

1. While yoga is linked to actor training through various practitioners such as Sulerzhitsky, Stanislavsky and Grotowski (Gordon 1987; Tcherkasski 2016), and still used by many actors and practitioners today, its place in actor-movement has also been questioned (Ewan and Green 2015: 1–2; Kapsali 2010). Some practitioners replace it with sequences that they believe have more to offer for the specific needs of the actor, such as Grotowski's The Cat (Wangh 2000: 57), or Ewan's Side Stretch or Swing-Stab-Release (Ewan and Green 2015: 293–4). These sequences already include much 'food' for the actor to work with expressively, and so in a sense are already Chekhovian, although they may still be usefully explored through the focus on a particular 'ground' such as rhythm, direction in space or radiating.
2. Laban and Chekhov resided at Dartington simultaneously for ten months in 1938. Unfortunately so far no evidence of exchanges between them during this time has been found in the archives, though as Laban spoke 'enthusiastically' about Chekhov's work it seems likely that such exchanges would have taken place (McCaw 2005).
3. See also 'The Necessity to Be Oriented' in *Lessons for Teachers* (Chekhov 2018: 156).
4. Lenard Petit, a Chekhov teacher who also trained with Decroux (a student of Suzanne Bing and Jacques Copeau), lists six archetypal gestures – in accordance with the six directions in space – from which infinite variations of psychological gesture can then be formed through changes of quality and rhythm (2010: 51). Cynthia Ashperger, meanwhile, lists nine Basic Psychological Gestures, providing some examples of the possible variations contained in each (2008: 320). While an understanding of the archetypal gestures connected to the cardinal directions (expand/contract, push/pull, rise/sink) are undoubtedly useful, Chekhov himself never provides a definitive list of Psychological Gestures, placing the actor's choice and creative agency before the need to categorize or provide a template for what is 'correct'.
5. Gordon gives as an example Chekhov's decision to replace Stanislavsky's use of the term 'relaxation' with the notion of doing any action with a 'Feeling of Ease', thereby offering 'an outward, positive image for the actor and [replacing] Stanislavsky's directorial command 'to relax'' (Gordon 1987: 126).
6. In 1946 Chekhov wrote to her from Hollywood: '"*My English is as bad as always, and it was only my confidence in you – that you would understand me – which gave me the freedom to express myself without any inner difficulties*"' (Hurst du Prey in Cariaccolo, MC/S4/36/H: 2).
7. The Cornish School in Seattle was to become an important influence and point of creative exchange in the instalment of the arts at Dartington that eventually led to Chekhov's invitation to work there. It was dedicated to 'the creative spirit in education', and music, dance, drama, puppetry and visual arts were incorporated here. The dance curriculum included: 'Dalcroze

eurythmics, Duncan-style dancing, ballet and modern dance as it was developing' (Nicholas 2007: 50).
8. Hurst du Prey was taught by Wigman while at the Cornish School. The synergies between Wigman's and Chekhov's approach are reflected in a shared belief in a 'higher-level *I*' that can be accessed by trusting and responding to one's creative imagination (Chekhov 2002: 86, 87) and the pedagogic imperative to emphasize students' creative agency. Like Chekhov, Wigman asked students to 'develop an individual way of fulfilling the movement', thereby aiming to achieve 'an enrichment of the whole person, physically and emotionally, through the practice of dance movement' (Santos Newhall 2009: 136).
9. Graham also emphasizes the importance of gesture as 'the real effort to communicate with another human being' (1991: 7). The Psychological Gestures of Opening and Closing can be seen to be embedded in her technique's focus on contraction and release, and echo Chekhov's ethos of constantly giving and receiving through the movement quality of radiating. Hurst du Prey danced as chorus lead under Graham's direction in Archibald MacLeish's play *Panic* on Broadway in 1935, and describes her affinity with Graham's work as linked to '*my love of gesture and love of poetry*' (Hurst du Prey in Kindelan, MC/S4/27/A 1977: 6–7).
10. Duncan also had a close friendship with, and influence on, Stanislavsky, a connection that dance and theatre history have often failed to mention, as discussed by Preston (2005).

# 5 Feeling space, making space

## Michael Chekhov's approach to theatre design

SINÉAD RUSHE

At his Studio in Dartington, as well as teaching the art of acting, Chekhov wanted the actors to understand the other aspects of producing a piece of theatre. He wanted them to engage with those elements normally considered outside their responsibility: writing, directing and designing. This was not only about empowerment; Chekhov believed that educating actors in this way would pave the way for more effective collaboration and that new models of making theatre would become possible if artists of different disciplines actively understood each other's work. '*This does not mean*', he clarified, '*that you write the lines with the author, but you must be with him with your full activity [. . .] we must develop in ourselves this feeling for everyone who is around us*' (TAITT: 14 January 1937).

In line with this collaborative approach, Deirdre Hurst du Prey, Chekhov's student and a performer, teacher and administrator at the Chekhov Theatre Studio recounts that actors had to 'design costumes, sets and lighting, create music and sound effects and direct' (Drama Review 1983: 90). Indeed, they also learnt to make costumes, be proficient in make-up and build simple sets and properties (The Chekhov Theatre Studio 1936: 24). To help with this, they were given lessons in chalk drawing and moulding clay by American expressionist painter Mark Tobey (1890–1976) and the Austrian sculptor Willi Soukop (1907–95) (Cornford 2013: 196–7). Many of Chekhov's own lessons also extended to a consideration of scenography, costume and **colour**. It is my aim in this chapter, therefore, to develop an account of the ideas and practices relating to theatre design that were developed by Chekhov in the process of training actors in his studio and their potential applications in contemporary theatre-making.

## 1 Overview: Scenography

Following the expanded definition outlined by Joslin McKinney and Scott Palmer, I understand scenography here not simply as the design of sets for the performance of dramatic works on stage 'but as a mode of encounter and exchange founded on spatial and material relations between bodies, objects and environments' (McKinney and Palmer 2017: 2). McKinney and Palmer outline three important aspects in contemporary scenography. In the first instance, it often facilitates 'spaces of encounter' between spectators and performers, as well as 'between spectators and other spectators, spaces, site and objects' (McKinney and Palmer

2017: 8). Moreover, its aesthetic dimension affects individual spectators on a sensual and emotional level and this, combined with the material dimensions of set, light and architecture, is as significant in the audience's understanding of any performance as other elements such as language (McKinney and Palmer 2017: 8). McKinney and Palmer's three interrelated concepts of relationality, affectivity and materiality are helpful as a way of understanding Chekhov's ideas on design.[1]

Chekhov's approach to scenography was original in two ways. First, he was not a designer. While he directed in his lifetime, he is known predominantly for his work as an actor and teacher. Furthermore, his practice at Dartington was focused on actors in training, rather than designers. This unusual situation invites us to consider not only what role actors fulfil in the design process and how they might use aspects of design in creating a role but also to what degree Chekhov's ideas are of value to theatre designers. What can designers and actors learn from each other's processes, and how might a more explicit collaboration between them, grounded in Chekhov's technique, enhance a production process?

I will begin by outlining key aspects of Chekhov's work on design at Dartington and follow it with an analysis of its limits as well as its merits. Then I will examine how we might adapt some of his ideas for a contemporary context, drawing on a series of practice-based workshops I led in collaboration with theatre designer Aldona Cunningham at the Actor's Centre, London; the Street Theatre, Canberra, Australia; and the Michael Chekhov New Pathways Symposium at Goldsmith's, University of London.[2] I will also draw on a series of interviews with set designers Alexa Reid, Andreas Skourtis, Rosie Elnile and Sarah Beaton; lighting designer Colin Grenfell; visual artists and painters Kai McCall and Gillian Carnegie; and costume supervisor, Karin Schuck.[3] I conclude this exploration with a case study of *Concert*, a dance-theatre production I directed in Ireland and France using some of Chekhov's ideas, particularly in relation to the sound design and its 'staging' which shaped the dramaturgy of the whole work.[4] *Scenography* is a process of conceptual drawing, by which the material and aesthetic world on stage is mapped. Dramaturgy, also a process of mapping, therefore inevitably intersects with it.

## 2 Design at Dartington

### 2.1 Scenography and gesture

At the Theatre Studio, it was important to Chekhov that students were given the opportunity 'to express original artistic ideas' (Chekhov 1936: 24). In addition to their regular classes in acting, students worked on original 'sketches' such as 'The Fishers' Scene', written in a range of versions by the student actors Paul Rogers, Iris Tree and Eleanor Faison (see Pitches 2013: 223 and the chapter by Fleming in this publication) and developed through a process of devising, improvising and rewriting. The students also worked on scenes from plays such as *Balladina* (a Polish tragedy by Slowacki adapted by Chekhov), *The Cave of Salamanca* (Cervantes), *Peer Gynt* (Ibsen) and *The Deluge* (Berger). The students assumed different roles for every project: those of director, scenographer, costume designer, lighting designer, writer and actor. At the outset, Chekhov impressed upon his students the importance of understanding the '*unifying idea*' (LTT: 17 April 1936) that underpins the play or scenario and their staging needed to communicate that guiding theme effectively.[5] Whether they were acting, designing, writing or directing, Chekhov taught them to begin this process by finding a *gesture* that would express the nature of this core idea: '*It is not enough*', he told them, '*to find the real, naturalistic, clever mise en scene. It must be speaking about the main idea [. . .] the mise en scene must do a gesture, just as everything must*' (TAITT: 16 March 1937).

Chekhov's tool of **psychological gesture** (or PG) is well known as a physical summary of the character's main motivating drive or will force; 'the PG reveals to you the entire character in *condensed* form' (Chekhov 2002: 68), he explains. It takes the form of a fully embodied gesture, executed with a particular tempo and quality and is governed largely by a particular **direction in space** (forward, back, up, down, left or right). If a character is motivated by generosity, for example, the PG might be a certain type of 'giving' gesture, the form of which is 'archetypal' and is never seen on stage. By archetypal, Chekhov means that it is a fundamental, distilled approach to movement. While the gesture may be a version of a 'giving' gesture, of which there are many kinds, the PG expresses giving in its most concentrated, intensified, essential form. While each actor will have his or her individual and nuanced approach to the gesture, all PGs of giving will broadly resemble each other: most actors will move in a forward direction and extend their arms and open their hands, for example. While Chekhov's PG is explored mainly as a character tool, at Dartington, students used it to cultivate a sensitivity towards scenography at large and to translate the guiding idea of their short production into a design (see Pitches 2013: 223 and Chapter 1 of this book).

When working on 'The Fishers' Scene', a simple scenario of a group of villagers waiting on the shore for the return of the fishermen after a terrible storm, the most significant point to convey, Chekhov explained, was '*the power of the sea, and the connection of people to this power*', and he criticized the students' design for having '*no connection with this power*'. While he reportedly sensed some kind of '*going out*' gesture in the set, he concluded that overall it was '*wrong*' because only one part conveyed this gesture, and the rest was '*frozen, dead, not movable*' (TAITT: 16 March 1937).[6] For Chekhov, the whole set must radiate inner vitality, and PG was the means with which to find it: '*we must create a setting by creating it with movement*', he insisted (TAITT: 16 March 1937).

He added two further clarifications: in the arrangement of set and props, the PG must have a clear predominant direction as well as be in formal harmony with the psychological **atmosphere** of the play. While he praised the choice of a spiral gesture for a presentation of *Balladina*, he could not determine whether it was going up or down and warned that '*there is a radical difference*' between these two directions. Similarly, he described the gesture of the play of *The Cave of Salamanca* as being '*like a champagne glass*' and argued that if the predominant gesture of any play is '*unhappy*', then structures that are '*happy and straight*' must be avoided (TAITT: 16 March 1937).

In all of this, Chekhov asserts one of his key design principles, that of unity between content and form: 'effective style', he stated, 'will not emerge unless there is a harmony among all the elements of the production and the play itself' (Kindelan 1985: 11). In this sense, he was in line with a series of pioneering theatre practitioners in the early twentieth century, such as Adolphe Appia (1862–1928), Edward Gordon Craig (1872–1966), and Bertolt Brecht (1898–1956) who, as McKinney and Palmer point out, questioned early assumptions about the decorative function of scenography and demonstrated 'how scenographic gestures created by the orchestration of design elements in themselves could make affective, profound and potentially transformative visual statements' (McKinney and Palmer 2017: 4–5). While Chekhov clearly thought along these lines also, his direct influences most likely came from his contemporary, the young director, Evgeny Vakhtangov (1883–1922), the visual artist and theatre designer Mstislav Dobujinksy (1875–1957) with whom he collaborated over many years (Listengarten 2015: 262) and the modernist scenographer Edward Gordon Craig (1872–1966), who designed the seminal production of *Hamlet* for the Moscow Art Theatre in 1912.

## 2.2 Exercises on gesture

As well as encapsulating the guiding idea of the play in a PG, Chekhov also used gesture to work with objects, props and images. He maintained that inanimate objects or structures (both man-made and naturally occurring) contain a hidden gesture or movement that is an expression of their internal life and that it is the duty of the artist to perceive that life force. Gesture, Chekhov argued, '*is to be found everywhere, not only in the human body. In nature, in living things and in dead things. In everything and everywhere, an artist can find and create psychological gestures which are not in immediate connection to the human body*' (TAITT: 7 February 1938). Hurst du Prey recounts how students were asked to discover a gesture 'in everything: a plant, a tree, a chair' (1983: 85); they went out into the gardens to 'feel the gestures of the trees' (Sharp 2002), to determine precisely how, for example, a cypress tree 'streams upward and has a quiet, positive, concentrated character' compared with that of an oak which rises 'upward and sideways' with a violent, uncontrolled, broad character' (Chekhov 1991: 39). As Tom Cornford points out, Mark Tobey's drawing lessons at Dartington complemented this practice; himself inspired by Chinese painter Teng Kwei, who observed 'that a tree is no longer solid, but a rhythm, a growing line', Tobey taught Chekhov's actors to 'experience' a painting and its 'directness of spirit', rather than simply looking at it (Cornford 2013: 196). In addition, Chekhov's students studied two-dimensional drawings of triangles and staircases to sense how they '*are acting, as it were, different parts, different characters. One has one will, the other, another*' (TAITT: 20 February 1940). Students first perceived the gesture, then created it in full-bodied movement and finally visualized it only, experiencing it as inner movement: '*to understand the gesture is nothing for us; we have to do this inside*', Chekhov explained (TAITT: 7 February 1938).

Here, we see one of Chekhov's key tools of characterization, PG, applied directly to material elements that traditionally belong to scenography. '*You are to experience this simple gesture*', Chekhov explained to his students, '*as though you were trying to develop a part*' (TAITT: 20 February 1940). They were to comprehend the strong, explicit identities of the different forms of staircases, chairs, trees and triangles in as rigorous a way as they might tackle character: as an objective, autonomous entity that operates on its own terms, with its own undeniable individuality, will and life. These materials may be inanimate, just as the image of a character is imaginary, but the question of their expressive vitality and affectivity is the same. This understanding is intended to help actors and designers determine the design that best conveys something of the guiding idea, to grasp, ultimately, whether a bed on stage '*must be heavy or low or wide or small*' or, in the case of *Peer Gynt*, whether the choice of bedclothes should be naturalistic and express the character, Asa's, poverty or convey instead something of *'the process of dying [. . .] while [Asa] is fighting with death'* (TAITT: 16 March 1937). In fact, the setting and props on stage function, for Chekhov, like characters, and the first stage in the work was to perceive the nature, psychology and gesture of each individual element; initially, students needed to understand what each element expresses in its own right before grasping how it relates to the whole stage picture. *'The setting is such an important shouting gesture for the audience'*, he explains, *'therefore the more we are responsible for the setting, the more we have the audience in our hands'* (TAITT: 16 March 1937).

Chekhov's personification or 'characterization' of space and objects is, in fact, how the scenographer and theatre-maker Alexa Reid approaches her work for site-specific and immersive performance, such as with the British theatre company, Punchdrunk. 'I agree with Chekhov,' she explained to me, 'that anything you place in a performative landscape makes a gesture and provokes the performer to move in relation to it in specific ways. I believe that audiences implicitly sense these kinds of resonances. There is a constant communication between object, space and performer on stage and while the balance may shift at any given point, their importance for me is equal' (Reid 2019). For Chekhov, to appreciate the detailed and unique characteristics or gesture of objects and settings is a fundamental starting point for effective performance and design. Once that is understood, in Reid's words, 'then we can begin to create a space or world that the audience can feel and participate in' (Reid 2019).

## 2.3 Scenographic composition

Another process Chekhov encouraged in his students involved understanding how to compose the various elements on stage in relation to each other, in a *'chorus of psychological gestures'* (TAITT: 16 March 1937). For Chekhov, this 'chorus' is created by the precise arrangement, including the location and proximity, of furniture, props and bodies in space and is as significant in conveying meaning as the acting. In addition to a study of musical composition and choral singing, regular exercises for the actors to understand scenographic relationality included three specific activities. The first was known as 'harmonious groupings', a group improvisation to strike a harmonious ensemble picture within which each individual pose aims to be as contrasting and original as possible (Autant-Mathieu 2009: 212–15). In the second, often accompanied by live music on the piano, the ensemble moved together symmetrically to a precise place in the room, followed by travelling together to a different location in the room, this time moving asymmetrically. The final exercise involved creating abstract compositions with their bodies while holding or placing boxes and structures, trying to find the *'desire'* and gesture of the structure they were improvising with and to move *'in harmony with this construction'* (TAITT: 4 October 1937). All this was intended to teach the actors how to *'incorporate'* the play not only through their voices and bodies, but *'through chairs and tables and objects which are standing here or there. This is [. . .] the psychological language of the space'* (TAITT: 16 March 1937). *'Movement as mise en scene'*, Chekhov explains, *'can continue its gesture in a wall, in a window, in a door, in a table'* and, for Chekhov, the actor must consider that her psychological movement and speech *'are connected with the window, for instance, and the window continues to act'* (TAITT: 16 March 1937).

Next, Chekhov's students explored how consciously exploiting positions on stage – the height of a piece of set, playing with depth, choosing stage left or right – are not simply physical or aesthetic choices; they can generate psychological meaning. A hero in a moment of high tension, Chekhov explains, must literally '*lose the ground*' (TAITT: 7 February 1938) and be placed high up; indeed, to increase the significance of any character for Chekhov means to retreat further back on stage, '*climb a little, and to the right*' (TAITT: 16 March 1937). Of course, this reflects the perspective of a Western spectator and presumes the direction of writing from left to right, as well as end-on viewing. Chekhov develops his point: downstage imparts '*intimacy*' (TAITT: 16 March 1937), while facing the audience directly, for Chekhov, means that '*the stage and everything on it recedes, and the actor is as if alone*' (TAITT: 11 September 1939). This downstage position, he suggests, is appropriate when we want to show the audience the character's introspective and moral thoughts, while standing in profile 'speaks of the mind' and 'calls forth a feeling of pride in thought' (Chekhov 2005: 98). These latter points perhaps offer more to contemporary immersive and site-specific practice where exploitation of proximity and intimacy is paramount. Whatever the staging context, Chekhov wanted actors to cultivate such a strong sense of composition that every movement, gesture or geographical position they make or take on stage becomes 'an artistic necessity' (Chekhov 1991: 154). Their designs and staging had to reflect this knowledge in equal measure and convey mastery of the material, spatial relations between actors, props and set.

## 2.4 Costume

In addition to creating their own set designs, the students at Dartington also had to invent and sketch costumes for the characters in their productions and realize them as far as possible within the simple means at their disposal. Chekhov's gift for drawing is well known, and creating caricatures of the characters he was working on formed an important part of his creative process as an actor. 'I retained a love of cartoons', he writes in his autobiography, 'I devoted myself to them, and I think that this played a not insubstantial part in my development as an actor' (Chekhov 2005: 25). It is striking that Chekhov's costume sketches are, in fact, three-dimensional *character* drawings: each is a semi-fantastical snapshot of the character caught in a moment in time, in thought, in action, in mid-speech, an expression of their individuality rather than simply a representation of what they are wearing.

Chekhov reflects Sir Toby Belch's lazy, carousing nature in *Twelfth Night*, for example, by sketching him lounging back in a chair, his hat tilted and his shirt loose and open (Figure 5.1). The excess of crimson material spilling messily onto the floor implies something of the character's excess and inability to contain himself. Feste's quick, self-deprecating and jesting spirit is expressed not only in the bright, chequered costume and acrobatic stance, but in the repeated image of the character in miniature, sitting underneath a larger version of himself; the extra-human fingers and multiple, bodiless heads on the shoulders suggest an otherworldly character who sees more than everyone else (Figure 5.2).

By contrast, Fabian seems down to earth, but his oversized shoes and hands as well as his flattened hat insinuate that he, too, is a prankster of sorts; his turned back, ruddy flesh, bulbous fingertips and rolls of folds not only contrast with the taut leanness of Feste but also evoke a somewhat dishevelled, relatively low-status character overall (Figure 5.3).

Fig. 5.1 Character sketch of Toby Belch by Michael Chekhov, photograph. CTS-DHDPA, MC/S8/1.

Chekhov taught the students to sketch people, behaviour and situations rather than costumes in an effort to capture the character's life and personality. As well as expressive coloured character drawings, their script notes reveal detailed sketches of stick figures doing physical actions ('*sweep across face with right arm*'), rhythmical actions ('*throw hands in the air one after the other*') and physical mannerisms ('*keeps his hands under his coat-tails*' and '*thinks of things with clenched jaws*') (TAITT: 25 July 1939). Imagining the role in bold, dynamic character montages was an extension of the students' embodied practice and inspiration and was considered as important as analysis in the psychological development of the role. The physical, aesthetic and material elements of costume had

Fig. 5.2 Character sketch of Feste by Michael Chekhov, photograph. CTS-DHDPA, MC/S8/1.

to become a conduit for and a manifestation of the emotional and psychological essence of the character.

## 2.5 Colour

Chekhov gave a lecture on colour to his students at Dartington, inspired by the theories of Rudolf Steiner (1861–1925), Albert Steffen (1884–1963) and, in particular, Johann Wolfgang von Goethe's (1749–1832) *Theory of Colours* (1810). As Jonathan Pitches points out, Chekhov takes from Goethe specifically the rejection of Newtonian optical theory in favour of psychological experience, the individual scientist's imagination and the observer's 'intuitive perception' (Pitches 2006: 13–17, 136–9).

Chekhov's aim was to teach students that using colours consciously and with care was a significant way to *'catch and hold the interest of our audience'* (TAITT: 15 March 1937). In a broad overview, he outlined that the colour of the set should express the atmosphere of the play at large, the lighting design needs to convey the changing atmospheres of the different scenes and moments within the play, and the colour of the costumes should communicate the specific **qualities** and moods of the characters. His approach to colour reflects his approach to style more generally, encouraging students to resist realistic, representational choices, and to exploit, instead, the symbolic and expressive use of colour.

## 2.6 Exercises in colour

Although Chekhov mentions an exercise of contemplating a landscape through coloured glass, his students mostly spent time observing actual colours in the studio or imagining them. The trajectory of study was as follows: to imagine the colour on its own *'without any connection to real things'*, to receive any impressions from it (qualities, direction,

Fig. 5.3 Character sketch of Fabian by Michael Chekhov, photograph. CTS-DHDPA, MC/S8/1.

associations with time or the elements), to imagine it *'flowing into unlimited space'* and determine the psychological gesture within it, and finally to *'try to be the colour'* (TAITT: 15 March 1937). They also observed combinations of colours side-by-side, noting whether one appears nearer, bigger or lighter than the other, if they are complementary or arouse any feelings. The aim was to awaken the students' *'natural reactions to colours'* (TAITT: 15 March 1937), transform them into PGs and to apply their findings in sketches, designs and mise en scènes.

In their work on 'The Fishers' Scene', for example, students drew up colour charts and identified different sections by colour: a red, yellow or grey moment.[7] Red corresponded to the section in the story called 'The Land' and the particular shades of carmine and scarlet, for example, were intended to evoke serious 'dignity' and 'love', respectively. We can sense the influence of Goethe here who asserts that red 'in its deep dark state' gives an impression of 'gravity and dignity', whereas 'in its light attenuated tint' conveys 'grace and attractiveness' (Goethe 2006: 173). In relation to the characters, red was to communicate *'assertiveness'* and the actors added a red handkerchief, shawl and blouse with a red pattern to the costumes to convey this (TAITT: 30 June 1937). Here, students employed colour consciously to translate their textual analysis directly into visual, scenographic possibilities. As Jonathan Pitches points out, colour was one of Chekhov's holistic techniques 'for bypassing the potentially dry intellectual process of play analysis' (Pitches 2013: 227) and stimulating a more rounded, kinaesthetic and imaginative response. It was part of an interdisciplinary curriculum that made aesthetic questions integral to the actor's education and promoted thinking beyond naturalism.

## 3 Critical analysis: Problems

Part of the focus of the practical workshops was to test-drive Chekhov's propositions and investigate them in the context of contemporary practice: do they hold true for twenty-first-century design and theatre-making, and if not, what kind of problems do they present? I'll discuss some of the problems and possibilities of Chekhov's ideas on colour, gesture and setting across the next two sections.

### 3.1 Colour

The first of Chekhov's proposals that proves difficult are his spiritual and moral affirmations on colour. He asserts, for example, that red and orange speak to us as *'God's wrath'*, that green and orange *'tend to make us egotistical'*, whereas black, grey and brown *'represent evil powers and evil influences'*. The more redemptive colours include yellow which *'leads us to spiritual self-realisation'*, blue which offers *'the quality of "God's mercy"'*, lilac *'calls up mystical feelings'*, while white radiates aspects of the *'highest part of the human being'* (TAITT: 15 March 1937).

Chekhov also asserts that colours have objective, physical and dynamic properties that stimulate particular effects. Red, he claims, has *'a gesture'* of *'activity and movement'*, and when there is some red on a green field or plane, the red *'begins to move'*. When red is coupled with blue, *'we get the feeling that red is nearer than blue'*, whereas when it is combined with yellow and blue, red *'endeavours to balance the two'* and also *'tries to fight the blue'* (TAITT: 15 March 1937). Less controversial, perhaps, is his affirmation that certain colours and combinations evoke precise emotions. Whereas yellow perceived on its own has the quality of *'joy and pleasure'*, if you add a little green to it, he states, it evokes *'the most dreadful feeling'*. That same green placed next to blue and yellow will restore balance whereas green-blue, green-yellow and blue-yellow combinations feel *'common and flat'* (TAITT: 15 March 1937).

All workshop participants and designers generally agreed that colours and tones do have some affective power. Cunningham and I asked them to observe silently large canvas panels one after the other, and in various combinations, each prepared and painted in one colour by Cunningham – red, yellow, blue, green, orange, purple and white. Everyone was free to move, sit quietly and contemplate, approach the panel or remain at a distance. In one exercise, scenographer Sarah Beaton noted how the contemplation of colour had an impact on the mood of the room; blue slowed people down, green provoked some sense of irregular rhythm and the ambience became lighter and more joyful when we contemplated orange. Visual artist Gillian Carnegie explained to me that for her exhibition of still lives, she chose a palette of muted, dirty greys and the overall effect created an environment of 'a certain calm distance' (Carnegie 2017). This was in contrast to an earlier work painted in monochromatic variations of sulphurous yellow where she intended to create an effect to challenge the viewer (Carnegie 2017).[8] Yet broadly participants concluded that the specific feeling an isolated colour provokes is often radically different, depending on the person and context. As Bauhaus artist Josef Albers (1888–1976) puts it, 'if one says "Red" [. . .] and there are 50 people listening, it can be expected that there will be 50 reds in their minds. And one can be sure that all these reds will be very different' (Albers 2006: 3); 'it seems good', he concludes, 'that we are of different tastes' (Albers 2006: 17).

However, it is challenging to see what some of Chekhov's moral associations with colour might offer in a contemporary, multicultural performance context. Lighting designer Colin Grenfell counters that many Western associations such as finding a correlation between purple and royalty or 'holiness', for example, 'far from being a genetically programmed response, relates to the simple fact that the dye was so expensive that only the elite could afford it' (Grenfell 2017). Similarly, theatre designer and film-maker Derek Jarman (1942–94) noted that often vermilion is considered 'the Queen of reds' because it is one of the most expensive natural minerals, costing as much as £250 for 250 grammes in 1994 (Jarman 2000: 36). Participants in the workshops agreed unanimously that responses to colour are determined by a whole series of factors that Chekhov does not mention: cultural, social and political background, historical and linguistic associations, age and gender. Chekhov also makes several references to *'flesh'* colour as having a gesture of '*disappearing on the edges*' or seeming to '*flow away*' (TAITT: 15 March 1937); it is clear that here, and in relation to the colour white as cited above, he is referring only to Caucasian flesh and offers no alternative perspectives.

Regarding stage lighting, seminal colour theorist Faber Birren (1900–88) has shown that there is some evidence that audiences pay more attention to colours in the centre of the visible spectrum of the light (yellow and green) than at its ends (red and blue), as well as to saturated rather than de-saturated colours (Birren 1969: 47). Richard H. Palmer, who writes on theatre aesthetics and lighting, describes tests that reveal how different coloured light can stimulate pituitary and pineal glands, influence blood pressure, heart and breathing rate, blinking, brain waves and muscular tension (Palmer 1998: 100–2). Specifically, red, Birren states, can increase levels of activity in regions of the brain controlling hormones, as do yellow and orange, whereas blue, by contrast, relaxes those areas (Birren 1978: 24), and it is interesting to note that some of these observations resonate with Chekhov's own statements. But, by and large, as lighting designer Yaron Abulafia points out, 'these findings are based on quantitative studies that have provided differing and controversial results' (Abulafia 2016: 94) and are not a reliable basis on which to assert a set of theoretical principles.

Visual artist Kai McCall explained to me that notions of 'objective' truths about colours are considered largely defunct in the analysis of contemporary painting. For him, a sense of movement in a painting is created through the relationship between colours and parts, and in particular between light and dark. Rather than prioritize colour or any sense of permanent significance within it, he thinks more about shaping tone across a composition. 'Colour is only at the service of the light envelope I have chosen to paint it in', he explains, 'and I want consciously to direct the viewer to the tonal dynamic within the work – a dramatic combination of highlights and dark tones, or the radiant subtlety of midtones – that's what contributes to its narrative' (McCall 2017).

Grenfell stresses the importance in his lighting of not privileging a particular meaning or dynamic in colour: '[S]ometimes', he told me, 'there is simply a visceral pleasure experienced from certain colour sequences and combinations on stage that operates at a non-verbal, subconscious level, which is equally significant. For the Tchaikovsky opera *Iolanta* (1892),[9] about a blind princess who recovers her sight, he lit the whole performance in monochrome with a very small frequency of light and opened out the whole spectrum of colour only as she began to see. 'It almost hurt', he told me, 'but it created the most extraordinary emotional reaction in the audience who suddenly began to experience the character's transformation'. The dramaturgy of the lighting design overall expressed Iolanta's physiological and emotional awakening; its success lay, above all, in the relationality of the colour choices.

While the question of colour's potential to *move* the audience by activating certain sensations appears relevant to designers, it tends not to be located in a specific colour per se. Little, it seems, is gained by assigning precise emotions to colours or insisting that they affect us all in a similar, collective way, as suggested by Goethe, who claims that 'a single colour excites, by a specific sensation, the tendency to universality' (Goethe 2006: 174). While certain ethnic or social groups may have shared reference points, we must be wary of using Chekhov's assumptions as the basis for a codified and essentialist approach to the use of colour. It is difficult to see how accepting prescriptive 'facts' about colour can teach us anything other than a learnt, automatic and unreflective approach. Artistic work requires a specific, individuated response to our stimulus and, in theatre and performance, designers, actors and directors need to work with creative rather than didactic principles.

## 4 Critical analysis: Possibilities for contemporary practice

### 4.1 Colour

In spite of the evident pitfalls of Chekhov's tendency to essentialize, practically doing Chekhov's exercises on colour did prompt some useful conclusions. I'll go through some typical responses from designers to elucidate. While Beaton normally uses colour consciously in her set designs to try to create atmosphere, Chekhov's exercise on contemplating colour made her consider how practically she might create a 'painterly' evocation of the atmosphere in the rehearsal room to influence the actors' work before the arrival of the set. Scenographer Andreas Skourtis found the colour exercise 'a brilliantly embodied, playful and immersive way to introduce designers to the impact of colour on the emotional world of the spectator beyond the first layer of aesthetics' (Skourtis 2017). It offers designers a way to learn how the effective use of colour juxtaposition, just by itself, can create experience and feelings, and communicate directly to the internal world of the spectator. 'This', explains Skourtis, 'is what good design should do'. Designer Rosie Elnile described how, while she does not relate to colour in Chekhov's terms, the exercise opens up an intensity of focus and attention to detail in the potential of one colour. In a recent design, she explored the use of a single colour; by transforming the entire theatre from a black box to a blue space, including light fittings, ceiling grid and seats for the production of *The Unknown Island* at London's Gate Theatre, she was 'trying to question the idea of blankness and things being invisible, like the black box of the theatre space. Normally, the audience are supposed to look just at the set and ignore the rest' (Elnile 2017).[10] Likewise, for the funeral scene in Cunningham's set for director Julia Bardsley's adaptation of Emile Zola's *Thérèse Raquin* 'the actors expressed no emotion in monotone voices', she explains, 'and all-red costumes in this moment functioned as the expression of a "psychological scream" within the space' (Cunningham 2017).[11]

The ability to perceive colour in a new light is the important point here, and the exercise of contemplating colour in isolation, detached from any context or meaning as a sort of total, embodied listening or receiving, paves the way for this. When Goethe looked at a flower, Chekhov explains, he '*looked at it as if he was creating it*' (LTT: 15 April 1936); his own proposition here cultivates a similarly heightened curiosity so that designers might use colours freshly, beyond their usual mediated and conditioned responses. This pure contemplation of colour might also help to cultivate an understanding of what McCall calls 'the vibrational effect' that is created by the relationship *between* colours, as well as their connection to the context of the whole work. Many of the designers and artists I shared these ideas with agreed that it is often there where colour's affective power lies.

## 4.2 Gesture and setting

In the workshops, we also explored Chekhov's practical exercises on settings; participants created PGs for a staircase, a low, three-legged stool, a coffee table, a bottle of water. They later did observation exercises of the same items placed in different positions in the room and stepped into the scene. We defined an end-on stage area, placed the objects and furniture in different configurations and considered silently whether each placement evoked a particular situation or an imminent event. One participant at a time stepped into each composition and later pairs played a scene using these physical objects as their set. We worked with scenes from Harold Pinter's *Betrayal* and also improvised silent scenarios.

In one workshop, Skourtis sensed 'the power of movement' within the still stage pictures he inhabited and explained that the exercise gave him 'a new way of articulating what designing for the theatre is all about: a process that creates dramaturgy, that is about movement and time'. In his teaching, he tries to raise awareness that the dynamics of spatial design are as much the designer's responsibility as the director's (Skourtis 2017). Chekhov suggests that '*perhaps the gesture of the whole scene requires that the chair will be low, with a low back. Then it will make harmony with the actor's acting, and the audience will feel much more receptive because of this small subconscious thing*' (TAITT: 7 February 1938). Chekhov's exercise teaches that design is not about creating an art object such as a painting; the set must facilitate life in the performers and what is actually happening on stage.

In my experience, actors are adept at adapting to the designs they work within; they are trained to relate to their surroundings and embrace the given circumstances of a production, after all. Yet we might ask how often do designers engage in acting processes, and how much is their training focused on realizing a director's or even a company's concept rather than, for example, learning to create environments with the kinds of psychophysical properties that inspire actors to play? If contemporary scenography is, according to McKinney and Palmer, 'multisensorial', 'no longer only associated with the static visual image' and is more 'the dynamic interaction of bodies, environments and materials' (McKinney and Palmer 2017: 8, 5), design practice and training needs to connect more fully with the actor's immersive, imaginative and kinaesthetic process. For Chekhov, it is the designer's job not only to '*feel our space*', but '*to make space from our feelings*' (TAITT: 16 March 1937). Cultivating a keen sensitivity to space is paramount, but equally crucial is the understanding that designers should create their work from an embodied practice. Design is not solely a mental activity, '*it is not a thing which we must find with our brain*', Chekhov insists, '*we must feel it*'; it is a '*psychological a, b, c*' (TAITT: 7 February 1938).

Working with Chekhov's PG brings designers into an immediately embodied relationship with their materials and closer to the kind of inhabited experience that actors engage in. As a result, scenographers might come into closer, 'felt' contact with space as 'psycho-plastic', to borrow theatre designer Josef Svoboda's phrase (1920–2002; McKinney and Palmer 2017: 8), and facilitate design choices that enhance both the inner and outer aspects of the actor's work. For Cunningham, the strength in Chekhov's exercises on gesture, setting and costume is the way they connect the designer directly with the actor, and what the actors might actually do or experience on the set. A different kind of collaboration might take place if designers intend their costume sketch, to take one example, to be an inspirational work of art, an artistic impression of the character herself as well as an acting proposition for the actor. '*If you have something on the stage*', Chekhov warns, '*which is not used for acting, it will be more and more disturbing*' (TAITT: 16 March 1937). He challenges designers to consider their work as activating the acting itself, plugging directly into and extending the actor's creative expression.

In her teaching, Reid encourages designers to work physically and practically with matter and materials and to get in touch with sensation. She invites students to explore the space with their bodies from the outset, just as she does in her own practice: '[W]hat is the sensation of walking down a particular corridor, for example, or why does one corner of the room feel uncomfortable, or how is the space already encoded with some sense of narrative or resonance?' (Reid 2019). She aims to harness these early experiences of the psychophysical impact of a space, and they become her guiding idea. By coaxing the designer into the terrain of the actor, she provides the basis for the kind of collaborative and interdisciplinary practice that Chekhov was trying to encourage. In my own show, *Concert*, the dramaturgy and scenography were created through a collaboration primarily between performer, director and sound designer. While we all brought our specific expertise, our roles in creation became less defined as we sought to determine the precise environment of our production, which was a world led by the music and sound design. Lighting and video design were developed at a later stage.

## 4.3 Case study: *Concert*

*Concert* is a solo dance-theatre show, performed by dancer Colin Dunne, that explores the music of the virtuoso traditional Irish fiddle player, Tommie Potts (1912–88). Co-created by Dunne, sound designer Mel Mercier and me in 2017, the premise of the production was for Dunne to 'dance' the one album Potts produced in 1972, *The Liffey Banks*. Potts's album, considered by many as iconic, was unique in the tradition of Irish folk music because it was never intended for dancing to; his tunes are short, without crescendo, and he introduces pauses, extra beats and rhythmic irregularity as well as (contrary to tradition) tunes in minor keys. One of our desires for the show was to help audiences appreciate the distinctive, idiosyncratic style and specificity of each Potts tune. In rehearsals, Dunne, Mercier and I explored the particular, unique qualities of each melody; we listened to it, listed our impressions and tried to understand its fundamental movement or gesture. We explored trying to find the PG of 'The Butterfly', one of Tommie Potts's signature melodies, and it became one of the climactic dances in *Concert*. Dunne associated the tune with a 'punchy, fighting' quality and its essential gesture that inspired one aspect of the choreography became that of a dogged, 'slippy', 'scissor-walk' that did not want to leave the ground.

Potts lamented certain limitations in the Irish folk tradition, in particular, a lack of melodic development and technical virtuosity. He played alone, never in public and his melancholic compositions resist the rousing jauntiness characteristic of much traditional music. It became clear to me that there was a gesture that encapsulated Potts's music at large: a movement upward, a reach for something beyond the ordinary, a yearning to elevate and lift off. This PG became a dramaturgical guide for us to shape the arc of the show into three sections: part one was entitled 'searching for Potts' and had a fragmented, broken, internal quality with the action taking place in isolated islands everywhere on stage; part two was 'finding Potts' and this was the 'concert' part of the show that the audience was perhaps hoping for: joyful, frank, playful, performed on a unified stage in the centre; part three was 'beyond Potts', and involved an experimental atmosphere, a new piece of music played by Dunne on piano and violin, rather than a piece of dance. This final part of the show was an attempt by Dunne to create something new through the encounter with Potts's material, to transcend both his own usual artistic responses and the traditional repertoire itself.

In his lighting design, Colin Grenfell introduced colour at two key moments into a palette that was largely cool white. The first was for a scene where Dunne listens to a jumbled mix of voice recordings of Potts on a cassette tape recorder, fast-forwarding and rewinding in search of a relevant motif. Grenfell described this moment as having a sonar-like quality, like a distant, submerged submarine, a sensation from the past, no longer corresponding to the world of reality; he translated this feeling into a green backlight, slowly fading up. The second colour choice was for the final scene of the show. Here, he chose a steely blue to express the closing atmosphere that he conceived as 'a breath and a world expanding'. While for most of the show we used disparate, contained and focused areas of light, Grenfell explained that in this moment he wanted 'to unify the spaces and bring them altogether' to create a sense of opening in the audience that was 'almost a sense of relief' (Grenfell 2017). While we didn't begin defining colours in any particular way, for me, green came to evoke a connection with Potts's past, and the blue ushered the audience into an evocation of the future and the legacy of this music for the generations to come. Grenfell's choices helped consolidate our three-part structure for the show that travelled through the past, present and future and helped create an almost Chekhovian form of our dramaturgy: sensory, embodied, affective.

Our research, which included film footage of interviews with Potts at home, led us to the conclusion that Potts's lonesome idiosyncrasy could not be conveyed in a 'concert' where Dunne 'serves up' the tunes with polished virtuosity. Rather, we sought an atmosphere that was intimate, home-made, almost domestic. It became an exploration of Potts's world at large rather than an interpretation of his album. Given also that Potts's music exists only as a recording, the way in which it was played back into the theatre and how and if it was manipulated or 'recomposed' became a crucial consideration for our dramaturgy and scenography overall. As a result, our design consisted of mobile islands or stages of various sizes and materials (thin hardboard, thick plywood, lino, rubber) that exposed Dunne's process itself, sites of exploration where Dunne 'encountered' and grappled with a particular tune in real time. A record player, a tape recorder, small hand-held speakers, a rifle mic and mobile speakers on the floor acted for Dunne as physical portals or conduits to Potts.

The figure of Dunne passing through various isolated 'stations' evoked something of Potts's own broken and solitary excavation of Irish music. Height featured only twice: we lit a flown speaker when the audience heard Potts's spoken voice for the first time, and Dunne created a vertical 'screen' from his various timber floor boards to show the first and only image of the man: a private film of Potts playing one of his most innovative variations. These isolated attempts at verticality were juxtaposed with the horizontal, earth-bound planes of flooring. Dunne, like Potts, attempted to take flight, but the moments were fleeting, unable to last. Chekhov's conception of scenography in its emphasis on inner gesture, the affective influence of colour and the dramaturgy of material stage elements underpinned our conception of the show.

## 5 Conclusion

Only by embracing Chekhov's ideas on scenography can we begin to grasp fully what he really intends with his collective, interdisciplinary theatre of the future. His ideal actor is well versed in design and only by mastering some fundamental design principles can Chekhov's acting technique be considered complete. We can also read Chekhov's approach as a provocation to scenographers. If good acting emerges from performers connecting wholly with their physical and aesthetic environment as an active part of their practice, good design requires designers getting inside the vitality of their materials, 'a meeting', as Simon O'Sullivan puts it, 'between material and sensation' (O'Sullivan in McKinney and Palmer 2017: 12). This involves designers undertaking experiential, embodied, psychophysical practice, like an actor.

Almost a century ago, Appia asserted that 'scenic art should be based on the one reality worthy of the theatre: the human body' (Appia 1993: 65). If Appia stresses mobility, the use of depth and horizontal dynamics and the three-dimensional quality of all elements on stage for a successful production, Chekhov emphasizes both the internal and external aspects of those elements as part of a psychophysical continuum. Actor, designer and director have shared responsibility for optimal 'scenic expressiveness' (Appia 1993: 57). This means that they need to be coaxed out of the safe confines and parameters of practising only within their discipline; '*we have to find another approach to the theatre*', Chekhov told his students, '*actor, designer, designer or author – each will be responsible for everyone*' (TAITT: 14 January 1937). Interdisciplinarity is the path towards greater creativity and a deeper understanding of the whole of the performance.

One obstacle to this in contemporary theatre rehearsals is that the relationship between actor and designer is often mediated by the director, and that, for understandably practical reasons, design decisions have already been made between them as the core 'creative team' before actors come on board. As Ric Knowles points out, this narrowly 'circumscribe[s] the options available to actors [. . .] long before they have begun fully to explore their roles' and kills the possibility of a 'design for a show to evolve alongside its other components' (Knowles 2004: 28). Actors are often obliged to justify choices that do not always make sense to them. If actors' input cannot be included in the early design process, they need to consider taking a more emboldened approach to any decisions that remain; designers and directors, in turn, must consider the psychophysical consequences for the actor as paramount in any scenographic choices they make.

Perhaps more importantly, however, it is time to think about new methodologies in acting and design training where actors and designers learn to inhabit each other's terrain and can help to expand the kinds of interdisciplinary, collaborative practice that occurs in many contemporary devising companies as well as international creative teams that date as far back as the iconic collaboration between Bertolt Brecht and his designer Caspar Neher. Such practice teaches how sharply design can heighten the live and fragile connection between the actor and spectator or, on the contrary, obstruct it. Educators need to pioneer investigative, interdisciplinary and psychophysical ways of teaching their craft, where actors designing and designers acting is considered less a temporary, extracurricular excursion and more a fundamental aspect of their creative practice. This doesn't mean abandoning expertise but rather laying the groundwork for more productive and informed conversations in the profession. Then we might see a theatrical landscape where actors and designers work alongside each other in close creative collaboration and where the actor-designer partnership could shape the production as fully as that of the director-designer.

## Notes

1. See also Deshpande Hutchinson (2018) and Julia Listengarten's chapter on Chekhov and the visual arts in Autant-Mathieu and Meerzon (2015: 253–67).
2. These workshops were on 14–15 May 2016 (The Actor's Centre); 27–30 July 2016 (The Street Theatre) and 10 September 2016 (Goldsmith's College). Aldona Cunningham is also Senior Lecturer in Theatre Design at Royal Central School of Speech and Drama, London.
3. Alexa Reid is a London-based cross-disciplinary artist who makes work in the margins between theatre, live art and installation. She has collaborated with Punchdrunk and ArtAngel on their site-specific and immersive projects and is a Lecturer in Performance Art and Theatre Making at Goldsmith's College. Andreas Skourtis is a London-based architect and scenographer and Senior Lecturer in Theatre Design and Scenography at Royal Central School of Speech and Drama, London. Rosie Elnile (Resident Design Assistant at Donmar Warehouse 2015–16) and Sarah Beaton (Linbury Prize Winner 2011) are both London-based theatre designers: http://www.sarahbeaton.com, www.rosieelnile.com. Colin Grenfell (TMA and Wales Theatre Award

winner) is based in Edinburgh, Scotland: https://lovely.lighting/. Kai McCall is based in Montreal: https://www.kaimccall.com/. Gillian Carnegie is based in London and was nominated for the Turner Prize in 2005. Karin Schuck is Costume Supervisor at the Royal Central School of Speech and Drama, London.

4. The show premiered at Centre National De La Danse, Paris on 28–29 March 2017 and was co-produced by Maura O'Keefe for Once Off Productions, Centre National De La Danse Paris, MA Scène Nationale/Pays de Montbéliard, La Comète/Scène Nationale de Châlons-en–Champagne and Dublin Dance Festival, with subsequent performances in 2018 at Festival Groningen; Tramway, Glasgow; The Pit, Barbican, London, and Baryshnikov Arts Centre, New York. It won the Gradam Comharcheoil TG4 2018 Award in Ireland. http://www.sineadrushe.co.uk/productions/concert/.
5. Chekhov wrote that he learnt this from Vladimir Nemirovich-Danchenko, one of the co-founders of the Moscow Art Theatre, whose 'genius', Chekhov wrote, 'lay in going directly to the crux of the matter and immediately finding the main idea, the guiding theme' (Chekhov and Leonard 1963: 45).
6. The student designer was Gretel Schreiber. In this particular critique, the author was Paul Rogers, the costume designer was Beatrice Straight, and the director was Deirdre Hurst du Prey. For a detailed study of this scene, see Pitches (2013: 219–36).
7. For a discussion of the colour scores, see Pitches (2013: 231).
8. The exhibition was at Cabinet Gallery, London, in 2016. Carnegie was nominated for the Turner Prize in 2005.
9. The production opened at Guildhall School of Music and Drama, London, in 2011.
10. The production was an adaptation from the novel *The Tale of the Unknown Island* by Nobel Laureate José Saramago and premiered on 11 September 2017, directed by Ellen McDougall.
11. The production was at Leicester Haymarket Theatre in October 1991.

# Section Three  Chekhov technique: Beyond the theatre

# 6 'If the new theatre is to have meaning, the audience too must play its part'

## Chekhov technique in applied, therapeutic and community contexts

CAOIMHE MCAVINCHEY

## 1 Introduction

The wide-reaching impact of Michael Chekhov's techniques has been evidenced in the testimony of theatre-makers though their professional practice, their teaching and in academic research (Ashperger 2008; Petit 2010; Autant-Mathieu and Meerzon 2015; Monday 2017; Rushe 2019). However, to date, the work of artists in socially engaged contexts has had little academic attention. In this chapter, I consider the ways in which Michael Chekhov's techniques have informed the work of artists working in a diverse range of applied contexts in different cultural settings. Drawing on the Michael Chekhov New Pathways praxis symposium, material from the Michael Chekhov Theatre Studio Deirdre Hurst du Prey Archive at the Dartington Hall Trust Archive and interviews with practitioners, I consider some of the ways in which applied, therapeutic and community theatre practices engage with what Anjalee Deshpande Hutchinson terms 'adaptations, re-imaginings and re-interpretations of the exercises' of Michael Chekhov combined with 'riffs' off the exercises created by others (2018: xv). This critical enquiry offers questions about the epistemologies that circulate in Applied Theatre practice, the influences that shape the work of artists working in socially engaged contexts and the role of higher education and training programmes in expanding the repertoire of approaches studied and disseminated.

Applied, therapeutic and community theatre practices operate in distinctly different theatre-making economies from commercial and professional theatre. This richly diverse spectrum accommodates work framed as Theatre for Health, Theatre for Development, Prison Theatre and Theatre in Education. It includes theatre practices with people who share particular experiences, for example, lived experience of homelessness, mental distress and exile, as well as work that may attend to a specific aspect of someone's identity, such as race, faith, age, gender or sexuality. Since the mid-1990s, theatre practices in educational, community and therapeutic contexts have increasingly been identified within the academy and, more recently, by theatre practitioners, funders and commissioners as Applied Drama, Theatre and Performance. Despite considerable debate and some resistance to the all-embracing nature of the term and subsequent obfuscation of any specificity, Applied Theatre is, as James Thompson writes, 'a useful phrase for a [drama/theatre/performance form] that claims usefulness' (2003: 14). The practices referred to in this chapter are both eclectic in range and specific in their application: they share characteristics of the participation of people who are not professional theatre-makers and an explicit intentionality, often to address issues of social concern, that shape the approach, content and audience for the work (Ackroyd 2000; Nicholson 2005). This brief overview of the field acknowledges not only the panoply of practices but how they are, necessarily, shaped by specific contexts, for example, the identity and dynamic of the participants, the duration of the project, the site it takes place in, the audiences who have access to it, the issues it addresses, the social imperative invested in by funding bodies and the wider political landscapes that shape it. What these practices also share is Chekhov's ambition for a theatre, declared in the Chekhov Theatre Studio Prospectus (1936): 'Modern problems are so serious, so intricate, and so tortuous that if a solution is to be offered in the theatre, the theatre must leave the ways of mere imitation and naturalism and probe beneath the surface' (12).

Internationally, there is a growing network of artists working in socially engaged contexts whose practice, informed by Chekhov, attends to 'modern problems'. Marjolein Baars is an actor and teacher who serves on the board of MICHA (the Michael Chekhov Association in the United States). As Artistic Director of tiny hero productions in Amsterdam, Baars has, since 2005, been developing work with people with dementia, their families and carers 'to create a network or "ensemble" in which all members play together and learn with and from each other by creating a learning environment'.[1] The project has had distinct phases, including research, training, a solo show, *Zwarte Gaten & Losse Eindjes* (2015) (*Black Holes & Loose Ends*) as well as publications, *Contact Maken bij Dementia: Het Oefenen Van Levende Communicatie in alle Fasen van Dementie* (2015) (*Making Contact With Dementia: Practicing Living Communication in all Stages of Dementia*) and *Dementie uit de Koffer: Vanuit Creativiteit Omgaan Met Dementie* (2012) (*Dementia Out of the Box: Dealing Creatively with Dementia*), supporting families, professionals and volunteers who live, work and care for people with dementia. Baars's extensive and socially responsive practice accommodates a wide range of practice – she has also worked as a social clown in hospital settings for many years. She contributed to the New Pathways Symposium in 2016, and her work is discussed in more detail elsewhere in this book. Jessica Cerullo, based in Washington, USA, is currently Artistic Director of MICHA, and her work as a performer, teacher and director of socially or civically engaged projects is informed by Michael Chekhov. Both Baars and Cerullo have been at the forefront of considering how Michael Chekhov's approach can inform social and civic practices, and together they led The Citizen Artist Session within MICHA's International Michael Chekhov Workshop (2017). Also in the United States, Peggy Coffey an actor, director and teacher, has acknowledged how her engagement with Chekhov was a catalyst for activism – the more she engaged with the technique, the more she engaged with the world: 'the technique led me to social engagement and a political commitment' (World Chekhov Teachers' Meeting 2018) which directly informed her community-based work following the mass shootings in Parkland, Florida, USA, in 2018.

In Berlin there is a strong community of artists, trained in Chekhov's methods, working in different community contexts. This includes Joerg Andrees, who organized the first

Chekhov conference in Berlin in 1992 with Jobst Langhams, founded the Michael Chekhov International Academy and is a faculty member of MICHA. Since the early 1990s Andrees has also worked in partnership with various practitioners in Germany in therapeutic uses of Chekhov's work, both within mainstream and anthroposophical mental health contexts, and worked closely with psychiatrist Dr Michael John in Sweden. Magdalena Scharler has collaborated with Syrian refugees and the development of the theatre company syn:format,[2] and Anna Katherina Andrees has developed an 'inclusion-oriented circus pedagogy' working with children, adolescents and adults with Down syndrome and other learning disabilities with the company, Zentrum für bewegte Kunste. V (ZBK; Centre for Moving Arts).[3] In Denmark, Jesper Michelsen is artistic director of both the Michael Chekhov Studio in Copenhagen and Glad Theater, a professional theatre and acting school for actors with disabilities which explicitly acknowledges the influence of Chekhov in attending to the body and the imagination in human development and creativity.[4] In Ireland, Declan Drohan's work with Quick Bright Things, an ensemble of actors with learning disabilities, was also informed by his training in Michael Chekhov's techniques. In Switzerland, in 2017, Bernadette Wintsch-Heinen and Mani Wintsch developed a long-term community project, based on *Peer Gynt* and informed by Chekhov, with a rural community in Switzerland drawing on Chekhov's work.[5] This brief selection of practitioners and projects provides a snapshot of diverse and innovative socially engaged practices, informed by adaptation, reimagining, reinterpreting and riffing on Chekhov's approaches to theatre-making.

## 2 Imperatives of theatre practice

The social and political possibilities of theatre, evident in these practices, resonates with the imperative outlined in the 1936 prospectus for the Chekhov Theatre Studio:

> It is the belief of the Studio that mankind's problems have shifted their ground in the decade and a half that has elapsed since the war; they are not only psychological but sociological. [. . .] The Studio believes that for some of the social problems besetting the modern world the theatre can offer at least a means of study and possibly a solution (15–16).

This acknowledgement of the interrelationship between the personal and the social, framed by a wider political context, shaped Chekhov's commitment to training actors who would take responsibility to connect *with* audiences rather than present work *to* them.[6] In Chekhov's *Lessons to Teachers* (which form part of the Deirdre Hurst du Prey archive), he carefully articulated a vision of work and the approaches to develop it that modelled rigorous collaboration between actors. The development of ensemble was a key aspect of this. Paul Rogers, who was nineteen years old when he went to the Chekhov Theatre Studio in 1936, reflected on the fundamental importance of ensemble in building a cohesive group: Chekhov dedicated so much time to this during training that Rogers wondered if the group would ever act at all (Sharp 2016). This sense of ensemble, self-awareness, interdependence and play was crucial to Chekhov's ambitions for the social practice of theatre. His commitment to make a new kind of theatre that recognized interrelations between the personal, social, spiritual and political, and connected directly with audiences, resonates with other theatre movements in the early and mid-twentieth century in the UK.

Although Applied Theatre is a relatively new academic term with a flourishing body of associated research, the practices aligned to it have a rich history, seeded in political theatre and radical pedagogy across the twentieth century. In *Applied Drama: The Gift of Theatre*, Helen Nicholson identifies three theatre movements that advocate the possibility of personal and social change: 'theatres of the political Left, which have been variously described as political, radical or alternative; drama and theatre in education; and community theatre' (2005: 8). While the political, social and economic contexts that theatre-makers operate in vary widely, these abundantly rich and distinctive areas of practice share a history of questioning social hierarchies and systems of power that circulate and construct society. This field of theatre practice is resolutely pro-social in its commitment to connect with people who are not theatre professionals in a wide range of contexts in order to bring the audience into direct contact with the theatre. These practices disrupt once-established ideas of who makes theatre, where it takes place and what it should be about, which, again, has strong resonances with Chekhov who 'believed that those who create Theater must take responsibility for the impact their productions have upon their audience. They must be willing to ask if what is being presented to the spectators has any value for them as human beings' (Powers 2006: xliii). This social ambition for theatre is reiterated in the language which introduced and framed Chekhov's Studio – that it's '*aim must be to find the connection to the whole world around us. [. . .] We are working for humanity and for society*' (TAITT: 1 February 1937). In this reconfigured power dynamic, Chekhov positions the actor – rather than the director or writer – at the centre of the theatre-making process, charging them with creative autonomy and critical responsibility. He provocatively claimed that '[t]he director, the stage designer, etc., are all accessories, but the actor is the theatre' (2006: 158). His actor-centred technique disrupts power relations and hierarchies in theatre as well as the world beyond it, critiquing structures of authority and power and echoing philosophies of key figures in education and theatre praxis across the twentieth century, including John Dewey (2011), Paulo Freire (1996), Dorothy Heathcote (1995) and Augusto Boal (2002), influential in specific areas of Applied and Community practice, particularly Drama in Education, Theatre in Education, Theatre for Change and Legislative Theatre. These approaches model democracy as an ethical practice, rather than political idea shaped by social and interactive processes open to all to participate, and position the actor/learner/participant at the centre of the process. This invitation to participate, to collaborate, to be part of the theatre-making process and the continued affirmation of the necessity of theatre-making as a way to reframe and navigate the world is explicitly articulated in 'A Memo to the Reader' in *To the Actor* (2006: 1), where Chekhov petitions practitioners to invigorate his approaches through their own practice:

> I need your help. The abstruse nature of the subject requires not only concentrated reading, not alone clear understanding, but *co-operation* with the author. For that which could easily be made comprehensible by personal contact and demonstration, must of necessity depend on mere words and intellectual concepts [. . .] the technique of acting can never be properly understood without *practicing it*.

This cooperation with the reader, this embodied consideration of ideas through practice, is both a generous invitation to test and adapt his work and also a directive – without the playful interrogation and alchemy of experience, the technique will become static. Effie

Makepeace, Zoe Brook, Hartley Jafine and Martin Sharp are artists working in socially engaged contexts who have embraced Chekhov's challenge. They have generously reflected on their experiences which inform key critical understandings developed in this chapter. Foregrounding the practitioners' voices, their critical reflections on 'cooperation' with Chekhov and 'personal contact' with participants, offers access to specific moments in their diverse practices and the nuanced, detailed blending and adaptation of Chekhov's techniques within it. Brief introductions to each of the four practitioners contextualize the place of Chekhov alongside other artistic, pedagogical and ethical approaches to give access to the particularity of the contexts they negotiate in their practice.

Martin Sharp is a producer and director for theatre, film and television. More recently, Sharp trained in existential psychology and psychotherapy and is increasingly interested in the therapeutic potential of aspects of Chekhov's technique. Sharp's connection with Chekhov goes back to the pivotal moment in 1993 when he was given a copy of *To the Actor*. For more than two decades, Chekhov's work has informed his thinking about art and life. During the Praxis Symposia, Sharp reflected:

> The Chekhov work runs as a parallel in my life [. . .] I was drawn towards the philosophic premise of what it is *to be*. In the world of existential psychotherapy, there's no essential nature of a human being, just an existential sense of being. With an existential sense of selfhood our supposed nature is constantly in flux, in a state of becoming, and therefore in a dynamic relationship with the world and others. When therapists talk about therapeutic interventions, they're usually referring to relational issues with someone or some people. So it's usually about how we are functioning as being-in-the-world, as Heidegger terms our unavoidable situation. So there is no position available to us that is not as a being-in-the-world, as open towards the world, in a state of social beingness if you like. So this state creates a sense of ourselves as manifestly *situated* in the world, and always in relationship towards others in the world [. . .] and we can manifest that in different ways; as being-for-another, which perhaps suggests our most intimate relational state. This is usually a state manifest between therapist and client within a therapeutic alliance. This opens out into a more communal, and social sense of self, as being-for-others [. . .] and for me there is an additional potential state of being-for-all-others, which is perhaps an aspirational state of consciousness with a unified global and ethical attitude towards all beings. It's an expansive position, and in Chekhovian terms could be considered as a psychophysical gesture towards the world as a totally inter-related, inter-dependent organism which includes all living organisms, but also could embrace so-called inanimate entities too. This can form a deeply integrative relational sense towards the world as a total holistic entity. This suggests to me a kind of Chekhovian consciousness that implicates a cognitive parity between the rational and imaginative faculties which can offer a vast landscape of meaningful narratives with which to engage and cohere around creatively as well as therapeutically. (2016)

Sharp is, with Sarah Kane, one of the co-founders of the Michael Chekhov Centre UK (now Michael Chekhov UK). He produced and directed the documentary, *Michael Chekhov: The Dartington Years* (2002), drawing on archival material and interviews with people associated with the Chekhov Theatre Studio, including 'the contact generation' (Paul Rogers, William Elmhirst and Deirdre Hurst du Prey) along with actors and directors whose work has been significantly influenced by this approach (such as Graham Dixon and Simon Callow).

Zoe Brook, along with Byrony Murray, founded Bazooka Arts in 2001. Bazooka Arts is a participatory arts organization, working in and with communities in the west of Scotland, primarily North Lanarkshire but also South Lanarkshire, Glasgow, East Renfrewshire and Ayrshire, in areas with higher levels of health inequality, isolation and unemployment. Some participants have been referred to the organization from health and social services or other statutory and voluntary agencies. It's mission is both ambitious for, and attentive to, the needs of the people it works with: 'We believe that creativity has the potential to act as a positive agent for personal, social and cultural transformation. This has led us to develop a person-centered approach to creative practice which is based on the principles of empowerment and equality' (www.bazookaarts.co.uk, accessed 12 December 2017). This commitment and care is illustrated throughout participatory arts practices which address people's lived experience including *A Time for Passion* (2015), a devised play with participants with longer-term mental health difficulties, including grief, depression and anxiety, commissioned for the Scottish Mental Health Arts and Film Festival which toured to regional community halls. Although Brook had studied Theatre and Politics, including Russian and Soviet theatre, she didn't encounter Michael Chekhov until she did Improbable Theatre's *Improbable Lessons* training which drew upon Chekhov's techniques, particularly **qualities of movement**. For Brook, who had also studied Dramatherapy and Alexander Technique, the Chekhov work gave her 'such an experience of embodiment' (2017) that she sought further training with Graham Dixon. Brook frames her work within a crucible of influences:

> I work across a continuum depending on the context. My community work is underpinned by therapeutic practice and what led me to Dramatherapy was Augusto Boal. When I was an undergraduate I studied Theatre and Politics – I was really interested in how theatre affects political change and that led me to Boal's experience about it being about psychology, particularly in first world contexts. Chekhov's work creatively accesses what the Boal work is trying to get to – it embodies empowerment. I liked the core of Boal's ideas but there was something missing and the Chekhov work helped me find out what that was (2017).

Brook's acknowledgement of embodied empowerment has strong resonance with Chekhov's imperative of '*contact with our being*' detailed in his classes (LTT: 11 April 1936):

> *There are two ways to speak to pupils: (1) From intellect to intellect, (2) From one's whole being to another whole being. The intellectual way tends to make one speak more quickly. [. . .] In our lessons we must emphasise the speaking and behaviour and the contact with our being.*

For Brook, Chekhov informs all aspects of her practice, particularly work with groups who have experienced adversity and trauma, and she has been actively engaged in disseminating Chekhov's techniques with Scottish Dramatherapists, the British Association of Dramatherapists and the therapeutic theatre company Theatre Tonic. Her practice is rooted in principles of equality and empowerment, 'That has always been the bottom line and it goes through the whole process – we make from people' (2017).

Hartley Jafine is an Applied Theatre practitioner who has been leading the use of theatre arts in healthcare and healthcare education in Canada. At McMaster University, Jafine teaches drama and arts-based courses in the Arts and Science programme, the

Bachelor of Health Sciences (Honours) programme and the School of Medicine. He is also a communication coach in the University of Toronto's Postgraduate Medical Education program and Interprofessional Arts-Based Educator at Baycrest, a research and teaching hospital specializing in long-term care. Jafine's research addresses the use of drama in healthcare training and environments, supporting healthcare professionals' engagement with patients and colleagues to improve clinical competencies, raise critical consciousness and build wellness. He has developed work in Canada, the United States, England, and at the Centre for Alternative Theatre Training (CATT) in Kosovo (2009) and The Netherlands (2018), an international and intercultural forum for advanced training for artists. Jafine's approach is informed by theatre, educational pedagogy, play and health sciences, particularly Brian Sutton-Smith's *The Ambiguity of Play* (1997), Donald Schon's *Reflective Practitioner* (1984), David Kolb's *Experiential Learning* (1983), Paolo Freire's *Pedagogy of the Oppressed* (1968), Postman and Weingartner's *Teaching as a Subversive Activity* (1969) and, in Improv Theatre, Kat Koppett's *Training to Imagine* (2012).

Effie Makepeace is a community theatre practitioner, artist and researcher who has extensive experience working in collaboration with grassroots organizations in development contexts in Malawi and India as well as with community-based organizations in the UK, including Cardboard Citizens, a theatre company that works primarily with and for people who have experience of homelessness. Effie's practice is informed by her undergraduate training in Drama and Theatre Arts at Goldsmiths (UK) and her postgraduate studies in Participation, Power and Social Change at Sussex University's Institute of Development Studies (UK). Her work facilitates community dialogue and debate through participation, access and meaningful engagement with groups, often sustained over years, in collaboration with organizations attending to specific social issues. Between 2012 and 2014, Effie worked with Nanzikambe, a Malawian grassroots organization addressing critical social issues, including HIV in prison, access to justice and violence against women. With Nirantar in India, she developed training programmes to support understanding of theatre as a research methodology and mode of dissemination of the research findings about young people's attitudes towards sexuality, gender, marriage and caste. Effie's practice is informed by Michael Chekhov and Augusto Boal, as well as education and development practices, including Training for Transformation, an education project in South Africa informed by Paulo Freire's pedagogy of the oppressed, teaching literacy through images made with the body. Anna Herrmann's and Sara Clifford's *Making a Leap: Theatre of Empowerment* (1998), Michael Rhod's *Theatre for Community, Conflict and Dialogue: The Hope is Vital Training Manual* (1998) and Clark Baim and Sally Brook's *The Geese Theatre Handbook: Drama with Offenders and People at Risk* (2002) are key critical sources.

In the following section of the chapter, I attend to the specific ways in which Sharp, Brook, Jafine and Makepeace reflect on the implications of a Chekhov-informed practice and how these observations offer insights to artists and students working within the wider landscape of socially engaged practice.

## 3 'An expansive position': Negotiating relational practices

In all applied, therapeutic and community theatre practices, people (participants and those who are facilitating the creative or therapeutic space) are in a constant state of negotiation and, potentially, cooperation – a fundamental relational practice identified by Chekhov in his entreaty to readers in To the Actor. In *Together: The Rituals, Pleasures and Politics of Cooperation* (2012), the sociologist Richard Sennett acknowledges that cooperation is not a given, nor a starting point but rather a craft which 'emerges from practical activity' (6) between people that requires 'the skill of understanding and responding to one another in order to act together [. . .] a thorny process, full of difficulty and ambiguity' (x). Applied Theatre practices, attending to a wide range of explicit intentions – from the therapeutic and personal to the social and political – are shaped by the implicit desires and fears of all involved: they are sites of difficult cooperation, of negotiation of the self in relation to others. Sennett proposes that interactions should be dialogical (as opposed to dialectical): expression should be subjunctive (as opposed to declarative); and social exchange should be empathetic (as opposed to sympathetic). Sennett's critical framework for affective relational practices resonates with Chekhov's techniques and how they facilitate the development of an expanded sense of self and different relational encounters with others, two fundamental and distinctive areas attended to by Sharp, Brook, Makepeace and Jafine in their reflections on practice. In 'Love in Our Theatre: Art or Profession?' Chekhov distils this commitment to engage in relational encounters with others through an expanded sense of self as love:

> Real and true love begins when we start loving every human being regardless of blood relationships or nationality, but only because it is another human being and we are able to love him without any specific reason, without the prefix of 'me' or 'mine'. *That* is the highest aspect of human love. (Chekhov and Leonard 1963: 19–20)

For Sharp, the practical philosophical considerations of what it is to be human – the selves that are in relational play as a person navigates the world – have strong roots in Chekhov's work. In the praxis symposium session, Sharp shared his experience of engaging with Chekhov to support a therapeutic practice, returning to his opening words in *To the Actor* (2006: 1),

> Our bodies can be either our best friends or worst enemies. It is a known fact that the human body and psychology influence each other and are in constant interplay. Either an undeveloped or muscularly overdeveloped body may easily dim the activity of the mind, dull the feelings or weaken the will. Because each field and profession is prey to characteristic occupational habits, diseases and hazards which inevitable affect its workers and practitioners, it is seldom that we find a complete balance or harmony between the body and psychology.

Sharp's offer to the participants in the praxis symposium was clear: 'I'd like to open a space in each of us so that we may become more acquainted with those hazards' (2016). This 'space in each of us' is, in Chekhov's terms, our heart, *'You must open your hearts. Without this gymnastics, without this heroic act, you will never get the artistic feelings. You must open your heart with tears and pain – but you must do it – otherwise your heart will be in a nice box, but nobody will see the jewel that is lying there'* (TAITT: 27 September 1937). To facilitate this, Sharp invited the group of artists and academics to work towards finding an equilibrium – moving around the space, moving towards space, being curious about the space, noticing things in it and what it triggers in their imagination.

As participants moved through space – finding different ways of travelling through it, backwards, sideways, hands on the floor, long sweeping strides, undulating, playing with height and tempo – they were encouraged to register the differences between these ways of moving, to find pleasure in this recognition of difference between everyday movement and the full-bodied psychophysical movement they were now exploring. Then Sharp encouraged people to 'start to bring yourself back into contact with the people in the room, start to make eye contact, give yourself a chance to register that person, trying to glimpse the expansiveness of their humanity, to make contact with them'. The language of making **contact**, registering, acknowledging the 'expansiveness' of another's humanity is fundamental to Michael Chekhov, as it is in person-centred therapeutic practices and approaches in the wider field of applied and community performance, where there is an imperative to acknowledge a person, their histories, desires and contradictions, without the need for someone to narrate them publicly.

Considerations about the conditions and power dynamics at play in relational encounters – specifically between the therapist and the client but also in teacher and student or facilitator and participant relationships – were explicitly addressed by Sharp, referring to Carl Rogers's (1959, 1994, 2014) articulation of the core conditions for successful therapy – 'the capacity to be empathetic; to be congruent in yourself as an individual and not to be put out of shape by something that happened; to have unconditional positive regard for the person and to try and create some sort of relationship to that person' (2016). The exercises Sharp shared with the group facilitated an embodied understanding of how these conditions could be activated and attended to. Crucially, Sharp acknowledged people's different capacities to 'tolerate intimacy' and offered exercises as structures for people to test and assess their tolerance of intimacy – how much they wanted to make themselves open to another, how willing they were to 'meet' the other person in their acknowledgement of themselves and of others. The following exercise demonstrates how this idea was explored in practice and demonstrates some of the skill required to develop, in Sennett's terms, the difficult craft of cooperation.

As the participants gathered at one side of the room, Sharp encouraged people to walk across the space and locate themselves in the space, depending on their level of identification to the following questions:

> If anyone who owns a pet.
> If anyone is a carnivore.
> If you are happy in the house you live.
> If you've ever been at somebody's death bed.
> If you've ever known somebody that's been in therapy.
> If you've ever had any therapeutic experience at all.
> If you consider yourself to be political.
> If you consider yourself to be on some sort of spiritual journey whatever that might mean to you.

While this exercise may be very familiar, the kinds of questions – addressing death, therapy, personal politics and spirituality – were less so, particularly in a context where people had only recently met. People moved across the space, witnessing each other, without comment. Once again, the idea of being open to recognizing the expansiveness of a person's humanity and being open to being seen by another, was not only talked about but felt, and this prepared participants for Sharp's following series of invitations:

> Go to the person in the room who you may feel might be the most difficult person in the room to work with.
> Find out who they are, why they are here.
> Find a space for the pair of you.
> In silence, just make eye contact.
> I want you to see them and let them see you.
> If you can tolerate it, see if you can be a bit closer.
> Imagine these people as children, with parents. Let your imagination explore.

The exercise ran for fifteen silent minutes after which the group was differently connected and configured in relation to themselves and to others. This invitation to be open, to see an other, to be seen by others, is informed by Chekhov's principles and techniques articulated in *To the Actor* where the need to find a way to connect to people is fundamental to the creation and negotiation of ensemble: 'The actor must develop within himself a sensitivity to the creative impulse of others. [. . .] An improvising ensemble lives in a constant process of giving and taking. [. . .] He tries to be aware of the *individual* presence of each. He makes an effort, figuratively speaking, "to open his heart" and admit everyone present' (2006: 41–2, emphasis in original). For Chekhov, these conditions of sensitization create a listening, attentive, acknowledging and responsive actor – a co-participant in the process of theatre-making.

Chekhov's invitation to open the heart demonstrated throughout Sharp's session in the praxis symposium, also resonates with Alison Jeffers who, in *Refugees, Theatre and Crisis: Performing Global Identities* (2012), examines a range of theatre practices with and about refugees. She engages with Emmanuel Levinas's ethical encounters to consider the possibility of artists and participants working 'alongside' the Other, face to face and, she proposes, shoulder to shoulder, without the need to be explicitly told anything or everything about a person or conversely to accept what is revealed through an encounter as an aspect of a person rather than the totality of their being (159–62). Sharp's approach, informed by his therapeutic work, strips bare the power dynamic between participants and the figure who leads a creative/therapeutic/pedagogic process (artist/ therapist/teacher) with participants/clients/students in contexts where people are asked to bring themselves – imaginatively embodied. This enables an expanded sense of self which, in turn, facilitates different relational encounters with others.

In the following section I consider how Brook, Sharp, Makepeace and Jafine have engaged with Chekhov's techniques to support the development of a boundaried space where participants negotiate the personal and the biographical through visualization techniques such as the **imaginary body** and work with **atmosphere**.

## 4 Embodied awareness

In my experience of working with groups in a range of institutional settings in Ireland, the UK and Brazil, including schools, pupil referral units, prisons and residential care settings, working through theatre can be, initially, a daunting and even unappealing prospect for participants. People are often apprehensive about 'acting', remembering lines, standing before an audience and their lack of training or skill as performers. In these contexts, it's imperative that the theatre-making approaches both attend to this concern and support people in bringing themselves, their experience and expertise to the process. In her reflections on her extensive experience of working in communities with high levels of health inequality, isolation and unemployment, Zoe Brook explicitly identifies the ways in which Chekhov's techniques, particularly visualization, **imaginary centres** and imaginary bodies have the capacity to support participants' radical engagement with their own bodies, their relationships with others and ignite a sense of agency. During the symposia, she led an exercise inviting participants to experience and reflect on their shifting sense of awareness of and attunement to their bodies, as well as the emotions evoked during the exercises. She offered the following prompts, giving time between them to allow participants to adjust and embody the imaginatively activated physical experiences:

> Move around the space, finding space, moving through space.
> Imagine that there's something pulling you forwards, it's compelling you forwards.
> The force disappears and you are moving through space again.
> Feel a magnet pulling at your back but you are trying to move forwards anyway.
> And then it releases and you move.
> Now you experience a pull from the front.
> Imagine you are being pulled from the back.
> Imagine you are being pulled from the ceiling.

After the exercise, participants offered detailed reflections, highlighting careful attention to shifts in their perception of the body, the space around them, their relationships with others and how this relates to their embodied imagination. The symposium's group of self-selecting artists and academics already had a hinterland and vocabulary for talking about theatre, but as Brook explained, the groups she works with, who don't have this expertise, also find a similar impact on their sense of embodied awareness. To demonstrate this, she made the distinction between an invitation to move the body through a command and an invitation to move the body through visualization, 'It worries me how little awareness people have of their own bodies, how limited their use of them is. If you say, 'stretch' then people huff. But if you say, 'imagine your arm is being lifted-up by a piece of string', there's full extension' (2016).

In my experience of working in institutional contexts, particularly prisons, I have witnessed participants' discomfort doing any kind of physical warm-up, however gentle this may be. People's bodies' capacity for mobility, to articulate a range of movement, is reduced because they have been, literally, confined within the prison and the strictures of institutional regime: the majority of their day is spent in cells with regulated movement between specific places assigned for particular activities: extra-daily movement is relegated to gym activity. The discomfort felt during warm-ups is an expression of people's awareness of their body's adjustment and movement outside of a limited range. Working with Chekhov, particularly imagining an external impulse which acts as a catalyst for gesture and extra-daily movement, allows people to think through their body rather than feel like their head is telling their body how to move. This apparently small but significant shift has radical implications:

Brook articulates the potential social and political efficacy of Chekhov's techniques when working in community contexts:

> I remember really clearly, in a women's health project, how powerful it was. We worked with a **quality of movement** exercise and people feeling present: people who hadn't felt present getting a perspective on when they are standing and noticing a space between themselves and somebody else, when they are actually in control of their actions and when they are not. [. . .] They also experienced how using thought processes to change your movement can impact on your emotions. They were exercising self-awareness, its power over what you do. The impact of trauma on people and adverse childhood experiences cuts people off from emotion, it numbs people. Chekhov's techniques seem to work for people that have been removed from themselves for a long time but not in a 'let's go back into this traumatic event': it's purely from a 'let's imagine that this is happening'. It allows them access body and emotion.

Brook's observations echo Chekhov's recognition:

> *Your body must be in a certain way a wise body. Our exercises, which are very simple, are giving to the body wisdom. This special kind of wisdom is what we are aiming at. [. . .] It is possible to go about our daily life and still keep these exercises in our consciousness. They will, in that way, become part of you.* (LTT: 23 May 1936)

Brook's and Chekhov's articulation of the power of the imagination in activating an individual's experiential sense of awareness and agency is an important proposition to facilitators working in applied and community theatre where ideas of agency and activism are often aligned to public articulations of change through practices influenced by the legacy of Augusto Boal, the Brazilian theatre director, pedagogue and activist who was founder of Theatre of the Oppressed and Legislative Theatre. While Boal's practices can be seen to be part of a lineage of direct responses to Chekhov's provocation in the prospectus for his theatre studio – 'If the new theatre is to have meaning, the audience too must play its part' – the means by which both practitioners address this, vary greatly. While Boal was directly involved in political action – from the Landless Workers Movement through to his election as a *vereador* (city councillor) in Rio de Janeiro (1993–7) – Brook's reflections on the ways in which aspects of Chekhov's work can be blended into an eclectic and responsive approach to working in and with specific communities, reveal a very different kind of political efficacy that opens up realms of agency and engagement for individuals in their negotiation of their selves in the world. Brook (2016) reflected:

> So many people that we work with cannot see the external world because the internal world is so overwhelming. If you can find the impulse outside of yourself, you can find a way not to be drowned by your inner life, by your emotion, by your experiences. To use your imagination that your whole body is being pulled by a magnet, or that your whole energy is coming from your knee, or that your centre is outside your body, is a new thinking with the imagination. Your imagination can give you an awareness of your body and the outside world through sensory imagination not just visual imagination. Your imagination becomes your agent for change.

Brook's experiences of working in and with specific communities in Scotland offers a helpful counterpoint to Effie Makepeace's reflections on her work with Nanzikambe, the

Malawian community organization. During this time (2012–14), she was working closely with co-facilitator Dipo Katimba and four groups of marginalized people, including prisoners and young women from two townships who were identified by the organization as vulnerable. The young women were seventeen to twenty-five years old: most had children and were single mothers, some were sex workers, all had dropped out of school. Makepeace introduced the distinct context for the practice, 'The work was framed as actor training, as learning skills – often this isn't foregrounded in applied and socially engaged work – but because it was actor training, the groups were developing an awareness of process, an awareness of learning. We worked with them for over four years and many of the group are now employed by Nanzikambe and other organisations' (2018). Unlike explicitly therapeutic practice, Makepeace's work, framed within the context of skills development, didn't address events in people's lives but rather called upon fantasy, story and memory, particularly when building characters:

> Some Applied Theatre processes explicitly support people to think about others, to put yourself in their shoes. We took some of those ideas and were rigorous in embodying that person. Chekhov talks about **crossing the threshold** and this supported people getting into character, to imagine that people are standing in front of you and you are, literally, stepping into the them [using the technique of the imaginary body]. We treated it like work – the exercises gave you permission to do that. In order for it to be realized, it needs to be rigorous: as a participant you can't half engage, you fully engage, you embody' (2018).

Again, the processes and principles underpinning Makepeace's practice resonate with Chekhov's idea of 'open-heartedness' in the development of ensemble, Sennett's acknowledgement of the need for empathy rather than sympathy in cooperation, Jeffers' proposal that participants and facilitators are 'shoulder to shoulder' in their consideration of the Other and Sharp's illustration of the ways in which he supports his clients to negotiate the psychotherapeutic space.

The Chekhov-informed training facilitated new skills, but there were particular challenges in negotiating linguistic and cultural differences, particularly in the linking of action and emotion. While Chekhov never talks directly of emotion, rather **movement qualities** or atmospheres that trigger sensations, he did refer to 'creative feelings [. . .] cleansed of the personal element' (undated [1944]: 38) and Makepeace's longer reflection echoes this distinction, offering insight into both the context of the work and the negotiated blending required to support the group:

> This particular group of young women we were working with were not used to talking about feelings and had less experience than the men in prison who had been in school longer, whose realm of experience was more. I knew from my own experience that moulding your body into a particular image can make you feel a particular psychophysical connection and, once you feel it, you can quickly go back there. I wanted see if that was possible with the group of young women but it was hard, partly because of language. The Chichewa language is a very rich language but doesn't have the same way of describing emotions as English which has specific words for each: in Chichewa the ways people feel are described in other ways. Not wanting to impose or ascribe English meanings we used examples of different emotions, trying to describe *this* kind of anger when you are

generally angry, *this* kind of anger when you are jealous to understand how this sensing of emotions worked. Even talking about imagination wasn't straightforward! Imagination was translated by Dipo as, 'someone creating a thought in their head of anything, or something, that could be or happen even if it's not really happening'! When we were working with emotions, we'd choose core emotions [. . .] then, drawing on Chekhov's imaginary centres, we'd try to place these emotions somewhere in the body, thinking about where it would be in the body and what it would it look like – would it be spikey, fluffy, red? People did start to talk about the heart being on fire, to use images that they were familiar with and placing them somewhere. It was tempting to want everything to work exactly as it had for me in my context in the UK, but this can never be the case. We found a way to use the same technique but revising our assumptions about emotion and imagination, and what they should look like. As a white, British practitioner this is especially important considering my presence in that space and country but also when using another European practitioner. What mattered was the process that the women were going through and them finding their own sense in it, and us then learning from that. (2018)

Makepeace's reflection on the challenges and limitations of working with Chekhov – of addressing the balance of influence with her practice – illustrates the ongoing need for artists and teachers to be alert and responsive to the overall needs of participants and the aims of each project in specific cultural contexts. It is imperative not to assume that ideas or practices can easily translate between cultures or even, potentially, generations, and this raises critical questions about equitable participation – an easy aspiration to articulate but a practically challenging ambition to be realized in applied and community theatre practices. For example, intergenerational work, particularly work in residential care homes, with primary school-aged children and older people, offers specific challenges to practitioners supporting people to negotiate different life experiences, different physical capacities. For some older people, arthritis or osteoporosis can impact severely on mobility and confidence. Working with Chekhov, through external impulses such as movement quality, **gesture** and atmosphere, can ignite imaginative and embodied responses supporting an engagement with gesture rather than a concern with dexterity in achieving a particular move that facilitates a more equitable participation, regardless of age, experience or ability. In Hartley Jafine's experience, this shift in focus from the internal impulse to the external catalyst:

> takes pressure off people to come up with something and allows them to step to the side of themselves, to be self-aware rather than self-conscious. It's authentic, based on person's own capacity rather than an ideal version that they may or make not reach (2018).

## 5 Authenticity, capacity and tolerance

The potential for Chekhov's techniques to address the delicate balance between self-awareness and self-consciousness is highlighted by Sharp in his therapeutic practice. While being careful to anonymize these moments of encounter, during the praxis symposium he identified specific ways in which Chekhovian influences enabled him to support people responding to traumatic situations through imaginary body and visualization techniques to articulate, through their bodies as well as through words, moments of personal crises and understanding: to find a way to either engage with or move through these moments in a way that was not re-feeling the psychological trauma of the events themselves. In the first example, Sharp reflected on a moment where, at the end of a session with a new client, the young man suddenly cried out in anguish and asked to be held.

> There's an ethical taboo that you don't touch people and yet this man was distressed. I gave him a moment to be upset and, so we could end a session without him feeling that his needs hadn't been met, or that he was shamed, I facilitated a way for him to unfold his body [from being collapsed over] and be in a sitting position, back in the room with me because he'd gone somewhere else. I don't know why it occurred, I was not consciously thinking, I know, I'm going to do some Michael Chekhov here – there was something intuitive in that space where he needed, somehow, to be met in the room.

Sharp, in finding a way to 'meet' the young man was, in Chekhov's words 'with' him. In *Lessons for Teachers*, Chekhov spoke with reference to teachers and students, but while the terms of the relationship differ – therapist and client – the imperative remains: '*You must always feel what is going on in your pupils. This is most important*' (LTT: 11 April 1936), there is a necessity to support students/artists/clients in '*the feeling that you are with them in what they are doing*' (LTT: 13 April 1936). In a later session with the same client, Sharp worked on developing trust, again drawing on Chekhov's attention to supporting through embodiment and use of gesture:

> We were across the room from each other and I invited him to see what it's like to create a space that feels right. I made a shape that was quite open and expansive, my arms were up, we made eye contact. There's something in that moment of expansion that says, 'I'm here for you.' I invited him to mirror, to meet me in a kind of openness. He was a tall man and he was clenched. Then quite awkwardly, he started to raise his arms a very little. That was his sense of open. So I lowered my arms to make it more tolerable.

Over the following months, Sharp continued to work with the client doing similar exercises until the man found himself in a position where he could, still hesitantly, raise his arms more fully, expanding and opening himself in a way that he felt able to. Returning to this gesture offered both Sharp and the client a visual articulation of his 'tolerance of intimacy' and how this shifted over time.

Sharp shared another example of working with a client where he engaged more explicitly with Chekhovian ideas of **psychological gesture**, imaginary centres and crossing the threshold. In this example, Sharp acknowledges the influence of Gestalt therapy, where there is a strong sense that the body will tell something: the therapist draws attention, but not judgement, to a specific gesture or posture and invites the client to question why they might hold themselves in a particular way. When one particular client spoke about her husband, Sharp noticed that her body started to show discomfort and when he asked why, she said, 'When I think about him, just inside [. . .] its spikey, icy, he makes me so angry.' Sharp invited her to physicalize the image and to give the image to him. When he asked how she felt no longer holding the image she said, 'It's fantastic'. He then asked her what he should do with this image and she told him that she couldn't leave it with him, 'so she took it back, and rather reluctantly put the image back inside her. It became clear that there was a strong image that she'd identified and that for a moment she'd had a feeling of what it was like not to carry that feeling, that object, that entity within her' (2016). In another session, when the client identified that she felt undervalued at work and wanted to address this but couldn't, Sharp invited her to use the imaginary body exercise and to imagine the woman who *could* address it, and inhabit her body with all its psychophysical characteristics. He recounted the exchange between them:

> *What would it be like to step into that?*
> She was hesitant.
> *Would you like to give that a go?*
> And she rather tentatively stepped in and took on this body and she started to walk around the room.
> *Talk to me, what does it feel like?*
> Good. Really good.
> *What would you say?*
> I'm going to talk to my boss, tell them to send me on that course and I deserve at least another two grand.
> *So you could do that?*
> Yes, of course I could, why not?
> Then slowly she slipped out of the character and said, *she* could do it, *I* couldn't.
> *But you know now what it would feel like to be that person.*

In this example, the woman was invited to cross the threshold, to step into and out of the imaginary body, to embody the person who had the capacity to undertake actions that the woman, at that moment, felt unable to. Sharp's reflections that, 'imagination, once expanded to fit some object will never return to its original size. She can never be the person who didn't know what it would be like to be in that body. You could never take that away from her' (2016), echo Brook's observations: 'Your imagination can give you an awareness of your body and the outside world through sensory imagination not just visual imagination' (2017). Both acknowledge the power of the imagination as an agent for change. Through the visualization techniques and imaginary body, Sharp's clients were facilitated in articulating something that may be challenging if not impossible to put into words, principles not dissimilar to aspects of play therapy. Fleming also connects Chekhov's work with play practices (2013) and discusses this in her chapter in this publication. In both examples, Sharp's experience of Chekhov allowed for a careful but radically expanded invitation to support his clients to find ways to embody, reflect and move through the physical manifestations of trauma. For Sharp, although he'd never want to see something framed as 'Chekhov Therapy Training', he acknowledges how Chekhov offers creative ways 'that get past the horrible shackles of supposed talking therapies, as if everything can be resolved in a talking way. I believe it can't' (2016).

Hartley Jafine's work in healthcare education supports medical residents who have been identified as requiring communication support and/or have failed oral examinations, which assess knowledge and the ways in which they present themselves in the role of a healthcare professional. Many of those referred to Jafine for coaching have been reported as 'having trouble commanding a room. They'll step into a room and don't have a presence. Or when they are explaining a treatment plan to a patient, they are not performing clearly or with any degree of confidence so a patient doubts their abilities' (2018). Jafine's one-to-one training with them supports them to take on a role that they can rehearse so that when they enter a space, they can command it, demonstrating knowledge and confidence. This sense of commanding the space includes the pragmatics of uncertainty, where a doctor may not know the answer to a patient's query but holds an atmosphere of 'comfortable uncertainty' while saying, 'I don't know but I will find out for you' (2018). For Jafine, this is where he makes explicit links between Chekhov and his training, addressing the reading of the patient's embodied gesture as well as their symptoms. This preparedness to enter the room, to cross the threshold of the clinical space, echoes Chekhov's 'Lessons for Teachers': *'As a teacher, you must be (1) active, (2) giving, (3) you must enter the room as a teacher. [. . .] 'Prepare your entrance. When you cross the threshold, you must be already concentrated on giving with as much love as you can feel'* (LTT: 11 April 1936). In the sessions, Jafine and the healthcare professionals 'reflect and talk about their biases and assumptions, based on gesture and how people hold themselves in a space, that impact clinical practice' (2018), referring to the embodied performance of both the healthcare professional and the patient. He encourages them to think about how their own body speaks volumes and what it says to patients, 'if they read a body as saying, 'I'm off to the next thing', it can prevent patients from talking to them as they are reading the body as not wanting to engage' (2018). To address this Jafine asks, 'What is the gesture that you want to perform to convey the role that you're about to play? How do you enter a space and perform without saying anything?' (2018). He supports the residents to attend to and read the bodies of patients, what they say through their gestures as well as their words and how this infuses the atmosphere of the space, 'How do they move? What are they doing in the space that might not have any relationship to what they are actually saying? How are they holding themselves? If they came in saying they are not feeling well, if they are holding their arm, what is their gesture saying to you?' (2018).

## 6 Space-making: Working with atmosphere

One of the areas of greatest potential for working with Michael Chekhov's techniques is specifically in relation to space-making and working with atmosphere. This is particularly challenging in many applied and community contexts where theatre projects take place in non-theatre spaces, in the rooms that happen to be available in community centres, village halls, churches, schools, an open shaded space in a prison yard: spaces where the sounds, smells and rhythms of institutional life are relentless and infuse the theatre-making space with a distinctive atmosphere. It is one thing to have a room to work in; it's another to create a space within it that runs parallel to its daily function. One of the most difficult environments I've ever worked in was a pupil referral unit in South East London with fourteen-year-olds who were excluded from school. Together with the visual artist, Yun Jung Ko, we worked with the young people for more than a year, meeting once a week on a Thursday afternoon in the dining hall. This venue offered an abundance of physical space but it reeked with the smell of the just-eaten lunch and echoed with the sound of pots and pans clanking as they were being washed up in the kitchen. The young people's concentration was easily disrupted and it took considerable commitment on all our behalves to create an alternative atmosphere within a room so strongly infused – aurally, visually and olfactorily – with a particular function. While an engagement with Chekhov's work on atmosphere could have supported a playful and rigorous acknowledgement of the impact of the circumstances, I am not entirely convinced that this would have been enough to subvert them. In the following section, I consider how engaging with Chekhov's atmosphere has influenced the site where the theatre-making takes places and supports people in reading, responding to or deflecting firmly established atmospheres within them.

In addition to the remedial one-to-one work within postgraduate medical education addressed in the previous section, Jafine has piloted a medical improv curriculum with residents in the Department of Family and Community Medicine at Sunnybrook Hospital, Toronto. This curriculum was part of their mandatory 'academic half-days'. Jafine reflects on a particular exercise that resonates with Chekhov's use of atmospheres: 'People are in a group and we ask two people to leave the room. When they come back they need to diagnose the space – to take the emotional temperature in the room. Linking this to a clinical practice setting, I invite them to think about it as improv – you can't prescribe what's going to happen when you walk into a room but you'll have to read this space quickly and respond' (2018). Jafine's blending of influences – including Chekhov, Koppett's work on improv and Kolb's work on experiential learning – support the healthcare professionals' capacity to diagnose, understand and navigate their encounters with patients.

While working in a very different economic and cultural context to Jafine, Makepeace's reflections on practice extend the possibilities of working with atmosphere in different socially engaged practices. In her critical reflections on her practice working with men in prison in Malawi, Makepeace highlights how adaptations of Chekhov's work impacted the ways in which a space, heavily inscribed with institutional authority, was shifted through the practice of movement qualities in different ways:

> I always do something based on **moulding, flowing, flying** and **radiating** but it's more of a game. We divided the ground into four squares – into earth, fire, water, air – and the group moved as an ensemble from one square to another. I remember thinking, 'the group is going to think, what is this?!' but they loved it. Another time, we got them to imagine walking through the different elements rather than embodying them. They said as they were moving through resistant substances, that that was their daily life, they could feel it and understand it. (Makepeace 2018)

This example of dividing a physical space into four areas, each with its own distinctive atmosphere related to the movement qualities, reveals the possibility of rewriting the established institutional atmosphere through theatre. James Thompson, in *Performance Affects: Applied Theatre and the End of Effect* (2011), encourages artists, academics and commissioners to attend not only to the impact and effect of socially engaged practices but to the *affect* these practices engender. Importantly, the practices and projects that Jafine and Makepeace have developed achieve their remarkable personal and social effects through a rigorous attention to theatre practices employed and the affect they produced. This repositioning of the lens and value-framework with which socially engaged theatre practices are viewed is critical to discourse, practice and training in the field and will be addressed more fully in the conclusion.

## 7 Conclusion: 'The agent of change is your imagination'

Theatre in Applied, Therapeutic and Social Contexts is extraordinarily diverse. However, each project shares a commitment to facilitate ways for people to meet and make work together. But as Martin Sharp, Zoe Brook, Hartley Jafine and Effie Makepeace highlight, for people to meet one another – to genuinely see and acknowledge the person before them, to be open to one another, to acknowledge the expansiveness of their humanity – demands care, rigour and playful responsiveness in order to cultivate the craft of cooperation.

In my research with artists and organizations working in socially engaged contexts, I attend to the ways in which people reflect on, identify and map who and what shapes their work. Genealogies of influence are often gloriously eclectic and, necessarily, personal: from formative moments as a child seeing a piece of theatre that cracks open a new world of possibility, through to conscious decisions to undertake a particular training, sometimes in theatre, sometimes in another discipline (such as dementia care, criminal justice, early years education) to support their understanding of the context they are working in; from the influence of a particular teacher at high school, training or university who encouraged them to interrogate the world through art, through to stumbling across a book that, because of the synchronicity of timing and a person's desire to find new ways to connect with audiences, has become pivotal in their personal and professional development. Each artist's work is informed by a patchwork of influences, not all of which carry the same weight or momentum. Together they inform an individual's approach rather than dictate a particular methodology. The question of influence and the recognition, assimilation and acknowledgement of how it informs each individual artist and their work, is something that may be talked about between artists informally but, too rarely, is made explicit within a wider public discourse about a specific project. It is interesting to note that, as with a wider body of socially engaged practice, the publicly available documentation about the work developed by Baars, Cerullo, Coffey, Scharler, Andrees, Andrees, Michelson, Drohan, Wintsch-Heinen and Wintsch referred to at the beginning of the chapter, identifies *who* the work is with (for example, adults with learning disabilities), *where* it takes place (for example, residential care homes), and *what* it seeks to do, socially and politically (for example, to develop an inclusive pedagogy). However, there is no explicit reference in this documentation as to the artistic or pedagogical influences which shape their artistic practices, including Michael Chekhov. This knowledge is shared informally between people through Michael Chekhov networks, including Michael Chekhov UK, MICHA and Michael Chekhov Europe (MCE), at the Michael Chekhov New Pathways Praxis Symposia (2016) that gave rise to this publication and the Citizen Artist Workshop at MICHA's International Michael Chekhov Workshop (2017). This articulation of influence between people and the absence of acknowledgement in print raises an epistemological challenge: how do people working outside of Chekhov networks find out about this work? How can artists working in socially engaged contexts be supported in testing and adapting Michael Chekhov's approach if they are not aware of the diverse and ambitious practices that exist? I approached a broad network of artists and academics working in socially engaged theatre in China, Japan, Australia, South Africa, Ireland, Canada and Jamaica and asked: are you aware of Michael Chekhov? Is your practice in any way influenced by his work? While many people had a fuzzy acknowledgement of Chekhov through undergraduate Drama programmes or independent reading, few acknowledged any experience or influence on their practice. This response was constructive in supporting my thinking about the content and structure of this chapter and what may be particularly useful to artists and students working in this area – from one-to-one therapeutic and coaching work through to large-scale community performance projects.

The other major influence on the shape and focus of this chapter was my experience of leading the MA Applied Drama: Theatre in Educational, Community and Social Contexts in Goldsmiths, University of London (2005–9). During this time, I was increasingly aware that the students – a wonderfully diverse group of students in terms of age, cultural heritage and experiences in arts, education, health and social care – were highly adept at talking about the government policies that shaped the landscape of socially engaged practices but sometimes needed support to develop a vocabulary to talk about the theatre practices tasked with this work in an equally rigorous way. We needed to spend more time attending to the Theatre in Applied Theatre. I had productive conversations with my then colleague, Cass Fleming, who, because of her significant experience as an actor-trainer, theatre director and producer working in a broad range of contexts from mainstream theatre to education and outreach departments in producing houses, understood the need for the students to extend their repertoire of theatre influences and blend these with their pedagogical theory and practice. She introduced the Applied Theatre students to Michael Chekhov's techniques. The impact was remarkable. Immediately, the students' focus shifted from the social expectations of the practice to the relational, dynamic and qualitative experience of the practice itself and how this could facilitate radical shifts in how an individual might see and navigate their world. The language of transformation, sometimes used in broad, optimistic brushstrokes, became more rigorous, careful and detailed as people reflected on the embodied experiences of participation rather than an intellectual understanding of it. Within the field of Applied Theatre, where work is usually funded by commissioners to realize a specific health, education, criminal justice or community development outcome, practitioners are often forced into talking about their work with reference to anticipated social outcomes, to speaking the language of policy. But this is only one kind of conversation, and it is imperative that artists and educators find a way to navigate this without limiting the parameters of their work and how it is perceived by those who have the power to commission and fund it.

Within the flourishing of Dramatherapy and specifically Applied Theatre programmes internationally – both university undergraduate and graduate programmes as well as continuous professional development training across the Southern and Northern Hemispheres – there is evidence of a keen interest from artists and students to understand the ways in which theatre may be engaged to 'probe beneath the surface' and address the 'serious', 'intricate' and 'tortuous' modern problems that people live and negotiate in their daily lives. The potential to extend and invigorate approaches to applied practice can only come to fruition if such training programmes attend to the 'theatre' in Applied Theatre. It is clear from the recent international surge in networks and publications about the ways in which Michael Chekhov's techniques are blended and adapted in professional and pedagogical practice that a rich body of experience and expertise exists in this field. There is now a confluence of circumstance that affords a unique opportunity to strategically support the articulation and expansion of Michael Chekhov technique in training and education through existing Chekhov networks and Applied Theatre programmes. Ultimately, Chekhov offers not only an approach to making theatre but a vocabulary to talk about it and why it matters. As Sharp reflects, 'Michael Chekhov gives a language to things that we sort of intuitively know – he gives us a creative vocabulary to talk to each other' (2016).

While it is impossible – and not desirable – to essentialize a nuanced range of applied, therapeutic and community practices in widely diverse social, cultural, economic and political contexts, there are some critical and creative imperatives, fundamental to this practice, that have informed the focus of the chapter: relational practice, space-making, the negotiation of the personal and the biographical, and the role of the artist/facilitator/therapist. Critical reflections of four practitioners who engage with Michael Chekhov's work – Zoe Brook, Martin Sharp, Effie Makepeace and Hartley Jafine – have illustrated the ways in which the politics, ethics and aesthetics of socially engaged practice are live, negotiated realities which ensure that 'the audience too plays its part' (Chekhov 1936: 18). Brook's (2016) reflections offer a closing provocation to artists working in applied, therapeutic and community contexts to explore the personal and potentially social and political implications of a Chekhov-informed, evolving, relational practice:

> The most important thing is to go into our bodies, connecting with our imaginations and to work from that place because that's where the power lies – that's the potential. [. . .] Through the Chekhov work, people begin to get a sense of their bodies, their bodies in space and their own sense of agency. If you don't know what your body is doing, what its relationship is to the outside, then you can't make changes. You can't make changes by trying to will it – it has to be through experience. The external impulse gives people an awareness of the outside world. When you begin to make contact with the outside world, when you see it, name it and you know it's *there*, then you know you are *here*. [*Brook placed her hand on her chest*]. You get a sense of where your power is through that.

## Notes

1. http://tinyhero.nl/ (accessed 12 December 2017).
2. See https://farbenbekennen.de/synformat/ (accessed 18 July 2019) for further information.
3. See the company website for further information: https://www.zbk-berlin.de (accessed 12 December 2017).
4. See the company website for further information: http://www.gladteater.dk/vaerdier-og-mal/ (accessed 12 December 2017).
5. https://www.buehne-moerel.ch/auffuehrungen/peer-gynt (accessed 18 July 2019).
6. Chekhov's commitment to engage with audiences with a wide range of theatre experience – as both audience and participants – was apparent in the work developing in and with the communities surrounding Dartington, for example, he opened the studio to children on Saturday mornings (Sharp 2002). The Studio also developed a devised/collaboratively written play for young audiences, *Troublemaker-Doublemaker* (1939).

# Cross-currents and conclusions

## CASS FLEMING AND TOM CORNFORD

## 1 Introduction

The chapters contained in this book focus predominantly on new pathways for Chekhov's techniques that have emerged primarily from practices developed in the UK. To have attempted a wider, comprehensive consideration of emergent developments in Chekhovian practices was beyond the remit of the research project of which this is the culmination. The 2016 New Pathways Research Event did, however, include a session of international exchange called 'Cross-Currents', which was chaired by Chekhov practitioner Gretchen Egolf and featured contributions from practitioners working in different parts of the world: Marjolein Baars (Netherlands), Ragnar Freidank and Joanna Merlin (USA) and Ulrich Meyer-Horsch (Germany). Joanna Merlin is the co-founder and president of Michael Chekhov Association (MICHA), and all four are faculty members of this US-based organization. The ideas and projects discussed by our counterparts beyond the UK intersect in numerous ways with the work explored in this volume. The aim of this final chapter, then, is to reflect on these intersections with practices outside the UK, to draw together some of the broader themes and conclusions of this book as a whole, and to look ahead to further possibilities for the extension of Chekhov's ideas into the future.

## 2 Cross-Currents 1: Marjolein Baars

Marjolein Baars, the artistic director of tiny hero productions in the Netherlands and vice president of MICHA, contributed to the Cross-Currents exchange via Skype from Amsterdam. As with the practitioners discussed by McAvinchey in Chapter 6 of this book, Baars has used Chekhov's techniques in health, social and community contexts for many years. Baars talked of her long-term work using Chekhov's methods in arts projects designed to help people living with dementia, their families and carers. In 2005 she started using and adapting Chekhov's techniques beyond the theatre in a project called 'Enjoy or Not (to) Enjoy', produced in an elderly person's home by The Suitcase Foundation. This project focused on developing art-related activities including singing, drawing and storytelling for people with dementia and their carers and families. Subsequently, it evolved into further projects and related training programmes from 2007 to 2009 for the same client groups: 'From Art to Craft' in old people's homes and 'How to Use your Art as a Craft', a programme of training for artists to apply their art in social and health care contexts. Among numerous activities, from 2009 to 2012 Baars and her collaborators were part of the European project 'Quality of Life: Using the arts to help people living with and affected by dementia' (Baars 2012) and extended the project 'From Art to Craft' into a care home and an institution for people with mental disabilities. Between 2013 and 2016, Baars continued working solo with The Suitcase Foundation on the project 'Living and playing in different realities' which had three strands: *Black Holes & Loose Ends*, a solo performance exploring the experience of dementia from different perspectives; a publication *Do-it-yourself Contact Suitcases*; a training programme for family members, volunteers, people with dementia and caretakers, and a do-it-yourself workbook, *Making Contact with Dementia* (2016). Baars explained how she used and transformed selected Chekhovian methods and principles in these projects. She drew, for instance, on the technique of **creative individuality** for the person with dementia. For the family members and caretakers, she designed training to explore the experience of dementia, which started with imaginative engagement, followed by an exploration guided by inner **gesture** (psychological gesture) to help them to better understand non-verbal communication, along with the ability to create or recognize **atmosphere**, and how personal and shared atmospheres relate to feeling/emotion. In addition, Baars drew on Chekhov's ensemble work, **play** and **improvisation**, in order to reframe what seem to be obstacles with communication as creative opportunities and to develop the notion of ensemble working practices in the health context. This training aimed to bring about change for the person with dementia, the family members and caretakers by adapting Chekhov's techniques to enact this change. In order to share her Chekhovian methodology more widely, Baars also developed a 'train-the-trainer' programme, so that staff at care homes can independently train colleagues, family members and volunteers.

In tandem with this work using Chekhov's techniques in relation to dementia, Baars also discussed her work in combining Chekhovian principles and practices with clown (which is also discussed in Chapter 1 of this book). When Chekhov explained to his students that artists have a *'responsibility for social life'* he argued that this can often be achieved using laughter and humour: *'to make people laugh, [is] to expand the human being. Laughter is like heat, like food, like a deep breath. Without humor the human being is not able to expand'* (TAITT: 16 January 1938). In 1991, Baars met Chekhov teacher Lenard Petit, who introduced her to clowning using Chekhov's principles and subsequently went to Russia on a Patch Adams Clown Trip, where she started social clowning. Since this time Baars has been using clown in health contexts around the world and from 2002 to 2004 organized clown trips under the name of 'La Troepe' to hospitals, refugee camps, old people's homes and institutes for people with mental disabilities in the Netherlands. She ran a Chekhov-based clown school in Amsterdam from 2002 to 2004 and currently works with clown at Michael Chekhov Studio in Brussels, with Belgium Contact Clowns, and with Sima, a school in Belgium for young people training to work in health care.

Baars feels there is great potential for the use of Chekhov's techniques in these health and social contexts and argues that you can use them to explore any social obstacle. She believes that the technique gives access to a creative language that enables practitioners to read and intervene in social situations. She argues that these benefits are extended by the capacity of clowning to find humour, explore the unknown without following rational logic, generate play and make mistakes. She also discusses the adaptations needed to use Chekhov's techniques beyond the theatre and explains that 'in using the technique you sometimes have to find equivalents for the language in the technique or use more 'normal' words, expressions, so it fits/matches the language of the target group' (2018). Baars strongly advocated for further work in this field in which practitioners use Chekhov's principles simply as a 'normal human being amongst others', exploring creativity in its broadest sense, beyond the theatre (2018).

## 3 Cross-Currents 2: Joanna Merlin and Ragnar Freidank

Joanna Merlin was a student of Michael Chekhov and is an actress, teacher and former casting director. She teaches in New York University's graduate acting programme at the Tisch School of the Arts and in 1999 she co-founded MICHA and took on the role of president. Since its inception, MICHA has trained thousands of artists and teachers from around the world in their annual two-week intensive programme. The organization has also translated and edited a version of Chekhov's *Lessons for Teachers* in English, German and Russian (Cerullo 2018) along with other materials and resources, including *Masterclasses in the Michael Chekhov Technique*, produced by MICHA in 2006. In 2016 MICHA introduced a Scholar Lab, which provides practitioner-scholars with the opportunity to continue their explorations of Chekhov's work with involvement from other practitioners, and a 'Theater of the Future: Open Space' event where artists can address complex issues facing their communities today. Ragnar Freidank is an actor, director, teacher, faculty and board member of MICHA. He trained as a mime and actor in Germany and studied Chekhov's techniques with Ted Pugh and Fern Sloan, with whom he has been collaborating in the Actors' Ensemble for the past twenty years. Freidank has taught extensively in the United States and is a faculty member of The New School in New York. With Pugh, Sloan and Merlin, he is co-founder of the Michael Chekhov School in Hudson, New York, a programme for performers and theatre-makers who train intensively in Chekhov technique.

Merlin and Freidank reflected on their recent teaching at the California State University two-week-long Summer Arts Programme, via Skype. They described the impact that their use of Chekhov's techniques had on the undergraduate students – many of whom were not Acting majors – that they worked with in that university programme. Merlin noted that using the techniques had brought about a significant change for many of the students in their social relations and everyday life, which was not the primary focus of the course but occurred through using the methodologies as a group. Over the course of the Summer Arts Programme, Merlin and Freidank supported the young people as they explored questions of identity and feelings of insecurity and self-consciousness through a creative exploration of a selection of Chekhov's methods and principles. The students became an ensemble, and this sense of contact and connection permeated their experiences beyond the studio, with Merlin reporting that it helped them to feel that 'it's okay to be me'. Freidank and Merlin noted that this feeling of connection, openness, agency and an increase in confidence is significant on a number of levels and was something that the students were able to take into other aspects of their studies in different subjects and their wider life. This would seem to show how teaching Chekhov's techniques can lead to students gaining an improved sense of well-being and a sense of their own agency in an indirect manner through creative engagement as an ensemble. This raises interesting questions about what these techniques may offer young people who have been socially marginalized and prevented from finding, taking and owning space. These aspects of Chekhov's method would appear to provide students with potentially transformative and empowering tools that can enable them to experience the agency to transform, change and challenge the world around them as well as themselves, points which resonate with the work of Zoe Brook discussed by McAvinchey in Chapter 6 of this book.

Freidank also talked about his experience of using Chekhov's techniques for various devised theatre projects, as did Chekhov (see Chapters 1 and 2). On one devised project, based on *A Midsummer Night's Dream*, Freidank used Open Space Technology (an approach to running meetings and conferences in which participants create and manage their own agenda) to help to create the show. Open Space Technology, originated by Harrison Owen, is also used by Improbable in the UK (whose co-founder and artistic director, Phelim McDermott, is probably the UK's most well-known exponent of Chekhov's work) and by MICHA, suggesting a number of important intersections between this practice and Chekhovian principles and methods. Freidank talked about the way in which Chekhov's techniques, in a devising context, seemed to 'live' in the actor-artists and enabled them to discover and use their own voices as creative artists, and not only actors. This correlated with the findings that Cornford and Fleming discuss in Chapters 1 and 2 of this book and supports the argument that Chekhov's techniques have a great deal to contribute to contemporary devised theatre and performance practice.

## 4 Cross-Currents 3: Ulrich Meyer-Horsch

Ulrich Meyer-Horsch is Co-founder of Michael Chekhov Europe (MCE), Artistic Director of the Michael Chekhov Acting Studio Hamburg and faculty member of MICHA. Meyer-Horsch delivered a short interactive paper entitled 'Listening', reflecting on its meaning in philosophical and practical terms, which he related to teaching Chekhov's approach in areas of conflict and crisis. He opened with a request that the audience participate in a listening exercise, paying attention to the sounds both outside and within them and into this silence he sang a German song 'Schweige und Höre', which asks its hearers to 'incline your heart's ear' (2016). He then asked us how we had listened drawing on the types of question posed by Chekhov in his lectures (Chekhov 2004): 'Did you listen primarily to agree or disagree? Did you listen with only half an ear while concentrating on something else? Did you listen with an open mind? Did you listen with your heart?' (Meyer-Horsch 2016). He went on to talk about the work of MCE in different parts of the world and explained their organization formed in Croatia in 2004, just after the Yugoslavian war, where 'you could still sense the open wounds' (2016). He talked about the political, cultural and spiritual crisis in Europe and argued 'national egoism has expanded over the whole continent. [. . .] Everybody wants to benefit from the other, but nobody wants to contribute anymore. Refugees, people in need, are seen as a danger. The political discourse is poisoned. People feel they have the right to shut up their opponents or smash them to the ground' (2016). In the Middle East Meyer-Horsch had worked in both Israel, with David Zinder and Olivia Rüdinger, and in Lebanon, where he heard 'the stories of war and fear, a history of three sibling religions fighting each other. There is an atmosphere of pessimism, but also a strong desire for healing' (2016). MCE's work with the university and theatres in Istanbul, Turkey, in 'a political climate of fear and suspicion' was also discussed. He also reflected on how a project he had directed in Taipei brought together actors from Taiwan, Hong Kong, mainland China, and Japan to develop an adaptation of Eileen Chang's 1943 novel, *Love in a Fallen City*, and learnt from this exploration of the Second World War 'how much the Chekhov work can help to heal the wounds of generations' (2016).

Meyer-Horsch argued that the central problem of our time is that we do not listen to each other but rather: 'We exchange opinions. We make statements [. . .]. Everybody wants to be right. We are no longer interested in finding compromises, which embrace the perspective of the Other. You are my friend or you are my enemy' (2017). He noted that this is a significant loss to political culture but also in our personal lives and that in Chekhov's terms this is a 'loss of the **feeling of the whole**'. Meyer-Horsch went on to argue that in his experience the relevance of Chekhov's work for social and political contexts is the way it can help us to relearn how to listen, as Chekhov put it: 'Try to listen to what someone is saying with your heart while asking your mind and your judgement to be silent for a time. You will always have time afterwards to analyze, agree, accept, deny or criticize – but start by listening with your heart' (Powers 2004: 44). Like Baars, Meyer-Horsch also highlighted the other aspects of this kind of love that Chekhov expounds, 'humour and the feeling of ease. If you can laugh at yourself, you will be able to open up for other perspectives' (2017). While working in Izmir, Turkey, during the 2016 military coup and civilian counter-coup, Meyer-Horsch and his colleagues explored a sequence of exercises which he terms 'Gestures of Listening', inspired by the work of Otto Scharmer, who has identified four essential layers of attention. He explained that in this work the ensemble develops **gestures**, with specific **qualities**, for each of these four levels:

1. Listening as downloading, or as I call it: listening as 'checking and filing'. In this mode of listening you simply reconfirm habitual judgements.

2. Object-focused or factual listening [is] a type of listening that makes us get vital information [. . .] you focus on what differs from what you already know. [. . .] You perceive with your senses and your *open mind*.

3. Empathic listening. For the third mode, we need '*to activate and tune a special instrument: the open heart, that is, the empathic capacity to connect directly with another person or living system*' (12). This skill comes close to what Chekhov calls 'listening with your heart'. [. . .] Your attention is with the other. You tune in to and sense from within with your *open mind and open heart*.

4. Generative listening. This fourth mode Scharmer calls '*listening from the emerging field of the future*' (12). In the communication, the sender and the receiver create together something entirely new; they generate a common future out of the space between them. They connect to something larger than themselves and go through a profound process of transformation. Here, our listening and understanding originates from the source of what wants to emerge, that is, from our *open mind, heart, and will* (2017).

Meyer-Horsch reported that in Turkey this work with gestures of listening transformed the 'cold atmosphere [into] to an atmosphere of warmth and hope' and that this experience

Fig. C.1 Seated participants in a 2016 New Pathways Praxis Symposium.

helped him realize 'how much we have to give as artists *to heal* a bleeding country' (2017). However, he stated:, 'I am not naïve. I am not saying we will solve the problems of the country. I am just saying that if we really *listen* to each other, we may be able to create a common future' (2017, emphasis original). Meyer-Horsch ended with an exercise where we imagined listening to the sound of a church bell, muezzin calling to prayer, songs in a synagogue and mother calling her child, his final words 'There is beauty in all of them (the **feeling of beauty**). We do have a common future' (2017).

## 5 Conclusions

In order to frame our conclusions, we return to the research questions that animated the project in the first place. We asked, initially, how practice researchers in theatre and performance can use archival materials to develop their practice and what questions this process raises for our understanding of artistic techniques and histories of actor training. All of the chapters in this book demonstrate, in various ways, that practice is a crucial approach to the exploration of archival materials. Its use remains, however, infrequent. Our findings in this project advocate strongly for the use of practice research methods to engage with records of practice, but not with the expectation that it will offer an authentic guide to historical practices. All of the contributions to this book use practice, instead, dialogically, and with a keen sense of its historically and socially situated nature. We have not brought Chekhov's archive into the training or rehearsal studio in the hope of direct, unmediated contact with his techniques but with a full acknowledgement of our differences and in the hope of creating a dialogue between the concerns of the present and the discoveries of the past. This is importantly distinct from the widespread understanding of actor training as a series of lineages, passed down from influential white men and limited to direct lines of descent. This was far from our approach, which sought instead to value differences and problems as much as agreements and solutions, and indirect and divergent relations to Chekhov's work as well as its more direct inheritance.

This approach to Chekhov's techniques shares something of the approach to the cultural transmission of Stanislavsky's system taken by Jonathan Pitches and Stefan Aquilina in *Stanislavsky in the World*, where they trace some occluded routes of Stanislavsky's influence across the globe, emphasizing that his system is and always has been 'a living culture', adapting itself to a wide range of localized conditions (2017: 21). Our conditions emerge more from the disciplinary and immediate social contexts of practice than the historical, cultural and geopolitical situations emphasized by Pitches and Aquilina's contributors. However, the differences between the contexts of the Chekhovian practices explored in this volume offer a fascinating case study of Chekhov's technique as another 'living culture' of practice, connected by shared principles but also animated by different emphases and by adaptations of Chekhov's methods, as well as by its combination with other approaches. Often, these adaptations and blends have been driven – as various contributors have observed – by problems, shortcomings and challenges, so this book stands, in part, as an argument for a dialogic and agonistic approach to working with histories of practice, driven not by authenticity to an imagined past but responsibility to the emergent challenges of the present.

One perennial challenge to which this book responds is how to work as an ensemble in an age of the individual. In spite of Chekhov's principled opposition to it, his techniques have proved far from immune to the assumptions of individualism: the most widely read version of his most famous book addresses itself, after all, 'to *the* actor', rather than the collaborative group to which the records of his teaching and directing at the Chekhov Theatre Studio, which have been our primary source, were addressed. As Chekhov put it, '[The Chekhov Studio's] *aim must be to find the connection to the whole world around us. [. . .] We are working for humanity and for society. [. . .] It means nothing to be an egotistical group. We will discover how to be useful to society, and we will grow in this way*' (TAITT: 1 February 1937). As we have seen, for Chekhov, this project was grounded in the ensemble principles that underpinned his practice and particularly the notion of making **contact** with others, whether members of the group, or of the audience, or simply another person encountered in everyday life. He explains that contact must be initiated by an offer rather than imposed: '*You invite the other person to enter your heart; you give him or her space; this is quite a different thing*' (26 November 1937).[1] The implicit requirement to expand ourselves in order to give space to the other relates closely to Chekhov's conception of love,[2] which he characterizes as a 'constant process of expansion' (Chekhov and Leonard 1963: 23–4), and which 'begins when we start loving every human being [. . .] without any specific reason, without the prefix of "me" or "mine"' (19–20). This is the root of Chekhov's sociopolitical beliefs and ethical principles:

> We cannot avoid the social responsibility of our life, whether we want to or not. We don't have to be political or diplomats but be social we must. [. . .] To be able to work as a social group, as an organism. We must feel each other. We will all suffer if one makes a mistake. In a good sense you must be responsible and live with the life of our present suffering humanity. (TAITT: 30 January 1939)

Chekhov's commitment to these principles extended to the design of his methods and exercises, which served as the foundation of his collaborative theatre-making practice. This included the conscious development of interpersonal skills and the ways in which these shaped the practices of his multidisciplinary creative teams. Chekhov's conception of love was evidently grounded in his commitment to Rudolf Steiner's Anthroposophy, and as Chamberlain points out, that '[t]he development of the actor's imagination is central to Chekhov's training [and] whilst this can happen without any understanding of Chekhov's relation to Anthroposophy, the cultivation of an ethos of compassion, love, patience and tolerance is essential' (2003).

We can see an example in Chekhov's *Lessons to Teachers*, when he explains that '*[t]he three essentials in a teacher's approach to her work are: WHO is giving. WHAT is given. HOW it is given. In other words, your work, your method, your being*' (LTT: 25 April 1936). In relation to the teacher's being, Chekhov believed that the teacher must '*display all the qualities which the pupil hopes someday to have, and much more, because she must lead the pupils to higher ideas, through the power of her understanding and her greater vision. [. . .] To do this the teacher must radiate a feeling of security, of understanding, of love, and of truth*' (LTT: 10 May 1936).

This attentiveness to the quality of the teaching relationship developed by Chekhov situates his practice in distinctly relational frameworks in Buber's (2004) sense of the term, based on mutuality and reciprocity. His ideas also anticipated both the feminist principle that the personal is political and the principles of radical pedagogy, articulated most famously by Paulo Freire in *Pedagogy of the Oppressed* ([1970] 1996). Freire sought forms of 'partnership' between teachers and students (56), whereby they might act as 'co-investigators' (87), and insisted upon the crucial function of love for this process: 'Dialogue cannot exist [. . .] in the absence of a profound love for the world and its people. [. . .] Love is at the same time the foundation of dialogue and dialogue itself' (70). As we have shown, Chekhov developed practical techniques and principles to enable such a dialogue, and his pedagogical, directorial and collaborative methods require facilitators of all kinds to commit to that process and thereby enable their participants to function as co-creators.

Some of the practical consequences of this commitment can be seen in the Chekhov Theatre Studio's dealings with playwright Henry Lyon Young, who was told in a 1939 letter from the Studio's manager about royalties for *A Spanish Evening* that '*the fact should be borne in mind that the play [. . .] owes its existence to Mr Chekhov, who worked at great length and with much care upon the M.S. and was, in fact, almost a collaborator*'. The letter goes on to point out that although Chekhov did not '*require royalties for himself, something should, of course, accrue to the Studio in respect of this work*' (Letter, 7 July 1939, MC/S4/45). This idea still goes against the grain of theatre-making today, in which rights and rewards for creative practice continue to accrue overwhelmingly to individuals, via a structure established in the interests of the most powerful among them, who are overwhelmingly writers and directors. Prioritizing the interests of relations among groups of collaborating artists would require as fundamental a restructuring of the theatre as a sector now as it would have done in Chekhov's time, and yet – as we have shown – such a reappraisal would evidently benefit emergent strands of collaborative and interdisciplinary practice in the contemporary theatre.

One of the ironies of contemporary Chekhovian practice is the extent to which a set of techniques that was so committed to interdisciplinarity in their inception has become assumed to be confined to the discipline of actor training. Contrary to this trend, we have drawn attention to numerous applications of Chekhov's techniques outside acting. Cornford explores the use of Chekhov's techniques for collaborative writing and dramaturgy; Fleming analyses Chekhov's techniques in processes of devising and directing; Mitchell considers the methods in the context of dance, choreography and actor-movement; Rushe investigates the techniques and principles in relation to theatre design, and Oram investigates their use in voice training. We have also sought to draw out the possibilities presented by Chekhov's work for exploring relationships between these disciplines. Tacitly, this process has also exposed the near absence of techniques and vocabularies for interdisciplinary creative practice in contemporary theatre practice. It is our contention that Chekhov's approach provides an unusually comprehensive and flexible basis for collaborations between disciplines, and we have offered numerous examples of these in practice. One clear potential consequence of these practices for training more widely would be to shift the focus from the atomized vocabularies of different specialisms to an inclusive technique that places emphasis on the relationships between them.

McAvinchey's account of applied, therapeutic and socially engaged applications of Chekhov's work also demonstrates the extent to which what Chekhov describes earlier as 'WHO is giving' and 'HOW it is given' can become 'WHAT is given' by shifting the context and focus of training in his techniques. In applied and therapeutic contexts, for example, approaches designed to address the way in which a director directs may become a much more central focus. As McAvinchey has argued, in these contexts, Chekhov's techniques offer the possibility for a rigorous and structured approach to shifting the focus 'from the social expectations of the practice to the relational, dynamic and qualitative experience of the practice itself and how this could facilitate radical shifts in how an individual might see and navigate their world'. The range of work analysed in her chapter, as well as that described in the 'Cross-Currents' earlier, offers a rich field of possibility for the use of Chekhov's techniques in applied, therapeutic and socially engaged contexts.

It is also clear from the research undertaken in this project that there are numerous possibilities for Chekhov's approaches to enable practitioners in all forms of performance to reconsider their practice as, itself, a means of social engagement. There is a political thread running through this book relating to the empowerment of participants as co-creators, which requires us to foster more dynamic, equal and horizontal structures and working practices in performance-making. This has been an important aspect of numerous developments in the working methods and ethics of acting schools and collaborative companies in the years since Chekhov's death. Chekhov's work offers further possibilities for such projects insofar as his techniques are designed to function as a shared language between all artists involved and to offer practical tools to achieve dynamic and egalitarian creative practices. As contributors to this book have noted, feminists and queer theorists have long been advocating for different models of communication and engagement, and clearly such arguments constitute a fundamental challenge to accepted principles and techniques in theatre-making. Chekhov's methods offer practitioners a vocabulary to respond to the challenge of differently configured roles and ethical responsibilities at a personal level. The recent publicity for the #MeToo campaign has widened awareness of the politics of interpersonal relationships in the theatre and film industry considerably and indicates the pressing need to train directors, in particular, to consider the personal attributes, qualities and skills they need to create a more equitable, respectful and safe space within which actors and other creative practitioners can work, and polyvocal processes within which different embodiments, identities, interpretations and expressions can coexist productively. We have found that a use of Chekhov's techniques focuses attention onto the politics of interpersonal relations and can also play a valuable role in achieving more diversity and equality in theatre-making.

Multiple contributors to this book have also noted challenges to and opportunities for Chekhov's approaches from decolonial and intercultural perspectives, in line with a wider movement in recent years that has sought to identify synergies between Chekhov's work and other philosophical, somatic and religious principles. Monica Cristini, for example, has argued that Chekhov's emphasis on imagination and concentration emerged prior to his encountering Steiner's writings, 'influenced probably by Eastern philosophies' (Cristini 2015). More specifically, Whyman has considered Chekhov's practice in relation to yogic philosophy (2008); Daboo in relation to Buddhism (2007) and the practice of Kathakali (Daboo 2015); Deshpande Hutchinson in relation to Hinduism (2018); while Brenan (2013) and Mroz (2015) have addressed its connections with Qigong and Yingyang Wuxing. Such synergies offer further possibilities for the intercultural elaboration of Chekhov's work in ways that exceed the scope of this project.

Finally, the New Pathways project, which engaged more than twenty practitioners and scholars, has provided a new model of practice research in the UK that has explored experimentation and exchange among historical, creative, embodied and scholarly knowledge(s), critical friendship and the development of new practices, understandings and critical discourses in a collaborative context. All of the authors of this book have continued to develop and diversify their practice and research in this field since 2016 and the Chekhov Collective UK has continued to exist as an organization seeking new and innovative uses of Chekhov's techniques in the twenty-first century.[3] Through this project, we have grown and

Fig. C.2 Participants in a movement exercise in a 2016 New Pathways Praxis Symposium.

diversified the Chekhov community in the UK and have started to build many more bridges to international friends working with these methods in other parts of the world. We look forward to further new pathways, experiments and international exchanges in the years to come.

## Notes

1. He explains that theatrical '*cooperation has many difficulties and obstacles*' as an art form and that at the studio they '*will develop the new technique to be cooperative in our creative work, but the feeling that we are obliged to create – not in solitude but in a group – is most important*' (LTT: 19 May 1936).
2. He names the most characteristic feature of this kind of love as 'its constant process of expansion' (1963: 23–4) and believes that this love should be extended even to the audience (1963: 22).
3. See https://chekhovcollectiveuk.co.uk/ for further information.

# Glossary of Michael Chekhov's terminology

For readers who are not familiar with Chekhov's techniques and principles, we have created this brief guide to some of his more commonly used terms. The first use in each chapter of terms included here appears in bold in order to signal the availability of these definitions. Since different practitioners use these terms in subtly different ways, and Chekhov himself varied their meaning somewhat as he developed his approach and used it in different contexts, these definitions should not be considered to be definitive or to contradict somewhat distinct emphases in the main body of the text. Instead, they are offered as a way of articulating our general understanding of these terms, which are central to Chekhov's work.

Two of Chekhov's publications, *To the Actor* (2002) and *On the Technique of Acting* (1991), are written as accessible handbooks and provide detailed descriptions of, and discussion about, these techniques and principles.

**Archetypes** – Chekhov uses the notion of archetypes in relation to gesture, movement qualities, characters from folk and fairy tales and myths, and various other techniques. He describes archetypal gesture as 'one which serves as an original model for all possible gestures of the same kind' (2002: 70). In effect, the archetypal aspect of his methods function as prototypes that enable artists to work with simple, clear and large starting points but which are transformed through the artists' creative individuality (their embodied imagination) and experimentation, preventing them from being reductionist. Chekhov expressed doubts about whether the term archetype best expressed his ideas (Ashperger 2008: 244), and he therefore suggested that practitioners of his technique might use different terms to express this idea.

**Atmosphere** – This is the feeling that belongs to a particular space and/or event that expresses its inner dynamic and rhythm. Chekhov believed that atmospheres exist everywhere and are continually changing. Changes in atmosphere relate to the overall dynamics of a performance and inspire certain qualities of movement, rhythms and relationships with space, and can enable the driving objective of a scene to be recognized and then shaped into a specific psychological gesture (Chekhov 1991: 33–4). Chekhov says that atmospheres are objective in their quality, though they do not necessarily inspire the same reactions in different people; therefore characters will have individual feelings within a shared atmosphere.

**Awareness** – Du Prey described this as a technique that required the actor 'being absolutely open to what is going on, so that it flows into you and takes you and lifts you and moves you' and notes that this must include every part of your being 'body, soul and spirit' (1978: 10).

**Beauty (the feeling of)** – This is one of the 'four brothers', the experience of radiance that Chekhov considered any work of art must possess; it is related to the movement quality of 'radiating', and is experienced intuitively and internally, and therefore emerges as a consequence of the artists being true to themselves.

**Centre (imaginary, ideal and archetypal)** – This is a point of origin of impulses of movement within the body and concomitantly 'the source of inner activity' (Chekhov 2002: 7). Work with a centre affects qualities of movement, direction in space, weight, posture, rhythm and inner sensation/experience. Chekhov believed that there are three archetypal centres: the head (which he related to thinking), the chest and arms (related to feeling) and the pelvis and legs (related to will) (1991: 52–3). He referred to the centre in the heart as the ideal centre. The technique known as 'the imaginary centre' includes the location of a point of origin anywhere within, or outside of, the actor's body, which may be given a specific form, size, material, temperature, colour or movement potential, triggering the process of developing a very specific movement language and related inner life. When used to develop characterization, the imaginary centre is an expression of the character's 'psychological makeup', with imaginative engagement and attention to inner sensation forming 'the link between the psychology and outer means of expression of the actor' (Chekhov 1991: 104). This technique also contributes to the analysis of a text, and an actor's imaginary centre will evolve over a creative process.

**Colour** – Chekhov worked extensively with colour as a technique at the Chekhov Theatre Studio in relation to his other methods such as character work, objective atmosphere and dramaturgy, in addition to the design of costume, set and lighting design. Chekhov was inspired by the theories on colour developed by Rudolf Steiner, Albert Steffen and Johann Wolfgang von Goethe.

**Contact** – For Chekhov, making contact is a necessary precondition for all aspects of his technique. This notion of contact applies to interpersonal relations with other artists and the audience, but also with space, architectural structures, settings, dramaturgy and any other aspects of a performance.

**Creative Individuality** – Chekhov argued that '[t]o create by inspiration one must become aware of one's own individuality' (2002: 85). He suggested that, in moments of imaginative inspiration 'the [everyday] of an artist undergoes a kind of metamorphosis' and that with this new, we can feel 'an influx of power never experienced in your routine life' (86). He argues that this higher-I 'puts you in a *creative* state' (87).

**Directions in Space** – Also referred to as archetypal directions, there are six fundamental directions in Chekhov's technique, forming three polarities: forwards and backwards, upwards and downwards, expanding and contracting. These underpin Chekhov's conception of gesture in particular.

**Divided Consciousness** – Later in a theatre-making process, after working with various 'grounds', Chekhov also encourages artists to develop a sense of what he termed the divided consciousness (the capacity to be both inside and outside of the performance), so that they have a clear sense of their relationship with the whole composition and simultaneously maintain strong, responsive contact with their fellow actors and – crucially – the spectators.

**Ease (the feeling of)** – One of the 'four brothers', this is the experience of naturalness and simplicity that Chekhov considered any art work must possess; it is related to the movement quality of 'flowing', and connected to releasing muscular tension and the breath.

**Flowing** – This is the archetypal movement quality associated with water; an easy, supported quality, as though the movement is carried on a current. Chekhov refers to the movement quality of flowing as floating in various sources, which can be a source of confusion. Flowing as a movement quality is distinct from 'floating', a sensation of upward movement, as though being lifted.

**Flying** – This is the archetypal movement quality associated with air; a light and unpredictable quality, triggered by an external impulse, as though the movement is a leaf caught by the wind.

**Flying over the play** – This is a technique that gives the cast an opportunity to move through or across a performance or part of it, in order to experience its composition and a sense of it as a whole. It can be done early in a rehearsal process using a score of atmospheres, for example.

**Form (the feeling of)** – One of the 'four brothers', this is the experience of solidity and clarity that Chekhov considered any work of art must possess; it is related to the movement quality of 'moulding'.

**The Four Brothers** – Chekhov considered that any work of art must have these four essential components, the feelings of beauty, ease, form and wholeness or entirety.

**Gesture** – One of Chekhov's most fundamental and synthesizing ideas, a gesture is a way of capturing the dynamic or experience of movement underlying all experiences or forms in the world; Chekhov believed that everything could be experienced as movement and used gesture to explore and express these movements, not only of people or their experiences or psychology, but of the forms of a plant, a tree, or even a chair (Hurst du Prey 1983: 85), as well as the dynamics of a scene, atmosphere, a text or a dramaturgical form. Chekhov notes that 'We can take any point in the method and turn it into a gesture' (1985: 108). The technique of 'psychological gesture' expresses the entirety of a character's psychology and experience in the embodied imagination through a movement of the whole body.

**Ground** – This is the technical basis for an exercise or improvised exploration in training, or a theatre-making or directing process, rehearsal or performance; the technique or idea upon which the performer concentrates and which serves as their guide. This principle catalyses and heightens the artists' creativity.

**Image (and visualization)** – Many of Chekhov's techniques relate to the visualization of various types of image; this may be of a character, a form, an imaginary centre or a pattern, and he designed exercises in which we visualize the transformation of an image (such as the growth of a tree). He perceives these images as having their own independent life and encourages artists to cooperate with it and then incorporate it.

**Imaginary Body** – This is a body-form that connects the actor's physical body and their image of the character. Chekhov asks that an actor inhabit the imaginary body and gradually learn from it how a character moves and experiences the world.

**Imaginary Centre** – see 'Centres'.

**Improvisation** – This is a core aspect of all of Chekhov's principles and techniques and the key to learning and subsequently applying each of his methods. It is also the freedom to invent and alter a performance within certain confines or on a certain basis or 'ground'; Chekhov believed that improvisation was an essential aspect of all performances.

**Juggler's Psychology** – For Chekhov, the centrality of improvisation in his approach required the development of a particular disposition, or state of mind, by both the actor and director/teacher to treat anything as potentially a springboard for improvisation/play and the generation of interpretative or original material. Chekhov termed this disposition and skill the juggler's psychology (du Prey 1978: 13).

**Moulding** – This is the archetypal movement quality associated with earth, a forceful, sculpting quality, as though the movement is pushing against the resistance of clay.

**Objective Atmosphere** – see 'Atmosphere'.

**Play and games** – Chekhov talks extensively about his techniques operating as 'games' to be played by actors, directors and theatre-makers and the significance of pleasure in his approach. The grounds chosen from within his technique determine the rules of these 'games'. The capacity to play relates to his notion of the Juggler's Psychology. He also used children's games in his training, making and rehearsal processes, for example, exercises such as throwing and catching a ball.

**Polarity** – Chekhov's term for a dialectical condition of inextricably connected opposition.

**Psychological Gesture** – see 'Gesture'.

**Qualities of Movement** – By 'quality', Chekhov simply meant how a movement is done: if the movement is a verb, the quality is an adverb. He took from Steiner the idea that there are four archetypal qualities, each associated with one of the four elements: moulding (earth), flowing (water), flying (air), radiating (fire). The archetypal movement qualities are discovered through an imaginative encounter with the four elements and their recognizable dynamic characteristics in the space around actors (Chekhov 2002: 13). There are, however, an infinite number of possible qualities of movement, just as there are infinite colours but a finite number of primary colours. All movement qualities necessarily entail a specific relationship with, and attitude towards, weight, time, space and flow, and consequently certain possibilities of relating to the world.

**Radiating** – This is the archetypal movement quality associated with fire, a movement that seems to emit heat and light. In Chekhov's concept of 'radiation', the actor consciously imagines 'that invisible rays stream from [their] movements into space, in the direction of the movement itself' (1991: 46–7). This is connected to the identification, location and channelling of an actor's energy (breath, life force, *prana*). Chekhov also perceives radiating as a form of 'giving' (2002:19); it is the way in which actors share their creative work with the audience and is the counterpart to receiving from others.

**Receiving** – This is the counterpart to 'radiating'; Chekhov believed that in addition to radiating their energy to others, actors, directors and teachers also had to be able to receive the presence of their partners, their actions and words, surroundings, atmosphere and the audience. 'To actually receive means to draw towards one's self with the utmost inner power the things, persons or events of the situation' (2002: 19).

**Rhythm and Tempo** – These terms are used in relation to inner/outer aspects of character, but also in relation to all of Chekhov's other techniques such as Gesture, Atmosphere and Movement Qualities. Rhythm was also an underpinning feature of his form of composition, dynamics, dramaturgy and performances.

**Spine** – This is the essence, or fundamental quality, or character of a thing, or a scene. A spine has to be felt and Chekhov notes there is no set law about its identification. Chekhov believed a spine can be a sensation, a feeling or an idea.

**Spying eye** – This is the process whereby actors/directors/teachers look back on their creation after working with a chosen ground to see where their spontaneous play has led them. Chekhov notes that the 'answer' or discoveries may come in the moment of acting (or devising) or afterwards, but using this principle avoids intellectual reasoning dominating the early part of the training, making or rehearsing process.

**Triplicity** – This is the compositional principle that everything has three parts or phases: an initiation, a development and a conclusion. It is connected to the principle of polarity because the polarized beginning and ending are connected by a transitional phase to make three parts.

**Wholeness or Entirety (the feeling of)** – One of the 'four brothers', this is the experience of completeness that Chekhov believed every work of art must have; it is associated with the movement quality of 'moulding'. Sometimes referred to as a sense of entirety.

# Bibliography

## Archival references

### The Michael Chekhov Theatre Studio Deirdre Hurst du Prey Archive

LTT: 'Lessons to Teachers' (MC/S1/7/A, April–June 1936).
TAITT: 'The Actor is the Theatre'.
   Volume 1 (MC/S1/7/A, October–December 1936).
   Volume 2 (MC/S1/7/B, January–June 1937).
   Volume 3 (MC/S1/8/A, July–December 1937).
   Volume 4 (MC/S1/8/B, January–March 1938).
   Volume 5 (MC/S1/9/A, 1938).
   Volume 6 (MC/S1/9/B, January–July 1939).
   Volume 7 (MC/S1/10/A, July–December 1939).
   Volume 8 (MC/S1/10/B, January–November 1940).
   Volume 9 (MC/S1/11/A, 1941).
   Volume 10 (MC/S1/12/A, January–April 1942).
Caracciolo, D. M. (1999), 'The Pencil: Memories of Dartington Hall and the English Origin of the Michael Chekhov Acting Method', (MC/S4/36/H).
Chekhov, M. (1937), 'Colour and Light: Mr. Chekhov's Criticism of March 15th 1937', (MC/S4/18/A).
Kindelan, N. (1977), 'Tape Recording of Deirdre Hurst du Prey', (MC/S4/27/A).
Young, H. L. (1941), 'Troublemaker-Doublemaker', typescript (MC/S6/8/E).

## Other archival sources

Chekhov, M. (undated [1944]), *Life and Encounters*, Ball, D. (trans.), collection of Michael Chekhov UK.

## Interviews

Baars, M. (2018), Interview with Cass Fleming.
Brook, Z. (2017), Interview with Cass Fleming and Caoimhe McAvinchey, 4 December 2017.
Carnegie, G. (2017), Interview with Sinéad Rushe, 22 August 2017.
Chambers, J. (2017), Interview with Roanna Mitchell, 6 July 2017.
Chen, K. (2018), Interview with Roanna Mitchell, 13 August 2018.
Cook, B. (2017), Interview with Roanna Mitchell, 17 March 2017.

Cunningham, A. (2017), Interview with Sinéad Rushe, 28 August 2017.
Cunningham, J. (2016), Interview with Roanna Mitchell, 26 June 2016.
Elnile, R. (2017), Interview with Sinéad Rushe, 5 August 2017.
Fenley, M. (2018), Interview with the Roanna Mitchell, 10 August 2018.
Frecknall, R. (2018), Interview with Cass Fleming, 20 November 2018.
Green, K. and Cornford, T. (2016), Interview with Roanna Mitchell, 6 July 2016.
Grenfell, C. (2017), Interview with Sinéad Rushe, 5 August 2017.
Jafine, H. (2018), Interview with Caoimhe McAvinchey, 22 May 2018.
Makepeace, E. (2018), Interview with Caoimhe McAvinchey, 6 June 2018.
McCall, K. (2017), Interview with Sinéad Rushe, 9 August 2017.
Mizenko, J. (2017), Interview with Roanna Mitchell, 7 July 2017.
Reid, A. (2019), Interview with Sinéad Rushe, 8 May 2019.
Rushe, S. (2017), Interview with Roanna Mitchell, 25 April 2017.
Skourtis, A. (2017), Interview with Sinéad Rushe, 4 August 2017.
Tringham, A. (2017), Interview with Roanna Mitchell, 7 July 2017.

## Published works

Abulafia, Y. (2016), *The Art of Light on Stage; Lighting in Contemporary Theatre*, London and New York: Routledge.
Ackroyd, J. (2000), 'Applied Theatre: Problems and Possibilities', *Applied Theatre Journal* (1), http://www.gu.edu.au/centre/cpci/atr/journal/article1_number1.htm (accessed 10 September 2010).
Ahmed, S. (2006), *Queer Phenomenology: Orientations, Objects, Others*, Durham and London: Duke University Press.
Albers, J. (2006, 1963), *Interaction of Color*, New Haven and London: Yale University Press.
Alexander, M. (1955), *The Use of the Self*, Kent: Integral Press.
Anderson, N. (2011), 'On Rudolf Steiner's Impact on the Training or the Actor', *Literature & Aesthetics*, 21 (1), 158–74.
Appia, A. (1993, 1899), *Texts on Theatre*, London and New York: Routledge.
Aristotle. (1999), *Poetics*, McLeish, K. (trans.), London: Nick Hern Books.
Ashperger, C. (2008), *The Rhythm of Space and Sound of Time: Michael Chekhov's Acting Technique in the 21st Century*, Amsterdam: Rodopi.
Aston, E. (1995), *An Introduction to Feminism and Theatre*, London and New York: Routledge.
Aston, E. (1999), *Feminist Theatre Practices*, London: Routledge.
Autant-Mathieu, M. C. (ed.) (2009), *Mikhaïl Tchekhov: de Moscow à Hollywood, du théâtre au cinéma*, Montpelier: L'entretemps éditions.
Autant-Mathieu, M. C. and Meerzon, Y. (eds) (2015), *The Routledge Companion to Michael Chekhov*, London and New York: Routledge.
Baars, M. (2012), 'Quality of Life: Using the Arts to Help People Living with and Affected by Dementia', http://www.destichtingkoffer.nl/dsk2015/wp-content/uploads/2014/11/quality-of-life-handbook-english-Netherlands.pdf (accessed 4 February 2020).
Baars, M. (2016), *Contact Maken bij dementia*, Amsterdam: De Stichting Koffer.
Baars, M., Frayman, C., and Gerner, P. (2012), *Dementia Out of the Box*, Amsterdam: De Stichting Koffer.
Baim, C. and Brook, S. (2002), *The Geese Theatre Handbook: Drama with Offenders and People at Risk*, Hook, Hampshire: Waterside Press.

Bainbridge Cohen, B. (2012), *Sensing, Feeling and Action*, 3rd edn, Toronto: Contact Editions.

Bazooka Arts, www.bazookaarts.co.uk (accessed 12 December 2017).

Bennett, J. (2010), *Vibrant Matter: A Political Ecology of Things*, Durham and London: Duke University Press.

Bennet, L. (2013), 'Inspired States: Adapting the Michael Chekhov Technique for the Singing Actor', *Theatre, Dance and Performance Training*, 4 (2), 146–61.

Bennett, S. M. (2013), 'The Dancer of the Future: Michael Chekhov in Cross-Training Practice', *Theatre, Dance and Performance Training*, 4 (2), 162–75.

Berry, C. (1973), *Voice and the Actor*, London: Harrap Ltd.

Berry, C. (1987), *The Actor and his Text*, London: Harrap Ltd.

Berry, C. (2000), *The Actor and the Text*, London: Virgin Books.

Berry, C. and Noble, A. (2010), *Text in Action*, London: Virgin Publishing.

Birren, F. (1950, 2013), *Color Psychology and Color Therapy; A Factual Study of the Influence of Color on Human Life*, Eastford, CT: Martino.

Birren, F. (1969), *Light. Color and Environment*, New York: Van Nostrand Reinhold Co.

Birren, F. (1978), *Color and Human Response*, New York: Van Nostrand Reinhold Co.

Black, L. (1987), *Mikhail Chekhov as Actor, Director, and Teacher*, Ann Arbor, MI: UMI Research Press.

Boal, A. (2002), *Theatre of the Oppressed*, London: Pluto Press.

Bogart, A. and Landau, T. (2005), *The Viewpoints Book: A Practical Guide to Viewpoints and Composition*, New York: Theatre Communications Group.

Brook, Z. (2016), 'Michael Chekhov in Applied, Therapeutic and Community Contexts: Michael Chekhov New Pathways', Goldsmiths, University of London, 10 September.

Brown, B. (2013), 'The Emergence of Studiinost: The Ethics and Processes of Ensemble in the Russian Theatre Studio', in J. Britton (ed.), *Encountering Ensemble*, London and New York: Bloomsbury, 49–60.

Brown, S. (2009), *Play: How It Shapes the Brain, Opens the Imagination and Invigorates the Soul*, New York: Penguin Group.

Buber, M. (2004), *I and Thou*, London and New York: Continuum.

Byckling, L. (2000), *The Theatre of Inspiration: A Critical Analysis of the Acting Theories of Michael Chekhov* [Russian language]. PhD. diss. University of Helsinki.

Byckling, L. (2002), Michael Chekhov as Actor, Teacher and Director in the West', *Toronto Slavic Quarterly*, 4, http:\\www.utoronto.ca/tsq/01/chekhovwest.shtml (accessed 10 September 2009).

Byckling, L. (2015), 'Michael Chekhov's Work as Director', in M. C. Autant-Mathieu and Y. Meerzon (eds), *The Routledge Companion to Michael Chekhov*. London and New York: Routledge, 21–39.

Caillois, R. (2001), *Man, Play and Games*, Barash, M. (trans.), Urbana and Chicago: University of Illinois Press .

Callow, S. (2002), 'Foreword', in M. Chekhov (ed.), *To the Actor*, London: Routledge, xi–xxiv.

Carnicke, S. (2009), *Stanislavski in Focus*, 2nd edn, London and New York: Routledge.

Carnicke, S. (2015), 'Michael Chekhov's Legacy in Soviet Russia: A Story about Coming Home', in M. C. Autant-Mathieu and Y. Meerzon (eds), *The Routledge Companion to Michael Chekhov*, London and New York: Routledge, 191–206.

Case, S. E. (1988), *Feminism and Theatre*, New York: Methuen.

Cattanach, A. (1992), *Play Therapy with Abused Children*, London and Philadelphia: Jessica Kingsley Publishers.

Chamberlain, F. (2003), 'Michael Chekhov: Pedagogy, Spirituality and the Occult', *Toronto Slavic Quarterly* (4) Spring, University of Toronto, Academic Electronic Journal in Slavic Studies.

Chamberlain, F. (2004), *Routledge Performance Practitioners: Michael Chekhov*, London and New York: Routledge.

Chamberlain, F. (2010), 'Michael Chekhov on the Technique of Acting', in A. Hodge (ed.), *Twentieth Century Actor Training*, London: Routledge, 63–80.

Chamberlain, F. (2013), 'Michael Chekhov's Ensemble Feeling', in J. Britton (ed.), *Encountering Ensemble*, London: Bloomsbury Methuen, 78–93.

Chamberlain, F. (2015), 'Michael Chekhov in England: Outside the Magic Circle', in M. C. Autant-Mathieu and Y. Meerzon (eds), *The Routledge Companion to Michael Chekhov*, London and New York: Routledge, 207–18.

Chamberlain, F., Kirillov, A. and Pitches, J. (eds) (2013), *Theatre, Dance and Performance Training: Michael Chekhov*, Special Issue 4.2.

Chambers, J. (2016), 'Chekhov, Laban and Steiner — Connections through the Body, the Spirit and Art', *Michael Chekhov Technique in the Twenty-First Century: New Pathways Praxis Symposia: 9–11 September, 2016*, London: Goldsmiths, University of London.

Chaskalson, M. (2014), *Mindfulness in Eight Weeks*, London: Harper Thorson.

Chekhov, M. (1983a), 'Chekhov's Academy of Arts Questionnaire', *The Drama Review*, 27 (3), 22–33.

Chekhov, M. (1983b), 'Chekhov on Acting: A Collection of Unpublished Materials', *The Drama Review*, 27 (3), 46–83.

Chekhov, M. (1991), *On the Technique of Acting*, New York: Harper Perennial.

Chekhov, M. (2000), *Lessons for Teachers of his Acting Technique*, Ottowa: Dovehouse Editions Inc.

Chekhov, M. (2002), *To the Actor*, London and New York: Routledge.

Chekhov, M. (2004), *On Theatre and the Art of Acting: The Five-Hour CD Master Class with Acclaimed Actor-Director-Teacher, Lectures Recorded by Michael Chekhov in 1955*. 4 CDs, New York: Working Arts.

Chekhov, M. (2005), *The Path of the Actor*, London and New York: Routledge.

Chekhov, M. (2006), *To the Actor: On the Technique of Acting*, by Michael Chekhov, London and New York: Routledge.

Chekhov, M. (2018), *Lessons for Teachers*, expanded edition, J. Cerullo (ed.), New York: Michael Chekhov Association.

Chekhov, M. and Hurst du Prey, D. (1985), *Lessons for the Professional Actor*, New York: Performing Arts Journal Publications.

Chekhov, M. and Leonard, C. (1963), *Michael Chekhov's To the Director and Playwright*, New York and Evanston: Harper and Row, 14–26.

Chekhov, M. and Powers, M. (1992), *Michael Chekhov: On Theatre and the Art of Acting: The Six Hour Master Class: A Guide to Discovery with Exercises*, with cassette recordings, New York: Applause.

The Chekhov Theatre Studio (1936), *The Chekhov Theatre Studio*, London: Curwen Press.

Cheney, S. (1969), *The Art of the Dance*, New York: Theatre Arts.

Citron, A. (1983), 'The Chekhov Technique Today', *The Drama Review*, 27 (3), 91–6.

Cixous, H. (2010), 'The Laugh of the Medusa', in M. Segarra (ed.), *The Portable Cixous*, New York: Colombia University Press, 27–39.

Clarke, A. (2009), 'Family Roles and Paternal/Maternal Genealogies within and between Psychophysical Performer Trainings and their Documentation', *Platform Postgraduate eJournal of Theatre and Performance Arts*, 4 (1), 25–43.

Clouder, C. (2003), *Rudolf Steiner: Education*, Forest Row: Sophia Books.

Coffey, P. (2018), 'Art in Society Presentation', *World Chekhov Teachers' Meeting*, Groznjan, Croatia.

Cornford, T. (2012), *The English Theatre Studios of Michael Chekhov and Michel Saint-Denis, 1935–1965*, Phd. diss., University of Warwick.

Cornford, T. (2013), 'A New Kind of Conversation': Michael Chekhov's 'Turn to the Crafts', *Theatre, Dance and Performance Training*, 4 (2), 189–203.

Cornford, T., Fleming, C., and Rushe, S. (eds) (2013), 'The Michael Chekhov Centre UK Past, Present and Future: An Inter-Generational Dialogue', an edited selection of interviews with Sarah Kane, Graham Dixon and Martin Sharp, *Theatre, Dance and Performance Training*, 4 (2): 316–24.

Cristini, M. (2015), 'Meditation and Imagination: The Contribution of Anthropsophy to Michael Chekhov's Acting Technique', in M. C. Autant-Mathieu and Y. Meerzon (eds), *The Routledge Companion to Michael Chekhov*, London and New York: Routledge, 69–81.

Cummings, S. T. (2006), *Remaking American Theater: Charles Mee, Anne Bogart and the SITI Company*, Cambridge: Cambridge University Press.

Daboo, J. (2007), 'Michael Chekhov and the Embodied Imagination: Higher Self and Non-Self', *Studies in Theatre and Performance*, 27 (3), 261–73.

Daboo, J. (2012), 'Michael Chekhov and the Studio in Dartington: The Re-membering of a Tradition', in J. Pitches (ed.), *The Russians in Britain: British Theatre and the Influence of the Russian Tradition of Acting*, London and New York: Routledge, 62–85.

Daboo, J. (2015), '"As the Shadow Follows the Body": Examining Chekhov's Creation of Character through "Eastern" Practices', in M. C. Autant-Mathieu and Y. Meerzon (eds), *The Routledge Companion to Michael Chekhov*, London and New York: Routledge, 282–96.

Damasio, A. (2000), *The Feeling of What Happens: Body, Emotion and the Making of Consciousness*, London: Vintage.

DeKoven, M. (2004), *Utopia Limited: The Sixties and the Emergence of the Postmodern*, Durham NC, and London: Duke University Press.

Dennis, A. (2002), *The Articulate Body: The Physical Training of the Actor*, London: Nick Hern.

Derrida, J. (1995), *Archive Fever: A Freudian Impression*, Baltimore: John Hopkins University Press.

Deshpande Hutchinson, A. (2018), *Acting Exercises for Non-Traditional Staging: Michael Chekhov Reimagined*, New York and London: Routledge.

Dewey, J. (2011), *Democracy and Education*, London: Simon and Brown.

Diamond, I. and Quinby, L. (eds) (1988), *Feminism and Foucault*, Boston: Northeastern University Press.

Dolar, M. (2006), *A Voice and Nothing More*, Cambridge, MA: MIT Press.

Duchen, J. (2014), 'A Great Playwright's Daughter Speaks', blog, http://www.jessicaduchen.co.uk/pdfs/other-2014/19-4-O'casey-jessica.pdf (accessed 27 October 2019).

Evans, M. (2009), *Movement Training for the Modern Actor*, London and New York: Routledge.

Evans, M. (2014), 'Playing with History: Personal Accounts of the Political and Cultural Self in Actor Training through Movement', *Theatre, Dance and Performance Training*, 5 (2), 144–56.

Ewan, V. and Green, D. (2015), *Actor Movement: Expression of the Physical Being*, London and New York: Bloomsbury.

Farb, N. A. S., Segal, Z. V., Mayberg, H., Bean, J., McKeon, D., Fatima, Z. and Anderson, A. K. (2007), 'Attending to the Present: Mindfulness Meditation Reveals Distinct Neural Modes of Self-Reference', *Social Cognitive and Affective Neuroscience*, 2 (4), 313–22.

Feldenkrais, M. (1980), *Awareness Through Movement: Health Exercises for Personal Growth*, London: Penguin.
Fleming, C. (2013), *A Genealogy of the Embodied Theatre Practices of Suzanne Bing and Michael Chekhov: The Use of Play in Actor Training*, PhD diss., De Montfort University.
Foucault, M. (1977), *Language, Counter-memory, Practice*, D. Bouchard (ed.), New York: Cornell University Press.
Freire, P. (1996), *Pedagogy of the Oppressed*, London: Penguin Books.
Frost, A. and Yarrow, R. (2016), *Improvisation in Drama, Theatre and Performance*, revised third edn, London: MacMillan International.
Fusetti, G. and Wilson, S. (2002), 'The Pedagogy of the Poetic Body', in D. Bradby and M. Delgado (eds), *The Paris Jigsaw*, New York: Palgrave, 93–101.
Gilmer, J. M. (2013), 'Michael Chekhov's Imagination of the Creative Word and the Question of its Integration into his Future Theatre', *Theatre, Dance and Performance Training*, 4 (2), 204–18.
Glad Teater Denmark, www.gladteater.dk/vaerdier-og-mal (accessed 12 September 2018).
Goethe, J. W. (1996), *Goethe on Science*, J. Naydler (ed.), Edinburgh: Floris Books.
Goethe, Wolfgang von (2006), *Theory of Colours*, Mineola, New York: Dover.
Gordon, C. E. (1957), *On the Art of the Theatre*, London: Heinemann.
Gordon, M. (1985), 'Introduction', in M. Chekhov, *Lessons for the Professional Actor*, New York: PAJ Books, 11–19.
Gordon, M. (1987), *The Stanislavsky Technique: Russia: A Workbook for Actors*, New York: Applause.
Gordon, M. (1995), 'The Castle Awakens: Mikhail Chekhov's 1931 Occult Fantasy', *Performing Arts Journal*, 49, 110–20.
Govan, E., Nicholson, H. and Normington, K. (2007), *Making a Performance: Devising Histories and Contemporary Practices*, London: Routledge.
Graham, M. (1991), *Blood Memory*, New York: Doubleday.
Grosz, E. (1999), 'Thinking of the New: Of Futures Yet Unthought', in E. Grosz (ed.), *Becomings: Explorations in Time, Memory and Futures*, Ithaca and London: Cornell University Press, 15–28.
Guattari, F. (2000), *The Three Ecologies*, Pindar, I. and Sutton, P. (trans.), London: Athlone Press.
Gutekunst, C. and Gillet, J. (2014), *Voice into Acting: Integrating Voice and the Stanislavski Approach*, London: Bloomsbury Methuen Drama.
Haffner, J. (2017), 'Musical Synthesis of the Michael Chekhov Technique: Integrated Training for the Singer-Actor', *Critical Stages / Scènes Critiques*, 15.
Hart, L. (1989), *Feminist Essays on Contemporary Women's Theatre*, Michigan: University of Michigan.
Hatton, N. (2016), *A Cultural Response to Dementia: Participatory Arts and Relationship-Centred Care*, PhD Thesis, Royal Holloway University of London.
Heathcote, D. and Bolton, Gavin (1995), *Drama for Learning: Dorothy Heathcote's Mantle of the Expert Approaches to Education*, London: Heineman.
Heddon, D. (2008), *Autobiography and Performance*, London: Palgrave Macmillan.
Heddon, D. and Milling, J. (2006), *Devising Performance: A Critical History*, Hampshire and New York: Palgrave Macmillan.
Heidegger, M. (1962), *Being and Time*, Macquarrie, J. and Robinson, E. (trans.), Oxford: Blackwell.
Henricks, T. S. (2015), *Play and the Human Condition*, Urbana, Chicago and Springfield: University of Illinois Press.
Herrmann, A. and Clifford, Sara (1998), *Making a Leap: Theatre of Empowerment*, London: Jessica Kingsley Publishing.

Huizinga, J. (1955), *Homo Ludens*, Boston: The Beacon Press.
Hurst du Prey, D. (1978), 'The Training Sessions of Michael Chekhov', in *Dartington Theatre Papers* (third series), Devon: Dept. of Theatre, Dartington College of Arts.
Hurst du Prey, D. (1980), 'The Training Sessions of Michael Chekhov', *Theatre Papers*, Series 3, no. 9, Dartington College of Arts.
Hurst du Prey, D. (1983), 'Working with Chekhov', *The Drama Review*, 27 (3), 84–90.
Hurst du Prey, D. (1985), 'Working with Chekhov', *The Drama Review*, 17 (3), 84–90.
Ingold, T. (2015), *The Life of Lines*, Abingdon: Routledge.
Jarman, Derek (2000), *Chroma*, London: Vintage.
Jeffers, A. (2012), *Refugees, Theatre and Crisis: Performing Global Identities*, Basingstoke: Palgrave Macmillan.
Kapsali, M. (2010), '"I Don't Attack It, But It's Not For Actors": The Use of Yoga by Jerzy Grotowski', *Theatre, Dance and Performance Training*, 1 (2), 185–98.
Kemp, R. (2012), *Embodied Acting: What Neuroscience Tells Us about Performance*, London and New York: Routledge.
Keogh, R. and Pearson, J. (2018), 'The Blind Mind: No Sensory Imagery in Aphantasia', *Cortex*, 105, 56–63.
Kindelan, N. (1977), *The Theatre of Inspiration: A Critical Analysis of the Acting Theories of Michael Chekhov*, PhD Thesis, University of Wisconsin, Madison.
Kindelan, N. (1985), 'A Solution for Children's Theatre: Michael Chekhov's "Psychology of Style"', *Children's Theatre Review*, 34 (2), 7–12.
Kirillov, A. (2005), Notes in Chekhov, M. *The Path of The Actor*, London and New York: Routledge, 203–28.
Kirillov, A. (2015), 'The Theatrical System of Michael Chekhov', in M. C. Autant-Mathieu and Y. Meerzon (eds), *The Routledge Companion to Michael Chekhov*, London and New York: Routledge, 40–56.
Kirillov, A. and Chamberlain, F. (2013), 'Rehearsal Protocols for Hamlet by William Shakespeare at the Second Moscow Art Theatre', *Theatre, Dance and Performance Training*, 4 (2), 243–79.
Kirkland, G. (1990), *The Shape of Love*, London: Hamish Hamilton.
Klee, P. (1963), *Pedagogical Sketchbook*, London: Faber and Faber.
Kolb, D. (1983), *Experiential Learning: Experience as the Sources of Learning and Development*, Upper Saddle River, NJ: Prentice.
Koppett, K. (2012), *Training to Imagine: Practical Improvisational Techniques for Trainers and Managers to Enhance Creativity, Teamwork, Leadership, and Learning*, Sterling, VA: Stylus.
Knowles, R. (2004), *Reading the Material Theatre*, Cambridge: Cambridge University Press.
Laban, R. (2011), *The Mastery of Movement*, 4th edn, revised by Lisa Ullman, Alton: Dance Books.
Lakoff, G. and Johnson, M. (1980), *Metaphors We Live By*, Chicago: University of Chicago Press.
Lakoff, G. and Johnson, M. (2003), *Metaphors We Live By*, Chicago and London: University of Chicago Press.
Lakoff, G. and Johnson, M. (1999), *Philosophy in the Flesh: The Embodied Mind and its Challenge to Western Thought*, New York: Basic Books.
Lampert, F. (2015), 'One Concept of Dance Improvisation: The Nine-Point Technique', *Creative Drama Journal*, 10 (2), 235–42.
Langman, D. (2014), *The Art of Acting: Body – Soul – Spirit – Word: A Practical and Spiritual Guide*, Forest Row: Temple Lodge.
Law, A. (1983), 'Chekhov's Russian "Hamlet" (1924)', *The Drama Review: TDR*, 27 (3), 34–45.
Lecoq, J. (2002), *The Moving Body: Teaching Creative Theatre*, London: Methuen Drama.

Lecoq, J. (2006), *Theatre of Movement and Gesture*, Abingdon: Routledge.

Leonard, C. (ed.) (1963), *Michael Chekhov's To the Director and Playwright*, New York and Evanston: Harper and Row.

Levy, E. (1979), *The Habima, Israel's National Theater, 1917–1977: A Study of Cultural Nationalism*, New York: Columbia University Press.

Linklater, K. (2006), *Freeing the Natural Voice: Imagery and Art in the Practice of Voice and Language*, London: Nick Hern Books.

Linklater, K. (2016), 'The Art and Craft of Voice (and Speech) Training', *Journal of Interdisciplinary Voice Studies*, 1 (1), 57–70.

Listengarten, J. (2015), 'Michael Chekhov and the Visual Arts: Influences, Synergies, Collaborations', in M. C. Autant-Mathieu and Y. Meerzon (eds), *The Routledge Companion to Michael Chekhov*, London and New York: Routledge, 253–66.

Lurie, A. (2009), 'Wisdom and Folly in Fairytales', *Guardian*, 14 October.

MacDonald, C. (2010), 'Conducting the Flow: Dramaturgy and Writing', *Studies in Theatre and Performance*, 30 (1), 91–100.

Marowitz, C. (2004), *The Other Chekhov: A Biography of Michael Chekhov, the Legendary Actor, Director and Theorist*, New York: Applause Theatre and Cinema Books.

Massumi, B. (2015), *The Politics of Affect*, Cambridge: Polity Press.

Massumi, B. (2017), *The Principle of Unrest: Activist Philosophy in the Expanded Field*, Open Humanities Press.

McCaw, D. (2005), 'Rudolf Laban and Michael Chekhov on Movement', presented at Theatre of the Future? Michael Chekhov and 21st Century Performance Conference, 4 August 2005, Falmouth: Falmouth University.

McCaw, D. (2011), *The Laban Sourcebook*, London: Routledge.

McCaw, D. and McDermott, P. (2005), *Space, Improvisation and Creativity*, DVD-Rom and accompanying notes, Exeter: Arts Archive / Palatine Project.

McConachie, B. A. and Hart, F. E. (eds) (2006), *Performance and Cognition: Theatre Studies and the Cognitive Turn*, London: Routledge.

McDermott, P. (2007), 'Essay 5: Physical Theatre and Text', in J. Keefe and S. Murray (eds), *Physical Theatres: A Critical Reader*, London and New York: Routledge, 201–8.

McEvenue, K. (2001), *The Alexander Technique for Actors*, London: Methuen Drama.

McKinney, J. and Palmer, S. (2017), *Scenography Expanded*, London: Bloomsbury.

Meerzon, Y. (2015), 'Staging the Spectator in Michael Chekhov's Acting Theory', in M. C. Autant-Mathieu and Y. Meerzon (eds), *The Routledge Companion to Michael Chekhov*, London and New York: Routledge, 123–37.

Merlin, B. (2001), *Beyond Stanislavsky: The Psycho-Physical Approach to Actor Training*, New York and London: Routledge, Nick Hern Books.

Mermikides, A. and Smart, J. (2010), *Devising in Process*, Basingstoke: Palgrave Macmillan.

Meyerhold, V. (1999), *Meyerhold on Theatre*, Braun, Edward (trans.), London: Methuen.

Meyer-Horsch, U. (2017), 'Gestures of Listening', *Critical Stages* [Online], 15, http://www.critical-stages.org/15/tag/by-ulrich-meyer-horsch/ (accessed 3 August 2018).

Milne, T. and Goodwin, C. (1967), 'Working with Joan', in C. Marowitz and S. Trussler (eds), *Theatre at Work: Playwrights and Productions in the Modern British Theatre*, London: Methuen.

Mitchell, R. (2014), 'Seen But Not Heard: An Embodied Account of the (Student) Actor's Aesthetic Labour', *Theatre, Dance and Performance Training*, 5 (1), 59–73.

Mittelsteiner, C. (2015), 'Georgette Boner and Michael Chekhov: Collaboration(s) and Dialogue(s) in Search of the Method', in M. C. Autant-Mathieu and Y. Meerzon (eds), *The Routledge Companion to Michael Chekhov*, London and New York: Routledge, 57–68.

Mizenko, J., Bloom, K., Adrian, B., Casciero, T. and Porter, C. (2018), *The Laban Workbook for Actors: A Practical Training Guide with Video*, London and New York: Bloomsbury Methuen Drama.

Monday, M. (2017), *Directing with Michael Chekhov Technique*, London: Bloomsbury Methuen Drama.

Mroz, D. (2015), 'Cycles of creation: Michael Chekhov and the *yinyang wuxing* cosmology', in M. C. Autant-Mathieu and Y. Meerzon (eds), *The Routledge Companion to Michael Chekhov*, London and New York: Routledge, 297–310.

Murray, S. (2010), 'Jacques Lecoq, Monika Pagneux and Philippe Gaulier: Training for Play, Lightness and Disobedience', in A. Hodge (ed.), *Actor Training*, 2nd edn, London and New York: Routledge, 215–36.

Murray, S. and Keefe, J. (2007), *Physical Theatres: A Critical Introduction*, London and New York: Routledge.

Murray, S. and Keefe, J. (2016), *Physical Theatres: A Critical Introduction*, 2nd edn, London and New York: Routledge.

Ngai, S. (2005), *Ugly Feelings*, Cambridge, MA: Harvard University Press.

Nicholas, L. (2007), *Dancing in Utopia: Dartington Hall and its Dancers*, Alton: Dance Books.

Nicholson, H. (2005), *Applied Drama: The Gift of Theatre*, Basingstoke: Palgrave Macmillan.

Nisbet, N. (2007), 'Interview: Jasmin Vardimon', *Article 19* [Online], January 6, http://www.article19.co.uk/interview/jasmin_vardimon_1.php (accessed 3 August 2018).

Oddey, A. (1994), *Devising Theatre*, London and New York: Routledge.

Oram, D. (2018), 'Losing Sight of the Land: Tales of Dyslexia and Dyspraxia in Psychophysical Actor Training', *Theatre, Dance and Performance Training*, 9 (1), 53–67.

Osbourne, T. (1999), 'The Ordinariness of the Archive', *History of the Human Sciences*, 12 (2), 51–64.

Palmer, Richard H. (1998), *The Lighting Art: The Aesthetics of Stage Lighting Design*, 2nd edn, Upper Saddle River, NJ: Prentice-Hall.

Petit, L. (2010), *The Michael Chekhov Handbook for the Actor*, London and New York: Routledge.

Pichlikova, L. (2017), 'Performing in Mask: Michael Chekhov's pedagogy, *Commedia* and Mime', *Critical Stages* [Online], 15, http://www.critical-stages.org/15/tag/by-lenka-pichlikova/ (accessed 3 August 2018).

Pisk, L. (2017), *The Actor and His Body*, 4th edn, London: Methuen Drama.

Pitches, J. (2006), *Science and the Stanislavsky Tradition of Acting*, London and New York: Routledge.

Pitches, J. (2013), 'The Technique in Microcosm: Michael Chekhov's Work on the Fishers' Scene', *Theatre, Dance and Performance Training*, 4 (2), 219–36.

Pitches, J. and Aquilina, S. (2017), *Stanislavsky in the World: The System and its Transformations Across Continents*, London: Bloomsbury.

Potts, T. (1972), *The Liffey Banks*, Audio LP, Dublin: Claddagh Records.

Powers, M. (2004), Accompanying booklet in Chekhov, M., *On Theatre and the Art of Acting: The Five-Hour CD Master Class with Acclaimed Actor-Director-Teacher, Lectures Recorded by Michael Chekhov in 1955*. New York: Working Arts.

Powers, M. (2006), 'The Past, Present and Future of Michael Chekhov', in M. Chekhov, *To the Actor: On the Technique of Acting*, London and New York: Routledge, xxv–xlviii.

Preston, C. J. (2005), 'The Motor in the Soul: Isadora Duncan and Modernist Performance', *Modernism/Modernity*, 12 (2), 273–89.

Radosavljević, D. (2013a), *Theatre-Making: Interplay Between Text and Performance in the 21st Century*, London: Palgrave Macmillan.

Radosavljević, D. (2013b), *The Contemporary Ensemble: Interviews with Theatre-Makers*, Abingdon: Routledge.

Rhod, M. (1998), *Theatre for Community, Conflict and Dialogue: The Hope is Vital Training Manual*, Portsmouth, New Hampshire: Heinemann.

Roach, J. (1993), *The Player's Passion*, Ann Arbour: University of Michigan Press.

Rogers, C. (1959), 'A Theory of Therapy, Personality and Interpersonal Relationships as Developed in the Client-centred Framework', in S. Koch (ed.), *Psychology: A Study of a Science. Vol. 3: Formulations of the Person and the Social Context*, New York: McGraw Hill.

Rogers, C. and Freiberg, H. (1994), *Freedom to Learn*, 3rd revised edn, Upper Saddle River, NJ: Prentice-Hall.

Rogers, C., Lyon, H. and Tausch, J. (2014), *Becoming an Effective Teacher: Person-Centered Teaching, Psychology, Philosophy and Dialogues with Carl R. Rogers and Harold Lyon*, London and New York: Routledge.

Rowbotham, S. (1977), *Hidden From History*, London: Pluto Press.

Rowbotham, S. (2011), *Dreamers of a New Day: Women Who Invented the Twentieth Century*, London and New York: Verso.

Rudlin, J. (2010), 'Jacques Copeau: The Quest for Sincerity', in A. Hodge (ed.), *Actor Training*, 2nd edn, London and New York: Routledge, 43–62.

Rushe, S. (2013), 'Diary of a Rehearsal Process: Rehearsing *Diary of a Madman* from the Michael Chekhov Perspective', *Theatre, Dance and Performance Training*, 4 (2), 304–13.

Rushe, S. (2019), *Michael Chekhov's Acting Technique: A Practitioner's Guide*, London: Bloomsbury Methuen Drama.

Saint-Denis, M. (1982), *Training for the Theatre: Premises and Promises*, Suria Saint-Denis (ed.), New York: Theatre Arts Books.

Santos Newhall, M. A. (2009), *Mary Wigman*, London: Routledge.

Schechner, R. (1993), *The Future of Ritual*, New York and London: Routledge.

Schneider, R. (2001), 'Archives: Performance Remains', *Performance Research*, 6 (2), 100–8.

Schon, D. (1984), *Reflective Practitioner: How Professionals Think in Action*, London and New York: Routledge.

Scott, J. W. (1999), *Gender and the Politics of History*, revised edn, New York: Colombia University Press.

Sennett, R. (2012), *Together: The Rituals, Pleasures and Politics of Cooperation*, London: Penguin.

Segarra, M. (ed.) (2010), 'Introduction: Hélène Cixous: Blood and Language', in *The Portable Cixous*, New York: Colombia University Press, 1–16.

Sharp, M. (2002), *The Dartington Years* (DVD), Michael Chekhov Centre UK/Palomino Films.

Sharp, M. (2016), 'Michael Chekhov in Applied, Therapeutic and Community Contexts: Michael Chekhov New Pathways', Goldsmiths, University of London, 10 September.

Shaughnessy, N. (2012), 'Participant Centred Pedagogy and the Affecting Learning Environment: LIFT 2011', in *Applying Performance: Live Art, Socially Engaged Theatre and Affective Practice*, Basingstoke: Palgrave, 209–24.

Shepherd, S. (2012), *Direction: Readings in Theatre Practice*, Basingstoke: Palgrave Macmillan.

Siegel, D. (2007), 'Mindfulness Training and Neural Integration: Differentiation of Distinct Streams of Awareness and the Cultivation of Well-Being', *Social, Cognitive and Affective Neuroscience*, 2 (4), 259–63.

Sigal, S. (2016), *Writing in Collaborative Theatre-Making: A Practical Guide for Writers and Companies*, Basingstoke: Palgrave.

Slowiak, J. and Cuesta, J. (2007), *Jerzy Grotowski*, New York: Routledge.

Šmidchens, G. (2007), 'National Heroic Narratives in the Baltics as a Source for Nonviolent Political Action', *Slavic Review*, 66 (3) Fall, 484–508.

Snow, J. (2012), *Movement Training for Actors*, London: Methuen Drama.
Sopotsinsky, O. (1978), *Art in the Soviet Union: Painting, Sculpture, Graphic Arts*. Leningrad: Aurora Art Publishers.
Spatz, B. (2015), *What a Body Can Do*, Hoboken: Taylor and Francis.
Spinoza, B. de (2020), *Spinoza's Ethics*, George Eliot (trans.), Claire Carlisle (ed.), Oxford: Princeton University Press.
Steedman, C. (2001), 'Something She Called a Fever: Michelet, Derrida, and Dust', *American Historical Review*, 106 (4), 1159–80.
Steiner, M. (1926), *Creative Speech*, London: The Rudolf Steiner Publishing Co., http://wn.rsarchive.org/RelAuthors/SteinerM/CreSpc_index.html (accessed 23 November 2017)
Steiner, R. (1959), *Speech and Drama*, New York: Anthroposophic Publishing Co.
Steiner, R. (1984), *An Introduction to Eurythmy: Talks given before Sixteen Eurythmy Performances*, Spring Valley, NY: Anthroposophic Press.
Stephens, S. (2012), *Three Kingdoms*, London: Methuen.
Straumanis, A. (ed.) (1979), *The Golden Steed: Seven Baltic Plays*, Illinois: Waveland Press.
Sutton-Smith, B. (1997), *The Ambiguity of Play*, New Haven: Harvard University Press.
Sutton-Smith, B. (2008), 'Play Theory: A Personal Journey and New Thoughts', *American Journal of Play*, 1 (1), 1–44.
Tcherkasski, S. (2016), *Stanislavski and Yoga*, Wroclaw and New York: Icarus and Routledge.
Thompson, J. (2003), *Applied Drama: Bewilderment and Beyond*, Oxford: Peter Lang.
Thompson, J. (2011), *Performance Affects: Applied Theatre and the End of Effect*, Basingstoke: Palgrave Macmillan.
Tiny Hero Productions, Netherlands, tinyhero.nl (accessed 12 September 2018).
Trencsényi, K. (2015), *Dramaturgy in the Making: A User's Guide for Theatre Practitioners*, London: Bloomsbury.
Trencsényi, K. and Cochrane, B. (eds) (2014), *New Dramaturgy: International Perspectives on Theory and Practice*, London: Bloomsbury.
Turner, C. and Behrndt, S. (2007), *Dramaturgy and Performance*, Basingstoke: Palgrave Macmillan.
Turner, V. (1982), *From Ritual to Theatre: The Human Seriousness of Play*, New York: Performing Arts Journal.
Wade, A. (1997), 'What is a Voice Coach For?: Training and the Rise of the Voice Coach', in M. Hampton (ed.), *Vocal Vision*, New York: Applause Books.
Wangh, S. (2000), *An Acrobat of the Heart*, New York: Vintage Books.
Whyman, R. (2008), *The Stanislavsky System of Acting: Legacy and Influence in Modern Performance*, Cambridge: Cambridge University Press.
Whyman, R. (2015), 'Russian Delsartism and Michael Chekhov: The Search for the Eternal Type', in M. C. Autant-Mathieu and Y. Meerzon (eds), *The Routledge Companion to Michael Chekhov*, London and New York: Routledge, 267–81.
Winnicott, D. W. (1991), *Playing and Reality*, London and New York: Tavistock / Routledge.
Worthen, H. (2014), 'For a Skeptical Dramaturgy', *Theatre Topics*, 24 (3), September, 175–86.
Wright, J. (2006), *Why is That So Funny?*. London: Nick Hern Books.
Zentrum für bewegte Kunst e.V (ZBK) (Centre for Moving Arts, Berlin, Germany), www.zbk-berlin.de (accessed 12 September 2018).
Zinder, D. (2002), *Body, Voice, Imagination: A Training for the Actor*, London and New York: Routledge.

# Index

abducting  33
Abulafia, Yaron  142
Actor's Centre  133
Actors' Ensemble, The  16, 176
Adams, Patch  175
Adler, Stella  15
Ahmed, Sara  87
Albers, Josef  142
Alexander Technique  110, 112, 158
Anderson, Neil  95, 97–8
Andrees, Anna Katherina  155, 171
Andrees, Joerg  16, 26, 62, 154–5
Anthroposophy  94, 181
Appia, Adolphe  134, 147
Aquilina, Stefan  180
archetypes, see Chekhov, Michael: techniques
Aristotle  30, 86
ArtAngel  148
Ashperger, Cynthia  26, 44, 130
atmosphere, see Chekhov, Michael: techniques
Autant-Mathieu, Marie-Christine  8, 9, 18–19, 123–4
awareness, see Chekhov, Michael: techniques

Baars, Marjolein  11, 13–14, 17, 62, 154, 171, 174–6, 178
Baim, Clark  159
Bainbridge-Cohen, Bonnie, see Body-Mind-Centering
Ballet Jörgen  126
*Bamboo Cutter, The*  33
Barba, Eugenio  62
Bardsley, Julia  144
Barr, Margaret  125
Baycrest  159
Bazooka Arts  4, 26, 158
    productions: *A Time for Passion*  158
Beaton, Sarah  133, 142–3
Belgium Contact Clowns  175
Bennet, Leslie  100
Bennett, Suzanne  107, 122, 126–8
Bernstein, Sidney  66
Berry, Cicely  99–100, 106
Bing, Suzanne  31, 45, 61–2, 107, 120, 130
biomechanics, see Meyerhold, Vsevolod
Birch, Alice  81
Birren, Faber  142
Black, Lendley  44
Boal, Augusto  156, 158–9, 164
Body-Mind-Centering  110
Bogart, Anne  62, 69–70, 74, 80–2
Boner, Georgette  9, 17, 22, 33, 124
    Lectures on the History and Development of the Theatre and Playwriting  37
Bostock, Tom  31
Brecht, Bertolt  15, 134–5, 148
Brenan, Matthew C  183
British Association of Dramatherapists  158
Brook, Sally  159
Brook, Zoe  12, 13, 25–6, 157–64, 168, 171, 173, 177
Brothers Grimm  33
Brown, Stuart  46, 49, 52
Buber, Martin  59, 181
Byckling, Liisa  4, 17, 38, 60

Cabinet Gallery  149
Caillois, Roger  46, 59, 62
California State University  176
Callow, Simon  15, 157
Caracciolo, Diane  18
Cardboard Citizens  159
Carnegie, Gillian  133, 142, 149
Carnicke, Sharon  17
Castlebuono, Francesca  63
Centre for Alternative Theatre Training (CATT)  159
Centre National De La Danse  149
centres, see Chekhov, Michael: techniques
Cerullo, Jessica  16–18, 154, 171

Chamberlain, Franc   13, 15, 20, 26, 29, 31–2, 44, 98, 104, 112, 181
Chambers, Juliet   12, 25–6, 107, 115–16, 118
Chang, Eileen   178
Chekhov, Anton   111
Chekhov, Michael: performances
   *The Inspector General*   124
Chekhov, Michael: productions
   *The Castle Awakens: An Essay in Rhythmical Drama*   33
   *The Government Inspector*   5
   *Hamlet*   79, 97
   *The Inspector General*   19
   *Twelfth Night*   60, 66, 137
Chekhov, Michael: writings
   'The Actor is the Theatre'   1–2, 17–18, 24, 29
   *To The Actor: On the Technique of Acting*   1, 19, 50, 72, 79, 93, 98, 111, 156–7, 160, 162
   *Lessons for Teachers*   18–19, 24, 115, 130, 155, 167, 169, 176, 181
   *The Path of the Actor*   137
Chekhov, Michael: techniques   5–7, 10–16, 18, 23–4, 30–1, 40, 50, 56, 60–1, 63, 64–5, 73, 81–2, 98–9, 103–5, 107–8, 111, 115, 118–22, 126, 141, 153, 157–8, 160, 162, 164, 166, 169, 172, 174–7, 180–3
   archetypes   6, 133, 185, 188
   atmosphere   6, 48, 50–1, 53–4, 56, 58–9, 65, 77–8, 81–8, 93, 100, 109, 126–7, 129, 134, 162, 165–6, 169–70, 175, 185–7, 189
   awareness   46–7, 186
   centres   6, 44, 53–4, 67, 73, 109, 114, 116, 129, 163, 166–7, 186
   Chart for Inspired Acting   93, 96
   Chart of Exploration   52–5, 57
   colour   109, 115, 126, 132, 139–46, 186, 188
   contact   7, 39, 83–4, 161, 180, 186
   creative individuality   7, 68, 108, 113, 175, 186
   directions in space   6, 73, 126, 133, 186
   divided consciousness   6, 47, 186
   dynamics   6
   ensemble   176, 180
   feeling of beauty   6, 73, 109, 114, 179, 186
   feeling of ease   6, 73, 109, 114–15, 130, 187
   feeling of form   6, 41, 73, 109, 114–15, 129, 187
   feeling of wholeness   6, 73, 76–7, 109, 114, 129, 178, 189
   flowing   73, 117, 123, 170, 187–8
   flying   73, 117, 170, 187–8
   flying over the play   57, 76–8, 187
   gesture   6, 34–5, 54–5, 67, 75–9, 81, 84–6, 95, 100, 109–10, 115, 118, 120, 124–30, 134–40, 144–6, 166–7, 175, 178, 185, 187, 189
   ground   41, 43–7, 49–56, 58–60, 62, 68, 114, 186–8
   image   6, 55, 59, 126, 187–8
   imaginary body   6, 44, 78, 109, 118, 162–3, 166, 188
   improvisation   6, 72, 77–8, 188
   juggler psychology   40, 46, 49–51, 59–60, 62–3, 188
   love   180–1
   moulding   73, 117, 121, 165, 170, 187–9
   play and games   44, 46, 48, 51–2, 54, 60, 63, 188
   polarity   6, 54, 73, 75, 81, 188–9
   qualities of movement   6, 51, 73, 75, 77, 81, 88, 107–31, 134–7, 141, 144, 146, 158, 164–6, 170, 185–9
   radiating   39, 102, 114, 117, 123, 128, 130–1, 170, 186, 188–9
   receiving   100, 189
   rhythm and tempo   6, 55, 58–9, 74–6, 79, 82, 86, 110, 120, 125, 127–9, 185–6, 189
   sketches   77–8
   spine   37, 42, 44–50, 52, 55–6, 58–60, 62, 114, 189
   spying eye   189
   triplicity   73, 75, 189
   visualization   163, 166–7
Chekhov Collective UK   4, 12, 13, 25–6, 31, 35, 55, 63, 183
Chekhov Theatre Players   1, 5, 17
Chekhov Theatre Studio   1–10, 13, 14–20, 22, 29, 31–3, 36–9, 41–2, 44–5, 47, 52, 62, 64–8, 71–4, 79, 83, 88–9, 93–7, 100, 104–5, 107–8, 113, 115, 122–4, 130, 132–9, 154–7, 173, 180–1, 186
Chekhov Theatre Studio: productions   17
   *Balladina I and Balladina II*   1, 33, 37, 43, 133–4
   *The Cave of Salamanca*   133–4
   *The Deluge*   133
   'The Fishers' Scene'   32–3, 47–8, 55–6, 78, 133, 141

*The Golden Steed* 33–4, 37, 77, 79–80
*The Lower Depths* 65
*The Old Jew* 65
*The Path of the Actor* 4
*Peer Gynt* 33, 65, 133, 135
*Pickwick Papers* 85, 87
*The Possessed* 13, 32, 78
*A Spanish Evening* 37, 52, 55, 65, 78, 181
*Two Kings* 33–4, 37
Chen, Kim 122, 125–6
Cixous, Hélène 36, 56
Clark, Michael 127
Clarke, Sian 31
Clifford, Sara 159
Clouder, Christopher 20
Clowning 3, 36–8, 62, 154, 175
Cochrane, Bernadette 69–71, 86
Coffey, Peggy 154, 171
colour, *see* Chekhov, Michael: techniques
Colvin, Jack 14
*Commedia dell'Arte* 3, 34, 36–8, 41, 52, 107
Common Ground Theatre 64, 73
*Concert* 133
contact, *see* Chekhov, Michael: techniques
Copeau, Jacques 31, 45, 61, 120, 130
Cornford, Tom 4, 12, 13, 22, 23–6, 61, 119, 122–3, 128, 135, 177, 182
Cornish, Nellie 9
Cornish School of the Arts 9, 18, 124, 130–1
Craig, Edward Gordon 134–5
creative individuality, *see* Chekhov, Michael: techniques
Cristini, Monica 183
Crowther, Alice 15, 17, 94–5, 102
Csíkszentmihályi, Mihály 46, 49
Cumming, Anne, *see* Mason, Felicity
Cummings, Scott 69
Cunningham, Aldona 12, 26, 133, 143, 144–5, 148
Cunningham, Julie 122, 126–8
Cunningham, Merce 127
Cutting, Blair 14

Daboo, Jerri 3, 14–16, 26, 31, 71, 97–8, 107, 122–3, 183
Dalcroze eurythmics 130–1
Dalton, Lisa 16–17
Dartington Hall 1, 4–5, 8–10, 15, 24, 66, 84, 115, 130, 173

Dartington School for Dance-Mime 125
Dasté, Marie-Hélène and Jean 45
Davies, Hannah 12, 13, 26, 64, 73, 80–1
Decroux, Etienne 120, 130
DeKoven, Marianne 69
Deleuze, Gilles 83, 86
Delsarte, François 5
*Demons*, *see* Dostoyevsky, Fyodor *The Possessed*
Derrida, Jacques 20–1
Deshpande Hutchinson, Anjalee 148, 153, 183
Devine, George 62
Dewey, John 9, 19, 156
directions in space, *see* Chekhov, Michael: techniques
divided consciousness, *see* Chekhov, Michael: techniques
Dixon, Graham 4, 13, 15, 25, 31, 94–5, 97, 99, 104, 106, 157–8
Dobujinsky, Mstislav 18, 76, 135
Dolar, Mladen 103
Dostoyevsky, Fyodor 13, 64
*The Possessed* 13, 64, 68, 73, 76
Dramatherapy 158
Dramaturgy 23, 35–6, 41, 54–8, 58–60, 64–89, 108, 125, 128–9, 133, 144–7, 182, 186–7, 189
dreamthinkspeak 81
Drohan, Declan 155, 171
Dublin Dance Festival 149
Dullin, Charles 120
Duncan, Isadora 124–5, 131
Dunne, Colin 146–7
dynamics, *see* Chekhov, Michael: techniques

Earhart, Amelia 35
*écriture féminine*, *see* Cixous, Hélène
effort, *see* Laban, Rudolf
Egolf, Gretchen 14, 17, 25–6, 174
Elmhirst, Dorothy 9, 17, 25, 77, 123
Elmhirst, Leonard 9
Elmhirst, William 157
Elnile, Rosie 133, 144, 148
Elwood, Derek 63
Emerson College 15, 26
Epner, Eero 68–70
Eurythmy 20, 33, 94–5, 98, 102, 107, 113
Ex Machina 62

Fairy Tale Committee 17, 33, 36
Faison, Eleanor 14, 133

Farb, Norman   102–3, 106
feeling of beauty, *see* Chekhov, Michael: techniques
feeling of ease, *see* Chekhov, Michael: techniques
feeling of form, *see* Chekhov, Michael: techniques
feeling of wholeness, *see* Chekhov, Michael: techniques
Feldenkrais Method   112
Fenley, Margot   122, 126
Filter Theatre   69
Fitch, Bryn   63
Fleming, Cass   4, 8, 12, 13, 16, 20, 22–6, 68, 107, 109, 113, 119–20, 168, 172, 177, 182
floating, *see* Chekhov, Michael: techniques
flowing, *see* Chekhov, Michael: techniques
flying, *see* Chekhov, Michael: techniques
flying over the play, *see* Chekhov, Michael: techniques
Fogarty, Elsie, *see* Royal Central School of Speech and Drama
Forsyth, William   129
Foucault, Michel   20–2
four brothers, the, *see* Chekhov, Michael: techniques
Foylan, Alistair   31
Freire, Paulo   156, 159, 181
Frecknall, Rebecca   31, 63
   *Summer and Smoke*   63
Friedank, Ragnar   13–14, 174, 176–7
Frost, Anthony   46

Garre, Sol   26
Gate Theatre   144
Gaunt, Michael   110
Genosko, Gary   89
George Brown College Dance department   126
Gestalt therapy   167
gesture, *see* Chekhov, Michael: techniques
Gillett, John   12, 26, 99–104, 105
Gilmer, Jane   98
Glad Theatre   155
Goethe, Johann Wolfgang von   114, 141, 143, 186
   *Theory of Colours*   139
Goldoni, Carlo   37
Goldsmiths University of London   4, 12, 26, 32, 148, 159, 172
Gordon, Mel   14, 44, 94, 130

Gorky, Maxim   65
Govan, Emma   36
Graham, Martha   18, 124, 131
Green, Katie   122, 128
Grenfell, Colin   133, 142–3, 146, 148
Grome, Melody Parker   63
Grosz, Elizabeth   61
Grotowski, Jerzy   15, 130
grounds, *see* Chekhov, Michael: techniques
Guattari, Felix   83, 89
Guidhall School of Music and Drama   149
Guildford School of Acting   26
Gutekunst, Christina   12, 26, 99–104, 105

Habima Theatre   60, 66
Haffler, Mark   100
Hagen, Uta   15
Halprin, Anna and Lawrence   62
*Hamlet*
   Claudius   79
   Hamlet   78
   Ophelia   78
Harkness, Alan   1, 98
Harkness, Mechthild   98
Hart, F. Elizabeth   103
Heathcote, Dorothy   156
Heidegger, Martin   88, 157
Heimann, Christopher   31
Henricks, Thomas   59
Hermann, Anna   159
Hilevaara, Katja   31
Hurst du Prey, Deirdre   1–4, 9, 14–15, 17–18, 21–2, 24, 29, 37, 40–2, 46, 68, 74, 93, 96–7, 106, 108, 110, 121, 123–5, 127, 129–32, 135, 149, 157, 185
Huizinga, Johan   59

Ibsen, Henrik   33, 65
   *Peer Gynt*   33, 65, 133, 135, 155
image, *see* Chekhov, Michael: techniques
imaginary body, *see* Chekhov, Michael: techniques
Improbable Theatre   15, 31, 62, 158, 177
improvisation, *see* Chekhov, Michael: techniques
Ingold, Tim   84–6
Institute for Rural Reconstruction (India)   9
Ivanova, Marina   17

Jacques-Dalcroze, Émile   5, 19
Jafine, Hartley   157–60, 162, 166, 168–71, 173

Jarman, Derek  142
Jeffers, Alison  162, 165
John, Michael  155
Johnson, Marietta  19
Johnstone, Keith  62
Joint Stock Theatre Company  69
Jooss, Kurt  10, 123
Jooss-Leeder School of Dance  24, 123
Jörgen, Bengt  126
juggler psychology, *see* Chekhov, Michael: techniques
Julie Cunningham & Company  127
Junti, Hannah  63

Kane, Sarah  3, 15–17, 25, 94, 97, 104, 106, 157
Katimba, Dipo  165–6
Kemp, Rick  111
Kilroy, Wil  16
Kindelan, Nancy  17, 96–7
Kirillov, Andrei  8, 38, 79, 97, 109–10
Knebel, Maria  15, 17
Knowles, Ric  148
Ko, Yun Jung  169
Kolb, David  159, 170
Koppett, Kat  159, 170
Krynke, Julia  12, 25–6
Kwei, Teng  135

Laban, Rudolf  9, 107, 110–11, 114–18, 123, 130
Lab Theatre  5
La Comète/Scène Nationale de Châlons-en-Champagne  149
Landau, Tina  74, 80–2
Lane, Kim  17
Langhams, Jobst  16, 26, 155
Langman, Dawn  106, 112
Leach, Bernard  9
Lecoq, Jacques  31, 45–6, 61–2, 109–11, 115, 120–1
Leeder, Sigurd  9, 123
Legislative Theatre  164
Leicester Haymarket Theatre  149
Lepage, Robert  62
Levinas, Emmanuel  162
Linklater, Kristin  100–3, 106
Listengarten, Julia  148
Littlewood, Joan  66
Living Theatre  69
London Academy of Music and Dramatic Art  98, 100, 106

London International Festival of Theatre  22
Lurie, Alison  33

MacAloon, John  46, 49
McAvinchey, Caoimhe  12, 13, 22, 24–6, 174, 177, 182
McCall, Kai  133, 143, 149
McConachie, Bruce  104
McDermott, Phelim  6, 15, 25, 31, 62, 177
MacDonald, Claire  70–1, 88
McDougall, Ellen  149
McKinney, Joslin  132–4, 145
MacLeish, Archibald  131
MacLellan, Joshua  31, 50–1
McMaster University  158
*Mahabharata, The*  33
Makepeace, Effie  156–7, 159–60, 162, 164–5–166, 170–1, 173
Marceau, Marcel  120
Marionette Theatre and Style  37
Marland, Saskia  63
Marowitz, Charles  19
MA Scène Nationale/Pays de Montbéliard  149
mask  36–8
Mason, Felicity  14–15, 17
Massumi, Brian  83
MAT First Studio  4
Mayo, Sue  22
Mee, Charles  69
Meerzon, Yana  8, 9, 148
Meisner, Sanford  15
Mercier, Joe  63
Mercier, Mel  146
Merleau-Ponty, Maurice  84
Merlin, Bella  15–16
Merlin, Joanna  13–14, 16–17, 44, 106, 174, 176
Meyer, Rudolf  34
Meyerhold, Vsevolod  111, 115, 118–19, 123
Meyer-Horsch, Ulrich  13–14, 174, 177–9
Michael Chekhov Acting Studio  177
Michael Chekhov Association (MICHA)  8, 13, 16, 26, 154–5, 171, 174, 176–7
Michael Chekhov Brazil  16
Michael Chekhov Canada  16
Michael Chekhov Europe (MCE)  13, 16, 171, 177
Michael Chekhov International Academy  26, 155
Michael Chekhov School  176
Michael Chekhov Studio  155
Michael Chekhov Studio Brussels  175
Michael Chekhov Studio London  8, 15, 26

Michael Chekhov Studio New York   18
Michael Chekhov UK (MCUK)   3, 8, 15, 26, 106, 157, 171
Michael Chekhov Workshop   16
Michael Tschechow Studio Berlin   26
Michelsen, Jesper   155, 171
mime   107, 120
Mitchell, Roanna   12, 13, 16, 18, 22, 24–6, 31–2, 81, 182
Mittelsteiner, Crista   22, 124
Mizenko, Juliet   118
Montessori, Maria   19
Morgenstern, Margareta   17
Moscow Arts Theatre   4, 10, 18, 70, 135, 149
moulding, *see* Chekhov, Michael: techniques
movement qualities, *see* Chekhov, Michael: techniques
Mroz, Daniel   71, 183
Murray, Bryony   158
Murray, Simon   45–6
Music Theatre programme, Melbourne   126

Nanzikambe   159, 164–5
National Michael Chekhov Association   16
National Theatre Studio   8, 31
Naughton, Phoebe   31
Naumburg, Margaret   19
Neher, Caspar   148
Nemirovich-Danchenko, Vladimir   18, 70, 149
New School, The   176
New York University   176
Ngai, Sianne   87
Nicholson, Helen   36, 156
Nietzsche, Friedrich   21
Nirantar   159
Normington, Katie   36
Nübling, Sebastian   66, 69
   *Three Kingdoms*   66–9

O'Casey, Sean   65
   *The Silver Tassie*   66
   *Within the Gates*   66
Oddey, Alison   30
O'Keefe, Maura   149
Once Off Productions   149
Open Space Technology   177
Oppenheim, Hans   9
Oram, Daron   12, 21, 24–6, 114, 182
Osbourne, Thomas   93
O'Sullivan, Simon   147
Overlie, Mary   62, 74
Owen, Harrison   177

Paidia   62
Palmer, Richard H   142
Palmer, Scott   132–3, 145
Palmer, Tania   69, 134
Performing Arts Festival Groningen   149
Performing Arts International   8, 25, 106
Petit, Lenard   16, 44, 62, 117, 130, 175
Pichlikova, Lenka   107, 120
Pinter, Harold   144
Pisk, Litz   110
Pit, The   149
Pitches, Jonathan   2, 26, 32, 47, 112, 114, 141, 149, 180
play and games, *see* Chekhov, Michael: techniques
Point Park University   98
polarity, *see* Chekhov, Michael: techniques
Postman, Neil   159
Potts, Tommie   146–7
Powers, Mala   14, 16–17, 20, 23, 93
Pratt, Caroline   19
Preston, C.J.   131
psychological gesture, *see* Chekhov, Michael: techniques: gesture
Pugh, Ted   16, 176
Punchdrunk   136, 148

Qigong, Zhi Neng   71, 183
qualities of movement, *see* Chekhov, Michael: techniques
Queen Mary University of London   4, 26, 32
Quick Bright Things   155

radiating, *see* Chekhov, Michael: techniques
Rainis, Jan   77, 79
*Ramayana*   33
receiving, *see* Chekhov, Michael: techniques
Reid, Alexa   133, 136, 145, 148
Reinhardt, Max   5
Reynolds, Eileen Carey   66
Rhod, Michael   159
rhythm and tempo, *see* Chekhov, Michael: techniques
Rice, Emma   69
Rider University   98
Roach, Joseph   121
Rogers, Paul   14, 47, 83, 133, 149, 155, 157, 161
Royal Academy of Dramatic Art   100
Royal Central School of Speech and Drama   4, 26, 95, 99, 101, 106, 148–9

Royal Court Theatre   62
Royal Shakespeare Company   99, 101
Rushe, Sinéad   4, 8, 11–13, 24–6, 45, 99, 102, 110, 118–20, 122, 182
   *Concert*   145–7

Saint-Denis, Michel   62
Saint-Exupéry, Antoine de   13, 35, 50–1, 58, 61
Santiniketan   9
Saramago, José   149
scenography   81–2, 132–7, 141–8
Scharler, Magdalena   155, 171
Scharmer, Otto   178
Schon, Donald   159
School of Dance-Mime   9, 18, 24
Schreiber, Gretel   149
Schuck, Karin   133, 149
Scottish Dramatherapists   158
Scottish Mental Health Arts and Film Festival   158
Segarra, Marta   36
Sennett, Richard   160, 165
Shakespeare, William
   *Hamlet*   78, 80, 135
   *King Lear*   79–80, 85
   *A Midsummer Night's Dream*   80, 177
   *Twelfth Night*   60, 66, 137
Shankar, Uday   5, 9, 71, 123
Sharp, Martin   4, 12, 13, 14–16, 25–6, 157, 159–62, 165–8, 171–3
Shdanoff, George   68, 76, 78
Shepherd, Simon   69
Shuttleworth, Holly   63
Sigal, Sarah   66, 69
Sima   175
singing   93
SITI Company   69, 74
sketches, *see* Chekhov, Michael: techniques
Skourtis, Andreas   133, 143–4, 148
Sloan, Fern   16–17, 176
Smith, Brian Sutton   159
Snow, Jackie   110
Soukoup, Willi   9, 132
Spatz, Ben   122
Speech Formation   94
spine, *see* Chekhov, Michael: techniques
Spinoza, Baruch   83
spying eye, *see* Chekhov, Michael: techniques
Stanislavsky, Konstantin   4, 5, 15, 18–19, 25, 70, 94, 99, 104, 112, 123, 130–1, 180
Steedman, Caroline   21, 95

Steffen, Albert   139, 186
Steiner, Rudolf   5, 15, 19–20, 25, 34, 38, 94–106, 112–13, 115, 139, 181, 183, 186, 188
Stephens, Chloe   63
Stephens, Simon   66–7, 69
Stoppard, Tom: *Rosencrantz and Guildenstern*   80
Straight, Beatrice   1, 4, 9, 14, 17–18, 22, 41–2, 47, 68, 96, 123–4, 149
Street Theatre   133
Suitcase Foundation, The   174–5
Sulerzhitsky, Leopold   4, 19, 130
Sungaard, Arnold   68
Sunnybrook Hospital   170
Sussex University   159
Suzuki, Tadashi   69
Svoboda, Josef   145

Tagore, Rabindranath   9
Tchaikovsky, Pyotr Ilyich: *Iolanta*   143
tempo, *see* Chekhov, Michael: techniques
Theatre Monkey   8
Theatre of the Oppressed   164
Theatre Tonic   158
Thompson, James   154, 170
tiny hero productions   154, 174
Tisch School of Arts   176
Tobey, Mark   9, 132, 135
*Tonetto Busetto*   33
Training for Transformation   159
Tramway   149
Tree, Iris   68, 133
Trencsényi, Katalin   69–71, 86
Tringham, Anna   120
triplicity, *see* Chekhov, Michael: techniques
*Tsar Saltan*   33
Turner, Victor   46–7

Ullman, Lisa   9, 107, 123
University of Bournemouth   26
University of Huddersfield   26
University of Kent   4, 26, 129
University of Toronto   159

Vakhtangov, Evgeny   4, 19, 38, 112, 123, 135
Vardimon, Jasmine   125
Victorian College of the Arts   98
viewpoints   62, 74, 80–3, 88
Visva-Bharati   9
voice   93–106

Wade, Andrew  99
Waldorf School  19
Warren, Iris  100–1
Weaver, Philip  31
Weingartner, Charles  159
West, Darron  69
Whyman, Rose  183
Wigman, Mary  18, 124, 131
Wintsch, Mani  155, 171
Wintsch-Heinen, Bernadette  155, 171
Worthen, Hana  72–3
Wright, John  15, 25, 31, 46, 62
Wuxing, Yinyang  71, 183

Yarrow, Ralph  46
Yeats, W.B.  66
Young, Henry Lyon  41, 65, 68, 80, 181
Young Vic Theatre  32
Young Vic Young Directors' Programme  8

Zapatista movement  81, 89
Zarrilli, Phillip  26, 31
Zentrum Für Bewegte Kunst  155
Zinder, David  26
Zola, Emile  144

www.ingramcontent.com/pod-product-compliance
Lightning Source LLC
Chambersburg PA
CBHW080549230426
43663CB00015B/2763